The European Commission a
of Europe
Images of Governance

D0546136

What kind of European Union do top Commission officials want? Should the European Union be supranational or intergovernmental? Should it promote market liberalism or regulated capitalism? Should the Commission be Europe's government or its civil service? The book examines top officials' preferences on these questions through analysis of unique data from 137 interviews.

Understanding the forces that shape human preferences is the subject of intense debate. Hooghe demonstrates that the Commission has difficulty shaping its employees' preferences in the fluid multi-institutional context of the European Union. Top officials' preferences are better explained by experiences outside rather than inside the Commission: political party, country, and prior work leave deeper imprints than length of service, directorate-general, or cabinet. Preferences are also influenced more by internalized values than by self-interested career calculation. Hooghe's findings are surprising and will challenge a number of common assumptions about the workings and motives of the European Commission.

LIESBET HOOGHE is Associate Professor of Political Science at the University of North Carolina at Chapel Hill. Her publications include editing *Cohesion Policy and European Integration: Building Multi-level Governance* (1996) and co-authoring *Multi-level Governance and European Integration* (with Gary Marks, 2001).

Themes in European Governance

Series Editors
Andrea Føllesdal
Johan P. Olsen

Editorial Board

Stefano Bartolini	Beate Kohler-Koch	Percy Lehning
Andrew Moravscik	Ulrich Preuss	Thomas Risse
Fritz W. Scharpf	Philip Schlesinger	Helen Wallace
Albert Weale	J.H.H. Weiler	

The evolving European systems of governance, in particular the European Union, challenge and transform the state, the most important locus of governance and political identity and loyalty over the past 200 years. The series *Themes in European Governance* aims to publish the best theoretical and analytical scholarship on the impact of European governance on the core institutions, policies and identities of nation-states. It focuses upon the implications for issues such as citizenship, welfare, political decision-making, and economic, monetary and fiscal policies. An initiative of Cambridge University Press and the Programme on Advanced Research on the Europeanisation of the Nation-State (ARENA), Norway, the series includes contributions in the social sciences, humanities and law. The series aims to provide theoretically informed studies analysing key issues at the European level and within European states. Volumes in the series will be of interest to scholars and students of Europe both within Europe and worldwide. They will be of particular relevance to those interested in the development of sovereignty and governance of European states and in the issues raised by multi-level governance and multi-national integration throughout the world.

Other books in the series:

Paulette Kurzer
Markets and Moral Regulation: Cultural Change in the European Union

Christoph Knill
The Europeanisation of National Administrations: Patterns of Institutional Change and Persistence

Tanja Börzel
States and Regions in the European Union: Institutional Adaptation in Germany and Spain

The European Commission and the Integration of Europe

Images of Governance

Liesbet Hooghe

CAMBRIDGE
UNIVERSITY PRESS

PUBLISHED BY THE PRESS SYNDICATE OF THE UNIVERSITY OF CAMBRIDGE
The Pitt Building, Trumpington Street, Cambridge, United Kingdom

CAMBRIDGE UNIVERSITY PRESS
The Edinburgh Building, Cambridge CB2 2RU, UK
40 West 20th Street, New York, NY 10011-4211, USA
477 Williamstown Road, Port Melbourne, VIC 3207, Australia
Ruiz de Alarcón 13, 28014 Madrid, Spain
Dock House, The Waterfront, Cape Town 8001, South Africa

http://www.cambridge.org

First published 2001

Printed in the United Kingdom at the University Press, Cambridge

Typeface Plantin 10/12 pt.   *System* LaTeX 2_ε [TB]

A catalogue record for this book is available from the British Library.

ISBN 0 521 80667 4 hardback
ISBN 0 521 00143 9 paperback

Contents

Figures

Tables

Preface

The study of the European Union (EU) has vacillated between being a vanguard for theoretical innovation and a feast for area specialists. The turn of the century has been a time of connecting these two worlds.

This book on preferences in the European Commission is written for both generalists and EU area specialists. For EU students, I explore the beliefs of decision makers at the heart of Europe about who should govern, how, and over whom. These questions have structured political competition in Europe's national states over the past century and a half. They now shape EU politics. Scholars have begun to map contestation among public, parties, and private interests. But how do office holders in the European Union's central executive and administrative body, the European Commission, conceive of European integration? What kind of European Union do top Commission officials want? Should the European Union be supranational or intergovernmental? Should it promote market liberalism or regulated capitalism? Should the Commission be an executive principal or an administrative/managerial agent? Should it be a consociational or a Weberian organization?

Between 1995 and 1997, I set up camp in Brussels in order to ask these people what they think of the integration of Europe. These 137 interviews constitute the empirical bedrock of this book. The leadership of the Commission holds diverse, not unitary views. Contrary to conventional wisdom, I find that top officials are divided as sharply as national parties, governments, and national publics. I show that the Commission does not succeed in shaping its employees' preferences, and this has much to do with the multi-level character of decision-making in the European Union. To understand Commission preferences one must understand how authority is exercised in the European Union.

This book is also written for generalists. Comprehending the forces that shape human preferences is the subject of intense debate in political science. I follow others in distinguishing between two basic contending theories of human motivation: a sociological paradigm that stresses how values shape preferences, and an economic paradigm that emphasizes self-interested utility. Trying to combine utility maximization and socialization may appear as fruitless as attempting to unite water and fire. They seem just too different. Yet interests *and* values motivate human preferences. So how can one do justice to both logics? In this book, I try to go beyond abstract debate to examine how each of these explains – or fails to explain – preferences. In what political circumstances, I ask, do values and interests motivate preferences? I show that the role of values and interests is contextual. To understand how values and interests shape preferences one must understand the particular contexts that make one or the other salient.

In writing this book, I have incurred many debts. The seeds were sown in conversations with my friend Hussein Kassim back in 1993, when we were both regular fixtures in the Junior Common Room of Nuffield College, Oxford. Encouraged by our mentor Vincent Wright, we contrived the ambitious plan to study the interplay between bureaucratic politics and policy-making in the Commission, and that, we decided, would require an analysis of the Commission as bureaucracy in combination with case studies in a variety of policy sectors. But, as Nuffield sent us off into the academic world, professional pressures got the better of our joint ambitions.

Two seminal books – Robert Putnam's classic *The Beliefs of Politicians* (1973) and Donald Searing's more recently published *Westminster's World* (1994) – persuaded me to listen intently to those who run the Commission. What began as an examination of a bureaucracy became a study of the preferences, beliefs, and roles of the people within. In the process, I gained not one but 137 collaborators: the top Commission officials who graciously parted with scarce time and frank insights during more than 180 hours of interviewing. This book would not have been possible without them. I thank them sincerely.

I received financial assistance from diverse sources. A Connaught grant from the University of Toronto (1994–5) provided seed money, and the Canadian Social Sciences and Humanities Research Council funded the lion's share of travel, accommodation, transcription and coding of the interviews, and data analysis through two three-year grants (1996–9 and 1999–2002). A Jean Monnet Fellowship at the European University Institute (EUI) in Florence (1996–7) allowed me to set aside precious time for research. The EUI provided a wonderful intellectual environment for soaking and poking in the data. This was the year that Yves Mény moved the Schuman Centre to the Convento, and I made extensive use of the new facilities, firing off letters, faxes, and phone calls to set up interviews in Brussels. As my friends at EUI will testify, my research activities provided essential intelligence on the robustness of the Convento's secretarial infrastructure. After I left, administrative expenses dropped considerably!

Brussels became a second home during months of interviewing. I thank the Katholieke Universiteit of Brussels for use of their facilities. Huguette answered many a Commission phone call on my behalf, and she unfailingly and unflappably sent (and resent) faxes to all corners in Brussels. If I did not miss appointments, it is because of her.

Over the years, I have benefited enormously from conversations, comments, and criticisms by many a colleague and friend. I cannot possibly mention, or remember, every single person who deserves my gratitude, but here I would like to single out those who shaped this end product perhaps more than they care to take credit for: Sven Bislev, Jean Blondel, Tanja Börzel, Jim Caporaso, Jeff Checkel, Stefaan De Rynck, Guido Dierickx, Morten Egeberg, Claus-Dieter Ehlermann, Adrienne Héritier, Simon Hug, Brigid Laffan, Mikel Landabaso, Larry Leduc, Andrea Lenschow, David Lowery, Neil Nevitte, Johan Olsen, Edward Page, John Peterson, Eberhard Rhein, Thomas Risse, Bert Rockman, Gerald Schneider, Pascal Sciarini, Don Searing, Marco Steenbergen, and Bernard Steunenberg. I presented parts of this work at numerous occasions, but I owe particular thanks to my colleagues at the European University Institute, the University of Toronto, and the University of North Carolina at Chapel Hill. I am also grateful to Michelle Cloutier, Gina Cosentino, Oded Haklai, Mike Harvey, Joshua Heatley, Andrew Price-Smith, Antonio Torres-Ruiz, and more than thirty student-transcribers at UNC-Chapel Hill and Toronto for invaluable research assistance. John Haslam, my editor at Cambridge University Press, guided this manuscript efficiently through the last stages by prodding me discreetly, but firmly, to notch it up yet one more time – and quickly.

Gary Marks lived my dreams, hopes, and anxieties about this book from the beginning. He shared and shaped every thought, every problem, and every small victory. This book is as much ours as is our co-authored work. With one small difference: the responsibility for its shortcomings are mine, and mine alone.

Prologue

European integration studies have found it difficult to produce cumulative research. Some may argue that cumulative knowledge is always hard to come by in area studies. Yet Europe has traditionally been a rewarding laboratory for scholars in search of answers to basic questions. Various subfields in political science – political parties, mass public opinion, welfare regimes, systems of industrial relations, public administration, public policy, social movements, or value change – draw empirically primarily from the "area of Europe".

Cumulative research in European integration studies has been an uphill struggle for several reasons. One is that European integration has often been perceived as a unique case. Despite Giovanni Sartori's warning that "he who knows only one country knows none" (Sartori 1991), many EU scholars have been reluctant to consider the European Union as one case within an *n* larger than one.[1] Ironically, the study of regional integration in Europe began as a distinctly comparative-historical enterprise. European integration occupied a secondary place to international integration in David Mitrany's functionalist theory (Mitrany 1966). Ernie Haas (1958, 1960, 1964) wrote about various forms of regional integration that were emerging in postwar Europe, including the Nordic Council, the Council of Europe, the North Atlantic Treaty Organisation (NATO), the Western European Union, and the predecessors of the European Community (EC), such as the European Coal and Steel Community. He also analyzed global forms of integration, such as the International Labour Organization, a study that had a strong influence on his formulation of neofunctionalism (Haas 1964). Karl Deutsch, another intellectual parent of regional integration studies, placed his work in a broad comparative-historical framework concerned with state and community formation in multinational empires. His examples were the Austro-Hungarian empire, national states such as the United Kingdom, Switzerland, or Italy, and

---

[1] This section is indebted to the forum published in the Review of the US European Community Studies Association (ECSA 1997). Forum (James Caporaso, Gary Marks, Andrew Moravcsik, and Mark Pollack).

international organizations such as NATO and the European Community (Deutsch et al. 1957). Philippe Schmitter (1970) elaborated this comparative regional integration framework with reference to Latin America, and Joseph Nye (1968) sought to apply it to other parts of the world.

Two real-world developments dealt a blow to this auspicious trend. By the end of the 1960s, it was clear that efforts at regional integration outside Europe had made little progress, and in many cases they had regressed. The collapse of the Bretton Woods system in the early 1970s reinforced this trend as the ensuing worldwide economic crisis ushered in a long decade of national protectionism. The second development was, strangely, the very success of the European Community. The extraordinary pace and depth of integration seemed to set this enterprise apart from faltering integration efforts elsewhere. Even when the rest of the world closed itself off from regional integration, the European Community stayed put and, despite much-publicized Eurosclerosis, enlarged its membership as well as deepened integration.

Regional integration theory fell victim to these twin developments. Ernie Haas (1975) explicitly confirmed its obsolescence; Karl Deutsch implicitly consented as he moved on to study security issues; and Philippe Schmitter redirected his intellectual energies to a distinctly national phenomenon – neocorporatism. This cleared the path for criticisms on the significance of European integration itself. Several leading comparative scholars and European integration students of the first hour led the attack (Hoffmann 1966; Inglehart 1967). This pushed the study of the European Community into the doldrums during much of the 1970s and the 1980s. A small group of students, most of them committed to the political idea of European integration, kept the field on the map. However, the bridges to regional integration studies were in disrepair, and this had consequences. European integration studies became a backwater of international relations. In comparative politics, the failure of regional integration theory coincided with the proliferation of major collaborative programs for crossnational data collection on household spending, welfare state development, public opinion, values, and elections. Comparativists were drawn to these new *national*-level data – and drawn away from European integration. The few remaining students of European integration were isolated; and European integration became a unique case. Reluctance to compare and contrast across time and space kept EU studies relatively insulated from developments in political science, and this impeded innovative theory building.

Another impediment to cumulative research is that few theorists have succeeded in translating their conceptual models into testable hypotheses. The earlier theorists, again, proved a partial exception, but their operationalizations led to complex, quasi-indeterminate models that were difficult to test. As the Haas–Schmitter neofunctionalist models and the Deutschian transactional approach were amended over time, they became unwieldy instruments of description (or prescription). In this respect the theorists reflected broader currents. Very few empirical EU scholars have devoted attention to systematic testing of competing theories against evidence. In a recent forum on the state of the discipline, Andrew Moravcsik (in ECSA Forum 1997) puts forth four reasons for this limited progress in theory testing:

- few studies rest on explicit hypotheses that offer standards of disconfirmation;
- few studies test alternative theories – most proffer evidence that supports their preferred explanation;
- few studies engage in comparative analysis – most are single-case studies or pick cases without much systematic attention to selection bias;
- few studies use "hard" primary sources.

One may argue that much of political science has regularly committed one or several of these "sins." The study of the European Union is no exception. But a greater impediment to cumulative knowledge may come from the quality of available data. In EU studies, comparative, publicly available, and replicable data remain scarce, and this hampers theory testing.

Theories of the EC/EU as a macro-system have traditionally been privileged over theories comparing elements of the EU with elements of other polities. Macro-theories are by nature more impervious to testing. One needs either credible competition from a rival macro-theory, or a means to carve up the larger theory into hypotheses pertaining to clearly delineated parts. Neither of these conditions was present in European integration studies – until the last decade of the twentieth century.

For a long time, the conditions for theoretical progress through theory competition were not ideal. Neofunctionalism was the only game in town until the early 1970s, and then it imploded under the weight of changing world politics and its own complexity – not as a result of competition with a superior rival theory. To the extent that scholars of the next generation were concerned with theorizing, state-centric or "intergovernmentalist" theories were hegemonic. Early intergovernmentalist theorizing was heavily indebted to neorealism, but it unraveled in the face of contradictory political events in the mid-1980s: the Single European Act and the subsequent resurgence of European integration. Just like neofunctionalism one-and-a-half decades earlier, neorealism did not put up much of a fight to uphold an unsustainable theory (for exceptions see Grieco 1995; Mann 1993; Mearsheimer 1990). A more sophisticated liberal intergovernmentalist model, rooted in institutional contractualism, supplanted neorealism (Hoffmann and Keohane 1991). But where was the rival theory? This lack of explicit dialogue between theoretical rivals is in stark contrast with what happened in the field of international relations, where controversies between neorealism and its opponents, and more recently between positivist and constructivist approaches, have defined the field.

Over the past ten years real competition among macrotheoretical models has emerged: liberal intergovernmentalism (Hoffmann and Keohane 1991; Martin 1993, 2000; Milner 1997; Moravcsik 1993, 1998), a revised neofunctionalist transactional model (Sandholtz 1996; Stone Sweet and Brunnell 1996; Stone Sweet and Sandholtz 1997), and multi-level governance (Börzel and Risse 2000; Jachtenfuchs and Kohler-Koch 1995; Marks 1992, 1993, 1996a; Marks, Hooghe, Blank 1996; Scharpf 1994). Each theoretical alternative has the ambition to compare the EU with other "cases" on specified second-order dimensions (Marks in ECSA Forum 1997). EU students are now invited to adjudicate among competing theories. At the same time, some scholars have argued that we move beyond competing macro-theories (Hix 1994; Peterson 1997a). Instead, they apply middle-range hypotheses drawn from comparative politics to the study of European integration.

The renewed fascination of comparativists with European integration is arguably the single most important development in European integration studies since the doldrums of the 1970s. Comparativists flocked back first of all to mine the new EU-level data-sets that began to accumulate from the 1980s. The most popular source is the European Union's own Eurobarometer initiative, which began only in 1974 to monitor public opinion in Europe on European integration using national surveys (Reif and Inglehart 1991). Other sources include election data (since the first direct elections for the European Parliament in 1979), parliamentary votes (since the early 1980s), statistics compiled by the Commission on the implementation of EU directives (since the late 1980s), and the growing number of European Court of Justice cases. This has allowed comparativists finally to plug the European Union into the field's mainstream theoretical models and methodologies, which generally require systematic data.

At the same time, methodological progress facilitated the "repatriation" of comparativists into European integration studies. The first generation of sophisticated quantitative analyses that transfused mainstream comparative politics did not lend themselves easily to modeling multilevel phenomena. For example, how could one estimate in one model the impact on policy outcomes in different countries of a common EU policy and common EU political process factors, combined with particular domestic politics factors, as well as potential interaction effects? This changed when, in response to methodological challenges in American politics, progress was made on multi-level statistical analysis in the early 1990s. Crossnational analysis had largely rested on the assumption that domestic arenas are insulated islands. The common EU factor was usually assumed to behave as a random part of the error term. With multi-level analysis, new possibilities have opened up for incorporating EU-level factors with domestic and subnational factors, and their interaction, in one and the same research design.

The renaissance of European integration studies in the 1990s owes much to the influx of first-rate comparativists. They have introduced the central debates of their field, such as different theoretical perspectives on democratization, social movements, political parties, election studies, public opinion, interest groups, public administration, public policy, legislative studies, or elite studies (Anderson 1995; Hix 1994, 1998; Lane 1997b; Mény, Muller, and Quermonne 1994). Unlike international relations scholars who focus on the single question of why states collaborate, and therefore tend to compare the one case of the European Union with other regional or global regimes, comparativists seek to understand the elephant by disaggregating European integration into component processes and events.

This study of top Commission officials is deeply indebted to EU research of the glorious early era, the doldrums years, and the recent renaissance in European integration studies. Like a growing number of EU scholars, I believe that serious mileage can be gained by integrating the study of the European Union into the various streams of political science.

1   Preference formation in the European Commission

Senior civil servants work in two worlds simultaneously: they make and take orders for routine actions in the hierarchical world of public administration, on the basis of formal rules, cost–benefit analysis, and expertise; and they mobilize support for contentious decisions in the non-hierarchical world of politics, through networking and arm-twisting.[1] Combining politics with expertise is indispensable in modern governance. Yet the relationship between these two worlds is delicate and contested, and senior civil servants, who are the interface between them, are directly affected.

Several institutional characteristics of the European Union exacerbate the tension between political agenda-setting and bureaucratic service (Hooghe 1997; Page 1997). In conjunction with the College of Commissioners, the officials of the European Commission have a constitutional obligation to set the legislative agenda because they have exclusive formal competence to draft EU legislation (except in foreign policy and some asylum and immigration issues). This competence sets senior Commission officials apart from their counterparts in national administrations. So they promote the policies of their directorate to private interests, politicians, public, and, last but not least, reluctant Commission colleagues. They direct negotiations between the Commission, on the one hand, and the Council of Ministers' working groups, the European Parliament, and interest groups, on the other. They broker legislative negotiations between the Council of Ministers and the European Parliament. Yet, as career civil servants, they also execute and administer political decisions taken by elected leaders. In that capacity, they provide administrative and managerial leadership to over 4,000 Commission administrators. Second, the mutual responsibilities of national governments and supranational institutions over legislation are contested. The European Union does not have

---

[1] Several researchers have studied hybrid bureaucratic and political roles for national administrations in advanced industrial societies (Aberbach, Rockman, and Putnam 1981; Campbell and Peters 1988; Christensen 1991; Ingraham 1998; Page 1985; Suleiman 1975; Suleiman and Mendras 1995; Wood and Waterman 1993).

a single political executive. The notion that the European Commission is merely an agent of national governments is complicated – and weakened – by competition among the European Parliament, the European Council, and the various functional Councils of Ministers. Interlocking competencies create significant scope for autonomy for senior Commission officials, though it also exposes them to the criticism that they are "a run-away bureaucracy" (Pollack 1997).

Commission officials are just one example of an expanding group of unelected appointees empowered to take authoritative decisions. Like public regulators, central bankers, intergovernmental negotiators, supreme court judges, and officials in international organizations such as the World Trade Organization, the World Bank, or the International Monetary Fund, Commission officials combine limited democratic accountability with authority that rests on expertise, partisan impartiality, and delegated competence. Unelected political actors walk a fine line between "being political" – which means making value-based choices – and "being an expert" – which is presumed to lift them above partisan choice. They undermine their legitimacy if they confound these roles. But this is sometimes difficult to avoid.[2]

In the complex setting of the European Union, Commission officials often find it impossible to resolve the tension between politics, expertise, and impartiality. As "guardians of the Treaties" endowed with unique powers of legislative initiative and considerable executive powers over an extraordinarily broad range of issues, they are intimately involved in making authoritative, that is, political, decisions (Noel 1973). As a body of unelected officials appointed for their expertise, the authoritative power of the Commission is second to none in contemporary advanced democracies. Yet, to the extent that their decisions are perceived as breaching impartiality, they are open to criticisms of partiality.

---

[2] A dramatic example is the US Supreme Court's final ruling in the presidential contest between George W. Bush and Al Gore of December 12, 2000, which split the Court along ideological lines. Leading commentators – left and right – decried the politicization of the Supreme Court. The Justices tread the political terrain with some trepidation. They prefaced their ruling with a reminder to the public of the delicacy of their task: "None are more conscious of the vital limits on judicial authority than are the members of this Court, and none stand more in admiration of the Constitution's design to leave the selection of the President to the people, through their legislatures, and to the political sphere. When contending parties invoke the process of the courts, however, it becomes our unsought responsibility to resolve the federal and constitutional issues the judicial system has been forced to confront" (*George W. Bush et al. vs. Albert Gore, Jr., et al.*, 531 U.S. 949 (Dec. 12, 2000).) In his dissenting opinion, however, Justice John Paul Stevens bluntly conceded that the courts had failed to walk the fine line: "Although we may never know with complete certainty the identity of the winner of this year's presidential election, the identity of the loser is perfectly clear. It is the nation's confidence in the judge as an impartial guardian of the rule of law."

Senior Commission officials have always been conscious of their vulnerable position at the intersection of politics and expertise. But their position has become more precarious as European integration has deepened. In June 1992, a sliver-thin majority of Danish citizens rejected the Maastricht Treaty, which laid the basis for a currency union by 1999 and devolved more national competencies to the European institutions. This sent a shockwave through the European political class. The initial rejection was reversed in the second Danish referendum in 1993, but the rules of the game had changed. The permissive consensus in favor of deepening European integration was shattered, and replaced by a constraining dissensus. The extent to which national sovereignty should be diluted and market integration should be complemented with European-wide political regulation is now a matter of dispute among governments, political parties, and citizens. The action has shifted from near-exclusive interactions between national governments and technocrats to encompass politics in the usual sense: party programs, electoral competition, parliamentary debates and votes, public opinion polls, and public referenda. Elitist decision-making has come to an end.

The Commission has taken the brunt of the blame for public unease with European integration. It reached its absolute low point in public esteem in Spring 1999, when the College of Commissioners resigned in the face of allegations of nepotism, fraud, and mismanagement of funds (see chapter 6). Subsequent investigations into management practices in the bureaucracy provided the context for a top–down reorganization of Commission services and a reshuffling of top officials. These brisk measures shook the confidence of many Commission officials to the core, and they did little to clarify the Commission's uneasy balancing act between politics, expertise, and impartiality.

Top Commission officials, then, are by no means above or beyond the fray of EU politics. Given the powers and responsibilities they have, they are drawn into debates on the chief issues facing the Euro-polity. And their role as the interface between politics and bureaucracy is directly affected by the transition in European governance from a largely functionalist, technocratic system for interstate collaboration to a European polity where objectives and decision rules are openly contested. Where do these people stand on the issues that shape the organization of authority in the European Union? What are their political preferences on European governance?

Questioning top Commission officials

In the European Union, a political struggle is being waged about first principles of political authority. It revolves around four enduring questions, which structure this book. How should authority be structured across territorial layers of government? What should be the scope of public authority in the economy? Should the European elite be democratically accountable? What role(s) should organized interests play in governing Europe? Let us examine these in turn.

What should be the primary locus of authority?

European integration has been undertaken on pragmatic grounds in pursuit of collective benefits and to minimize transaction costs. Yet, it inevitably raises questions concerning the proper allocation of authority. National sovereignty has been eroded (Caporaso 1996; Hooghe 1996; Marks, Hooghe, and Blank 1996; Peterson 1997a; Risse-Kappen 1996; Sandholtz and Zysman 1989; Sbragia 1993; William Wallace 1996). Is this outcome desirable, or should it be reversed? Should member states and the Council of Ministers be strengthened, or should supranational institutions such as the European Commission and the European Parliament be bolstered? In the language of students of European integration, should the EU be *intergovernmental* or *supranational*? This echoes debates about federalism in societies with center–periphery tensions (Elazar 1987; Sbragia 1992, 1993).

What should be the scope of authoritative regulation?

Should the European Union promote *market liberal capitalism*, based on the Anglo-American model, or should it support *regulated capitalism*, rooted in the continental European Rhine model (Hix 1999; Kitschelt, Lange, Marks, and Stephens 1999; Rhodes and van Apeldoorn 1997; Streeck 1996, 1998; Streeck and Schmitter 1991; Wilks 1996)? The conventional left/right cleavage, which emerged out of the industrialization of Europe in the nineteenth and twentieth centuries, reflects contrasting views on the role of the state in the economy (Lipset and Rokkan 1967; Page 1995). This cleavage, the most widely present fissure across European societies, has now spilled over into the European arena.

What should be the principles of authoritative decision-making?

Should the European Union be *democratic*, like its constituent member states, or should it be *technocratic*, like other international organizations for economic cooperation? Political contention on this question goes back to the mid-1960s, when Jean Monnet's method of piecemeal problem solving was thwarted by French president Charles de Gaulle, partly on

grounds of defending national democracy against supranational technocracy (Dinan 1994; Duchêne 1994; Hooghe and Marks 1999). Until the
mid-1980s, decision-making was elite dominated, but it has since been
prized open by wide-ranging public debate (Greven and Pauly 2000;
Schmitter 1996, 2000; Helen Wallace 1993, 1996).

How should EU public interest be reconciled with national pressures?

The European Union is a heterogeneous polity. It knits together some
twenty nationalities; it mobilizes competition and cooperation among a
diverse array of societal groups; and it creates interaction among social,
economic, and territorial institutions from fifteen countries. How should
Commission officials conceive of the public interest? Should they consider themselves architects and guardians of a common European interest
that transcends national, cultural, social, and territorial particularities?
Or should the EU authorities act as agents of particular stakeholders in
European policies – public and private interest groups perhaps, and, last
but not least, national interests? Should an elite speaking for the general
European interest lead Europe, or should its elites be responsive to contending national interests? The debate between these conceptions echoes
the tension in national states between demands for pluralistic responsiveness to societal interests and a more *dirigiste* state tradition, in which
bureaucracies are viewed as valuable instruments for continuity in a fluc-
tuating political environment (Aberbach, Rockman, and Putnam 1981;
Dogan and Pelassy 1984; Mény 1993; Page 1985, 1995; Suleiman 1975,
1984).

These questions are fundamental for all democratic polities, and they
frame debate in the European Union. They bear directly on the role
of the Commission and its top officials. And in turn, top Commission
officials, by virtue of their considerable powers in EU decision-making,
are central voices in that debate. Yet we have had no clear idea about the
preferences of top officials.

Researching preferences

Preferences pose a serious research challenge to social scientists. They
cannot be observed objectively, unless one engages in in-depth structured
interviewing. How have social scientists tackled this problem?

One response has been flatly to reject the significance of preferences. In
the 1970s and 1980s, research on political preferences was largely aban-
doned because they rarely seemed to predict behavior (Searing 1991).

As Robert Putnam once put it, "values and beliefs [were] discarded from political analysis as froth on the mouth of madmen or froth on the waves of history" (Putnam 1976: 103). The psychoanalytical school perceived values and beliefs merely as rationalizations for emotional impulses, while Machiavellians or Marxists claimed they simply cloaked self-interest or class interest. However, the perceived gap between behavior and preferences has less to do with perfidious or contradictory behavior on the part of the objects of study – human actors – than with poor conceptualization and weak methodology on the part of social scientists. For example, many studies focus on case-bound or time-specific preferences rather than on *basic* preferences, that is, generalized beliefs and evaluations about social and political life (George 1979). That is why this book does not focus on top officials' preferences in relation to the Commission's most recent anti-trust decision or the European Parliament's vote on the reform of the structural funds. Instead, it seeks to understand their basic preferences on the four questions of European governance listed above.

Some scholars are skeptical about the value of researching preferences because they harbor unrealistic expectations about their causal power. They place the bar too high. Preferences are general guidelines – heuristic aids to action – not a set of algorithms. They are context-sensitive propensities to action. Preferences should therefore be placed in a causal chain that includes situational, institutional, and interactional factors (George 1979; Putnam 1973; Scharpf 1997b; Searing 1994). Basic orientations serve as "bounded rationalities" or "prisms" through which individuals conceive and respond to objective facts. They profoundly influence, but do not determine, action.

This book describes and explains the basic preferences of top Commission officials. My point of departure is that this is an empirical rather than a deductive endeavor. If preferences help to shape action, then it makes little sense to infer them from action.[3] It is better to research preferences as directly as possible. Structured elite interviews enable one to gain information about preferences that is *independent* of how actors behave. I chose to ask top Commission officials – more than 200 of them – a common set of questions designed to capture basic dimensions of EU governance. Of these, 137 obliged.

This is an empirical enterprise, but it raises conceptual issues of general interest to comparative politics. What motivates elite actors to take

---

[3] Some researchers have been tempted to shortcut the measurement problem by inferring preferences from action. This is the approach implied by the notion of "revealed preferences" in economics. As Fritz Scharpf notes, "whatever may be its status in economic theory, if used as a methodological precept in empirical policy research, it could produce only tautologies instead of explanations" (Scharpf 1997b: 60).

certain positions? How do they form preferences? Most social science explains actions, and, in doing so, explanations often assume preferences to be given – exogenous. But this begs the question why humans have certain preferences in the first place. Understanding the sources of human motivation – the forces that shape human preferences – is the subject of an intense debate that spans diverse theoretical approaches. My aim is to contribute to a theory of preference formation.

Interests and values

EU governance has calculable consequences for the role of the Commission, and for top Commission officials' jobs. Top officials find it difficult to keep silent on the chief issues facing the Euro-polity because they are politicians; their power of initiative involves them intimately in political decisions. Yet, as unelected officials appointed for their expertise, they are presumed to be above the political fray. If they do not handle these tensions well, they may weaken their legitimacy. Commission officials rarely admit it, but their professional lives are at stake in the changing EU polity. It seems sensible for them to take these implications to heart when forming preferences on EU governance. This is what rational choice would predict because it expects rational individuals to act and think in ways that maximize their self-interest.

The idea of the rational, self-interested person has deep roots in Western political thought, and it is a key assumption underlying much social science (Mansbridge 1990). Yet we know that human motivation is complex (Elster 1989, 1994). There are many occasions when individuals' preferences cannot be explained by self-interest – unless one is willing to stretch the concept of "rational self-interest" beyond common usage.[4] Why do some rich people vote for leftist parties that favor income redistribution? What explains the anonymous bravery of thousands who, during World War II, rescued Jews from Nazi persecution in Europe?[5]

---

[4] On conceptual stretching, see Sartori (1991) and Collier and Mahon (1993).

[5] In her book on altruism, Kristen Renwick Monroe seeks to shed light on what motivates ordinary people to risk their lives for others (Monroe 1996). One of her case studies concerns rescuers of Jews under Nazi occupation. She finds that altruists share a particular "perspective, a feeling of being strongly linked to others through a shared humanity and [this] constitutes such a central core to altruists' identity that it leaves them with no choice in their behavior when others are in great need" (Monroe 1996: 234). They adhere, in other words, to values that predispose them to adopt a universalistic worldview. Conventional rational actors do not hold these values. Monroe shows that altruism is not simply a function of socio-cultural or socio-demographic characteristics, or of an economic incentive structure. Her study contributes to the debate about human motivation in that it demonstrates that self-interest is ill suited to explain some human motivations such as altruism.

More often still, rationality – understood as maximizing self-interest – fails to account for variation in the preferences of individuals with similar interests. Why, for example, do Swedes, Danes, Norwegians, or Finns give five to seven times more of their income to developing countries than do equally wealthy US citizens?[6] And why are farmers across the European Union invariably among the most Euroskeptic, even though they have been by far the greatest beneficiaries of EU largess over the past fifty years (Gabel 1998c)?

There is more than one way to bring order to, or categorize, the rich palette of human motivations. Jon Elster, for example, distinguishes three sources of human motivation: rationality (or self-interest), emotions (or passions), and social norms (Elster 1994: 21). In similar vein, Donald Kinder argues that the primary ingredients of political preferences are material interests, group sympathies and resentments, and principles (Kinder 1998: 800). People have preferences because they see benefit in doing so, because they feel emotionally compelled to, or because they believe it is the proper thing to do. Other researchers propose more complex categorizations (for discussions, see Chong 2000; Sears and Funk 1991). These categorizations can be grasped in terms of two basic contending theories of human motivation, an economic model that emphasizes utility maximization as mechanism for preference formation, and a sociological model that stresses socialization.

Utility maximization versus socialization

Utility maximization. Utility theory maintains that individuals are motivated to maximize their utility and that they adjust their preferences accordingly.

The notion that human behavior is governed primarily by utility maximization is particularly strong in economics, and it has gained ground in political science under the denomination of rational choice or public choice (Downs 1967; Moe 1990, 1997; Niskanen 1971; see also Chong 2000). There is much debate among rational choice scholars about what constitutes maximization and what can be put into the utility function,

---

[6] Scandinavian countries give on average 0.74 percent of their GNP as official aid to the developing world – ranging from 0.33 percent in Finland to 1.01 percent in Denmark – against 0.11 percent for the United States. These figures for 1997/98 are drawn from data on aid to third world countries published every year by the Organisation for Economic Co-operation and Development (OECD). There is a widespread belief that the United States does badly in governmental aid but makes up for that through generous non-governmental charities. But this perception does not have a basis in reality. The OECD figures for non-governmental aid show that the United States is on a par with Scandinavian countries: 0.03 percent of GNP against an average of 0.025 percent for the Scandinavian countries.

but two principles seem relatively uncontroversial. The first is rationality, that is, individuals make decisions consistent with reasonable calculations of costs and benefits. The capacity to calculate may be limited by the amount of information available and by external constraints, but the key is that individuals act consistently in relation to their calculations. The second is egoism, that is, that outcomes for oneself weigh more heavily than outcomes for others. However, some utility theorists stretch the definition beyond self-interest.

There is no consensus on a third idea, material hedonism, which says that utility maximization depends primarily on the acquisition of material goods (Sears and Funk 1991). This is a restricted notion of what individuals put in their utility function: it includes material interests, especially money, but not non-material interests, such as social prestige or feelings of moral contentment (Chong 2000; Elster 1989; Levi 1997b; Sears and Funk 1991).

When one conceives of human motivation primarily in terms of maximizing utility, then this has clear implications for one's understanding of preference formation. First of all, utility maximization presumes that individuals act consciously and deliberately. They calculate the costs and benefits of alternatives, and any choice they make is intentional. In Jon Elster's words, "rationality is a variety of intentionality" (Elster 1989: 7). Secondly, utility maximization assumes that rational individuals show no loyalty to existing norms, practices, or preferences when these no longer serve their interests. They adapt preferences to external constraints, and they do so because they expect that such an adaptation will have desired consequences, that is, it will make it easier for them to realize their goals. In the most general way, actors want to make the best of a constrained situation. Unlike Don Quixote, they are reasonable in that they do not seek to tilt at windmills. This reflects what John March and Johan Olsen have called "the logic of consequentiality" (March and Olsen 1989: 160). Thirdly, it follows from this that political preferences are not very stable. Individuals may update their preferences quite frequently, depending on the incentive structures they face.

Socialization. The core idea of socialization theory is that individuals acquire preferences by internalizing norms, values, and principles embodied by the groups or institutions that are important to their lives. This view emphasizes the centrality of group ties and longstanding personal dispositions, which organize individual preferences and shape behavior (Converse 1964; Johnston 1998; Kinder 1998; Rohrschneider 1994, 1996; Searing 1969, 1986; Searing, Wright, and Rabinowitz 1976; Verba 1965).

The notion that group ties and values – longstanding, deeply anchored dispositions – govern human behavior has a strong foundation in
sociology as well as in psychology (Glenn 1980; McGuire 1993). It is the
dominant paradigm among students of political attitudes and preferences
(Kinder 1998). How these dispositions become anchored as part of an
individual's identity and how they shape this person's preferences and behavior towards new objects or issues are matters of debate. Yet scholars in
this socialization paradigm concur in seeking explanations in sociological
and psychological processes – not in human instinct for rationality.

Individuals develop preferences for social reasons that cannot be attributed to direct material incentives or coercion. The absence of a strong
association between self-interest and preferences is the key difference
between a socialization and a utility maximization model. Socialization
directs the individual away from the self to the socializing group. The
original meaning of the word "to socialize," after all, is "to render social,
to make fit for living in society [or in the particular group]" (Conover
1991: 131).[7] This notion of a non-material, social basis of preferences is
crucial for the socialization perspective.

Another widely shared notion is that socialization is a gradual, in-
cremental process. Individuals typically internalize values or preferences
through innumerable encounters with particular political norms or practices. Socialization takes time (Verba 1965). The longer one is exposed
to particular stimuli, the more one is likely to absorb these influences
(Kinder and Sears 1985; Glenn 1980).

To be sure, socialization is not always gradual. It is occasionally brought
about by dramatic single episodes. One-time, powerful events – wars,
historic elections, or protests – may jolt individuals into changing political

---

[7] A critical issue in the socialization literature, which bears on my topic indirectly, concerns
the micro-processes of socialization. Through what processes are norms and values transmitted? Socialization scholars generally distinguish four processes, which range from the
self-conscious to the subconscious. At one end of the continuum stands persuasion, or
social learning, whereby individuals are convinced through self-conscious cognition that
particular norms and causal understandings are correct and ought to guide their own
behavior. Second, social influence refers to the process whereby individuals' desire to
maintain or increase social status or prestige induces them to conform to group norms.
The group rewards an individual's behavior with back-patting and status markers or punishes it with opprobrium and status devaluation (Checkel 1998; Johnston 1998). Some
scholars are reluctant to consider social influence or pressure as a genuine socialization
process because it does not necessarily require that individuals actually change their preferences. Social influence is "public conformity without private acceptance" (Johnston
1998). A third process is social mimicking, whereby an individual "inherits" or copies
norms and behavior without putting much conscious thought into it (Beck and Jennings
1991; Johnston 1998). Finally, attitude crystallization refers to a largely subconscious
process whereby individuals extend deeply held, stable attitudes to new attitude objects
through cognitive or affective processes (Converse 1964; Sears and Valentino 1997).

preferences. The open, still unshaped minds of young adults appear to be particularly susceptible to this type of socialization (Sears and Valentino 1997). It is not impossible for adults too to be "shocked" by such events, and to embrace a different value system as a result of it. However, this usually demands an "exacting and unusually powerful social situation" (Kinder and Sears 1985: 724).

There is less agreement on how internalized dispositions guide preference formation on new political objects, that is, the psychological processes underlying political judgment. Some scholars conceive of these processes as primarily cognitive, others as emotive/affective. The former conceive of people as "cognitive misers" who have limited capacity for processing information and who therefore must use cues or prior knowledge to reach judgments on new objects (Conover and Feldman 1984; Taylor 1981). The latter scholars emphasize the emotive/affective aspects of political judgment (Sears 1993; Sears and Funk 1991). Yet common to these explanations is the psychological notion of belief or affect consistency, which maintains that individuals' quest for consistency in beliefs or affects is a basic human desire (Sears 1993; Sears and Funk 1991).

The leading cognitive model, the on-line model, assumes that people keep summary evaluations ("running tallies") of important political processes or principles. They use these to spontaneously evaluate new objects and, although they regularly update their tallies, they quickly forget the details that prompted the updating in the first place (Lodge and Steenbergen 1995). So dispositions – running tallies – are not immutably fixed; they are incrementally updated, and yet they provide cognitive guidance to individuals in evaluating new experiences.

David Sears' symbolic politics theory is the most prominent example on the emotive side (Sears 1993; Sears and Funk 1991). The model holds that people acquire stable affective responses to particular symbols through socialization.[8] These dispositions influence preferences on new political objects in the following way. Each political object is composed of one or more symbols, and these symbols determine which dispositions are invoked. Individuals automatically transfer the internalized affects from these invoked symbols to the new object.[9]

---

[8] The strongest dispositions, namely party identification, political ideology, and racial prejudice, are called symbolic dispositions, and they may last a lifetime.

[9] Cognitive and affective models also see eye to eye in that they emphasize the prevalence of non-rational over rational processes. David Sears summarizes the contrast with a rational perspective: "The rational choice view depicts a deliberate decision maker objectively evaluating costs and benefits. The cognitive miser approach sees a cerebral being desperately trying to husband his or her limited psychic energy in the midst of a torrent of information. The symbolic processor is reacting in a gut-level, automatic manner to emotionally evocative political and social objects" (Sears 1993: 137).

When one conceives of human motivation primarily in terms of living by predispositions, this has clear consequences for preference formation. First of all, a socialization perspective presumes that individuals react instinctively to cognitive cues or affects. People follow established traditions and conform to social norms in a relatively reflexive fashion. They do not calculate probable costs and benefits (Sears 1993). Second, the centrality of socialization means that individuals show considerable loyalty to internalized norms, practices, or preferences. Individuals hold on to these, even when they cease to serve their interests. What motivates them is, in March and Olsen's terms, "a logic of appropriateness" (March and Olsen 1989). They ask: Who am I? What group am I part of? So what is the proper thing to do? They do not ponder on what is in it for them. That is why the controversy between the two paradigms is often presented as a conflict between values and interests (Chong 2000; Sears and Funk 1991). The implication of this is that basic preferences are perceived to be relatively stable, even rigid. They do not adjust easily to changing circumstances; rather, individuals have a tendency to integrate new political objects or situations into familiar value systems.

Utility maximization and socialization perspectives tap distinct, yet complementary sources of human motivations. Explanations for preference formation that privilege one above the other produce parsimonious models, but the truth is that both interests (utility) and values (socialization) are part and parcel of human life. Why would we, then, want to exclude one or the other?

A model of interests and values

For many years, the attempt to combine utility maximization and socialization appeared to be as fruitless as combining water and fire. Their ontological and epistemological foundations seemed just too different. Yet, recent work by Dennis Chong has carved out a path for a genuinely integrated approach to preference formation (Chong 1996, 2000).

Chong, one of a handful of political scientists with active research in both traditions, identifies some key weaknesses of each approach. Chong's main critique of the socialization model is that it does not provide a convincing account of value or norm formation, that is, how group norms originate and why they differ, why people conform to group norms, why groups put so much effort into imposing their norms on others, and when values or norms change (see Chong 2000: 36–7; 1996: 2082). Socialization theory emphasizes the generality and stability of attitudes, and underemphasizes conflict over ways of life. "A static model built on relatively fixed dispositions encounters difficulty explaining changes in norms and values" (Chong 2000: 45). Chong makes a case for treating norms and values strategically, and he identifies ways in which interests and rational decision-making support values and norms. His main argument is that current dispositions are often based on past strategic calculations. Or, to put it differently, the reasons for internalizing norms in the first place often have to do with rational interest.

In fairness to the socialization perspective, considerable work has been done to specify the conditions under which internalized dispositions may change (e.g. Glenn 1980; Searing, Wright, and Rabinowitz 1976; Sears and Valentino 1997). Research specifying the micro-foundations of the socialization model, such as the on-line model and the symbolic politics model, brings to light the psychological processes by which change in dispositions occurs. However, these explanations rarely reserve a space for interest. Chong's argument, in contrast, is that rational calculation enters into and shapes socialization.

Chong criticizes the rationality assumption in the utility model because it does not specify how norms, practices, and values – internalized through socialization – facilitate rational decision-making. The idea of bounded rationality, popularized by Herbert Simon, creates an opening to bring values into rational decision-making. Bounded or procedural rationality is relevant for "a person who is limited in computational capacity, and who searches very selectively through large realms of possibilities in order to discover what alternatives of action are available... The search is incomplete, often inadequate, based on uncertain information and partial ignorance, and usually terminated with the discovery of satisfactory, not optimal, courses of action" (Simon 1985: 295). Human processing of information under these imperfect conditions has been a major topic in cognitive psychology (Kinder 1998 presents an overview). Chong, like cognitive psychologists, starts from the assumption that individuals are fallible humans with myopia or plainly limited brains. In this context, norms, practices, values, and group ties become indispensable. They provide powerful cues to help people figure out their utility and choose among alternatives.

It is true that many rational choice analyses now routinely examine limitations to available information and constraints on information processing. Yet norms, values, and dispositions appear in these models as disturbing factors that derail rational calculation, or they are relegated to a residual category (for discussions see Kato 1996; Nørgaard 1996; Weingast 1995; Yee 1997). Chong presents an argument in which norms and values become an integral part of rational calculation.

Chong goes on to develop a general model of preference formation "that combines a social psychological model in which identities and values are socialized through socialization with an economic model in which belief and value formation are motivated by external or instrumental benefits" (2000: 7). Preference formation depends on two factors: (a) the costs and benefits (material and social incentives) of present alternatives, and (b) dispositions, which have themselves been formed by past investments in values, group identities, and knowledge. So short-term and long-term factors combine to explain a political preference on a particular object.

This model of preference formation constitutes a breakthrough. It identifies dependencies among apparently incompatible paradigms. The model also has a simple structure. Preference is the function of two independent variables: strength and direction of dispositions for each alternative, and cost/benefit calculations for each alternative. The key task, then, is to estimate parameters for each variable. Furthermore, the model offers a plausible interpretation of complex human motivation. The sociological perspective conceives of individuals as social beings – *homines sociologici* – who live their lives to a large extent in the shadow of effective social norms and values. Utility maximization suggests that individuals are self-interested beings – *homines economici* – who consciously calculate the costs and benefits of their actions and preferences. In Chong's model, the question is no longer whether individuals live in utilitarian cocoons or sociological cages (Searing 1991). Rather, the task is to understand the interplay between socialization and utility maximization and to specify the conditions under which the balance between the two varies. When, for example, do career concerns weigh more heavily than ideology for top Commission officials on basic issues of EU governance? Are officials more likely to be mindful of their career when they choose between a supranational or intergovernmental Union than when the choice is between a neoliberal or regulated European economy? Does it depend on where they work in the Commission, their nationality, and their length of service in the Commission? What makes values trump interests, or vice versa? These concrete questions raise conceptual and methodological issues, which now need to be addressed.

An empirical approach

How can one develop a scientific, that is to say falsifiable, theory of preference formation?

Workable concepts. A testable, falsifiable model requires definitions that unambiguously separate key concepts from each other. This necessitates some hard choices and, though these choices are inherently debatable, they should also be transparent. A model that examines the relative impact of utility and socialization should avoid slippery concepts.

The trickiest issue concerns the boundaries of *utility*. What could a rational individual reasonably seek to maximize? At the heart of utility theory *stricto sensu* is a definition of rationality that emphasizes the maximization of economic self-interest, often expressed as money (Kato 1996; Yee 1997). In rational choice jargon, this is the thick version of rationality. It transfers the notion of rationality used in the neoclassical economic model to the analysis of politics. Rational interest is defined in terms of (a) the material wellbeing and (b) individuals' own personal life (or that of their immediate family). Both definitional conditions are contested.

Margaret Levi represents the opposite pole of the debate when she recommends using a thin variant of rationality in which individuals act consistently in relation to their preferences. In this view, any kind of object or value could be maximized, including economic self-interest, economic group interest, non-economic interests, power, security, status and respect, ideas or norms, an interest in pleasure, or an interest in developing a coherent understanding of society. There is no reason, then, to stick to the assumption that individuals are self-interested; they could seek to maximize the utility of their family, their community, their party, or their country. The only methodological requirement is that researchers should define the value *ex ante* (Levi 1997b).

If one were to adopt a thick notion of utility, one would focus on whether Commission officials could draw personal financial benefit from a particular attitude. Were one to adopt a thin notion of rationality, the utility function of Commission officials could encompass personal power, the power of the Commission, the status of their nationality, or maximizing the European Public Good.[10]

A thin version of utility maximization can easily produce tautology: whatever people do becomes a revealed preference.[11] A thin notion is also at odds with the common sense understanding of rational interest. Moreover, by refusing to exclude the most unambiguous non-self-interested goods, it opens the door for nonsensical arguments in which heroic acts are explained in terms of altruism, or philanthropy is presumed to be motivated by the desire to maximize the pleasure of being good. This confounds values and interests.

---

[10] For example, the two founders of public choice, Gordon Tullock (1965) and Anthony Downs (1967), interpreted self-interest broadly to include suprapersonal values of various sorts, for example regarding good policy or the public interest (Moe 1997: 457 fn.1). As I argue below, this amounts to rather creative conceptual stretching of the neoclassical definition of self-interest.

[11] This is why Levi advises researchers to specify the utility function *ex ante* (Levi 1997b:24).

It seems therefore sensible to limit utility maximization to material interests. Many rational choice analysts restrict utility to an individual's own material interest. However, I propose to broaden this to include material group interest. It seems reasonable to extend the motivation of utility maximization to individuals acting on behalf of their groups when these individuals share in expected group benefits.

Where does this leave us? Following Levi's suggestion, I define *ex ante* what is included in the utility function of top officials. The single most important thing that should jolt a top official into strategic preference formation is a concern for his (or her) professional career. Top officials work in an environment where competition for attention from principals, agenda setting, resources, prestige, influence, and promotion is harsh. To be ignored or bypassed by their principals once or twice may publicly taint an ambitious official; to be demoted to a peripheral service is equivalent to semi-permanent exile; to be sidetracked to an advisory position off the normal hierarchical line usually means premature career death. Top Commission officials cannot easily be fired, and they earn very handsome salaries. Yet, barring these, there is considerable scope for the College of Commissioners to affect top officials' professional careers and so one may expect rational officials to take this into account when forming their preferences.

My definition of utility maximization focuses on material interests beyond the neoclassical concern with individual wealth maximization. I expect rational Commission officials to be motivated primarily by individual career concerns. Yet I think it also likely that they may maximize group benefits. For example, it seems sensible to categorize a top official whose preferences reflect opportunities to maximize economic payoffs for his country as motivated by utility maximization. After all, he can reasonably expect that he (and his family) will share in the benefit.[12] I do not wish to rule out a link between material group interest and material individual interest.

Defining utility maximization broadly has a strategic advantage for hypothesis testing. It gives utility factors the greatest possible chance to be picked up in a contest with socialization variables. This is important because socialization theory has long been the dominant paradigm in the study of political attitudes and preferences (Chong 2000; Kinder 1998). Utility maximization is a newcomer.

---

[12] The reader may be surprised that I mostly use masculine pronouns when referring to Commission officials. To use "she or he" would create a false impression of gender balance in an institution where only 6.5 percent of top Commission officials are female. Instead, I employ feminine pronouns only occasionally to reflect the extreme gender imbalance in the top layers of the Commission bureaucracy.

Operationalizing *socialization* is more straightforward. Socialization theory suggests that a top official's preferences on EU governance reflect internalized norms, values, and principles embodied by the groups or institutions that have been important in his life.

Most theorists conceptualize socialization as a gradual process that takes considerable time. They also expect experiences in childhood or young adulthood to be more formative than experiences later in life, for example at mid-career. Yet it is possible that "exacting and unusually powerful" (Kinder and Sears 1985: 724) one-time events may jolt top officials into internalizing particular preferences, although these occurrences should be rare. For example, one might expect the resignation of the Commission in 1999 to constitute such an event. However, socialization requires, most of the time, sustained exposure to consistently transmitted norms and values. Socialization variables should therefore be sensitive to time.

Utility maximization presumes that top officials are guided by tangible, immediate career benefits, whereas socialization implies that top officials' preferences reflect intangible, longstanding dispositions that were internalized through participation in groups or institutions over time. This way, the two basic logics are unambiguously distinct.

Testable hypotheses. It is one thing to be able to recognize alternative human motivations when one encounters them. The next step is to hypothesize circumstances in which one may expect socialization or utility maximization to shape top officials' preferences on basic issues of EU governance.

My guiding hypothesis is that top officials' preferences are rooted in experience. However, not every experience shapes their calculations or dispositions to EU governance. What is needed is an approach that enables one to distinguish relevant from irrelevant experiences. Of the many opportunity structures encountered by top officials, which induce them to adjust their preferences to further their career? And which internalized values are likely to shape their preferences on EU governance?

A focus on institutional rules allows one to think systematically about the contexts in which utility or socialization take place.[13] The concept of institution or institutional rules is simpler, yet more general, than

---

[13] This ties in with the resurgent study of institutions in rational choice and the literature on socialization and learning. Rational choice institutionalism and historical or sociological institutionalism conceive of individuals as rule bound (for overviews, see Aspinwall and Schneider 2000; Hall and Taylor 1996; Ostrom 1986, 1991; Thelen 1999). That is, in explaining preferences and behavior, they give analytical priority to the particular institutional rules that constrain individuals at a given time.

opportunity structures, incentive structures, reference groups, socialization agents or schools, churches, and family – often employed by utility maximization or socialization perspectives to describe particular contexts.

What are the relevant institutional contexts for top Commission officials? It seems reasonable to expect top Commission officials to be influenced by multiple institutional contexts simultaneously. Why is that so?

In a simple world, a single institution would mold top officials' preferences. If the Commission were a strongly bounded institution with perfect control over top officials' working life, it would be Commission interests and values that shape its employees' preferences. The question would then be *how* top officials acquire Commission preferences. Is it because the Commission is an effective socialization agent (a process of value transfer), or because it controls top officials' careers (a process of strategic calculation and adjustment)?

Yet the Commission lacks the insulation to mold its employees' preferences uniformly. Top Commission officials have diverse cultural and educational backgrounds and very different professional experiences. So they start as a diverse bunch; and the Commission's way of working permits them to remain heterogeneous. The Commission is a compartmentalized bureaucracy, where many directorates-general resemble self-governing statelets. This makes it possible for top officials – the bosses of these statelets – to mold the norms and habits of their own small world to their own image, and thus to persevere in being different. Socialization scholars tell us that such institutional conditions are not conducive to creating a homogeneous, single-purposive service. This contrasts sharply with many national administrations in Europe.

Second, the Commission's grip on the professional lives of its top employees is subject to national governmental and, in a number of cases, partisan control. National governments or political parties can and do influence Commission officials' careers indirectly. They monitor closely whether the Commission abides by the agreed national quota for senior positions. They often draw up a shortlist of candidates for high-level positions that are reserved for candidates from outside the Commission (*parachutage*), and they may have de facto "right of first refusal" for such positions. Finally, they usually enjoy ties with the personal cabinets of the commissioner of their nationality or party allegiance, and these cabinets are the brokers in Commission personnel policy. These flaws in Commission control over its own employees do not induce rational top officials to adjust their preferences to the Commission's, as a cursory analysis of their utility function would suggest.

Third, the wider political context influences top Commission officials deeply. As noted above, Commission officials are players in a multi-level political system in which authority is shared vertically across territorial levels and horizontally between several EU and national institutions. In many (now most) policy areas, no institution – not the Commission or the Council or the European Parliament, not national governments – can take authoritative decisions unilaterally (Hooghe and Marks 2001, appendix 1; Pollack 1995, 2000; Schmitter 1996). Top officials need to be attuned to national governments, political parties, and the public, as well as to the European institutions – and not only, or even primarily, to the Commission. The European system of multi-level governance plugs top Commission officials into multiple institutional contexts.[14]

These observations shatter the notion of the Commission as a unitary institution capable of controlling the preferences of its employees. What comes into view is a multi-layered institutional context, where institutions smaller than the Commission, such as the cabinet or the directorate-general (DG), loom larger, and institutions outside the Commission, such as political parties, national administrations, or national political systems, come closer. Top Commission officials' preferences on European governance are likely to be shaped by experiences inside and outside the Commission.

We now have the building blocks for a testable model of preference formation in the Commission. By combining type of institutional context with logic of influence, it is possible to pin down a limited number of plausible influences on top Commission officials' preferences. These are presented in figure 1.1.

Preference formation in the Commission

Figure 1.1 summarizes how the life and career paths of top officials may shape their preferences on EU governance. The cells in figure 1.1 apply socialization and utility maximization to institutional contexts inside the Commission and institutional contexts outside the Commission. I have two general expectations:

---

[14] There is a growing literature on how a system in which authority is diffused across territorial levels – a multi-level polity – influences the preferences and behavior of public opinion (Anderson and Gabel 2000), political parties (Bomberg 1998; Hix 1999; Marks and Wilson 1998, 2000), trade unions (Ebbinghaus 1999; Ebbinghaus and Visser 1997; Turner 1996), social movements (Imig and Tarrow 1997, 2001; Marks and McAdam 1995; Tarrow 1995, 1999), firms and business representation (Coen 1997; Greenwood 1997), national and regional governments (Hooghe 1996; Marks 1996a,b; Marks et al. 1996), structures of interest intermediation (Falkner 1996, 1999), and policy networks (Kohler-Koch and Eising 1999). It seems reasonable to assume that top Commission officials' desires and deeds too should be affected by their involvement in various institutional settings of this multi-level system.

Logic of influence (causal mechanism)	Source of influence (type of institutional context)	
	Type I Inside the Commission	Type II Outside the Commission
Socialization	Length of service in Commission Length of service in DG/policy area Cabinet experience	Experience in national administration Experience in political system Political party identification
Hybrid category	Delors factor ↓	Parachutage ↓
Utility maximization	Years to retirement Position in DG/policy area	National economic interest Character of national network Size of national quota

Figure 1.1 Top officials and preference formation on EU governance.

1. Basic preferences on EU governance are likely to reflect a mix of socialization and utility factors. Most people are, most of the time, both rational and moral.
2. These preferences are likely to be shaped by experiences *outside* as well as *inside* the Commission. The Commission and its components (DG and cabinet) constitute merely one part of a multi-faceted institutional environment, which also includes national political parties, national administrations, national networks for socializing in Brussels, or national political systems. Let us examine these.

Commission – socialization vs. utility maximization

We have unmasked the Commission as a weak institution, but it would be rash to dismiss it altogether as a potential influence on top officials' preferences. A typical top official clocks workdays of close to ten hours, five or six days a week, and that should give plenty of time for socialization or utility calculation.

The prevailing assumption in much work on European integration is that the Commission is pro-integrationist. This assumption characterizes the first major theory of European integration, neofunctionalism.

The theory argues that supranational actors care about the provision of a variety of collective goods that would not otherwise be provided, and this brings them to want to shift authority to the European level (Haas 1958; Lindberg 1963; Lindberg and Scheingold 1970; Sandholtz 1996; Sandholtz and Stone Sweet 1998; Schmitter 1969, 1970; Stone Sweet and Sandholtz 1997, 1998). So the Commission embodies certain predispositions, and one may expect top officials to internalize these values while working for the Commission.

Many new institutionalist students of European integration concede that Commission officials' motivations are more complex, but they maintain that supporting pro-integrationist positions is usually the most important (Pierson 1996; Schneider 1997; Steunenberg 1996; Tsebelis and Kreppel 1998).[15] So parsimony leads them to emphasize that Commission officials are primarily motivated to defend the Commission's institutional interest in deeper integration, and they do so out of rational self-interest. This utilitarian line of reasoning builds on public choice theories that argue that bureaucrats support bureau-maximizing strategies – budget expansion, more bureaucratic discretion, or better status and work conditions – because that maximizes their own career benefits (especially when they are unlikely to retire soon) (Blais and Dion 1991; Calvert, McCubbins, and Weingast 1989; Dunleavy 1991; McCubbins, Noll, and Weingast 1987; Moe 1984, 1990; Niskanen 1971; Ringquist 1995; Wood and Waterman 1991, 1993).

Policy area/DG – socialization vs. utility maximization

Departmental divisions in the Commission are more marked than in national bureaucracies (Peterson 1999; Richardson 1996). David Coombes, an early student of the Commission, described the institution as a collection of feudal fiefdoms (Coombes 1970). So it is plausible that parts of the Commission shape top officials' views.

---

[15] In a recent article, George Tsebelis and Geoffrey Garrett advance a more nuanced view (2000). They speculate on two reasons why the Commission – and, by implication, Commission officials – may *not* take integrationist positions. One refers to recruitment rules. One might expect the Commission to side with the less integrationist Council, because it is the latter that appoints the Commission (though the 1999 Amsterdam Treaty and the 1999 Commission resignation crisis have given the European Parliament the constitutional power *and* the political authority to vet these appointments.) The second argument brings in left/right ideology. Tsebelis and Garrett argue that the "technocrats in the Commission would tend to be quite conservative on most regulatory matters, and hence they would be more likely to side with the Council when it was dominated by right-wing governments" (Tsebelis and Garrett 2000: 31); in other words, they would prefer less to more integration for ideological reasons. I take up both factors, and reformulate them to examine variation *within* the Commission in pro-integrationist preferences.

This expectation finds support in a diverse literature, which is best known under the denomination of "new governance." The main argument is that authority is increasingly compartmentalized in specialized public–private policy networks – technical groupings such as networks for health and safety in the workplace, for clean air, information technology, product standardization, or banking. Although functionally narrow, these networks are often territorially inclusive, as they incorporate specialists from supranational, national, regional, and local levels (March and Olsen 1984; Mazey and Richardson 1993; Peters 1994; Peterson 1995a, 1997a; Richardson 1997, 1998; for an overview see Hix 1998). The tendency to cluster authority in policy networks is strongest in federal or multi-level polities and in technical policy sectors (Hix 1999; Majone 1995; Peterson and Bomberg 1999). Scholars have found the European Union to be a propitious arena for policy networks (Börzel 1997; Héritier 1996, 1999b; Jachtenfuchs and Kohler-Koch 1995, 1997; Kohler-Koch 1996; Majone 1994a,b; Rhodes, Bache, and George 1996; see also Pollack 1995; Radaelli 1999).

Policy networks connect top officials with their functional counterparts in the national or subnational governments while insulating them from the Commission as a whole. A top official charged with social policy may then have little in common with his colleagues in a market-making directorate-general. There are two ways to hypothesize about how this social world may impact on his preferences. According to socialization theory, values acquired over years of experience in social and redistributional issues are likely to trump new experiences, for example, were the official to move to competition policy. In contrast, utility maximization would expect that where someone works at time t is more important than what he did previously. Preferences are adjusted to the exigencies of the job at hand.

Cabinet socialization

Cabinets are the heart and soul of Commission politics; they are where national interests, party political priorities, European political goals, and technocratic policy-making meet. This requires from cabinet members a distinct set of attitudes.

It is possible that officials self-select: they become members of a cabinet because they already have the values and attitudes that make a cabinet member successful, and their cabinet experience reinforces prior internalized values. It is also possible that cabinet members learn these values on the job. The bottom line is that officials with cabinet experience are likely to have different preferences on key issues of EU governance from those who have not.

Experience from a national administration

Top Commission officials negotiate day in day out with many actors, but none are so prominent as the representatives of national governments *par excellence*: national civil servants. It is the role of national civil servants to speak on behalf of their country. There is, then, a good chance that national civil servants bring to the negotiating table concerns – values and interests – that go against Commission concerns.

Divergence between supranational and national concerns is the core assumption of liberal intergovernmentalism. The thrust of this theory is that the EU is an instrument for national governments to maximize the national economic benefits of international cooperation while minimizing the loss of national sovereignty (Garrett 1992; Hoffmann 1966, 1982; Moravcsik 1993, 1994, 1998; Milward 1992; Milward and Sørensen 1993; Streeck 1996; Taylor 1991, 1996). National civil servants are expected to voice these concerns, and, given that more than half of top Commission officials were at one point national civil servants, it is possible that national interest still guides them in the Commission.

National economic interest – motivation for maximizing utility

National economic interest may also shape top officials' preferences on EU governance in a more direct fashion. If EU politics is all about countries' economic interest, it seems rational for Commission officials to act as agents of national governments. They would work to maximize EU funding for their countries, or to push for policies that benefit their countries.

National interest is consistent with a group conception of utility maximization. It presumes that top officials are motivated to maximize their country's economic interest, and thereby increase their own utility.

Learning in a political system

"What an individual believes about the political process is learned from observation of that process" (Verba 1965: 533). Socialization theory predicts that growing up and participating in a particular political system shapes political values. The imprint of socialization in a particular national setting can remain even when the individual moves to a different system (Rohrschneider 1994, 1996).

Identifying with a political party

Ideology and party identification reflect and structure the political preferences of ordinary citizens (Converse 1976; Kinder 1998; Sears 1993; Weisberg 1998). Socialization research demonstrates that they are yet more powerful for political elites and opinion leaders (Jennings 1992; Zaller 1992). Hence, it is likely that party identification shapes top officials' preferences on European governance.

A series of recent articles reveals that EU politics is structured by a left/right ideological dimension imported from domestic politics, and a newer territorial dimension pitting nationalism against supranationalism (Caporaso 1996; Hix 1999; Hix and Lord 1997; Hooghe 1998; Hooghe and Marks 1999; Hooghe, Marks, and Wilson 2000; Marks and Steenbergen 2000; Marks and Wilson 2000; Risse-Kappen 1996; Sbragia 1993; Thomassen and Schmitt 1999). This work demonstrates that political parties are central in framing contention in the European Union (Hix 1999, 1998; Marks and Steenbergen 2000; Marks and Wilson 2000).

Utility maximization and nationality

No person is born a European. Commission officials enter the Commission as French, Italian, Danish, or Greek – not as Europeans. Moreover, exclusive national citizenship is the norm. It is possible to change one's nationality – though that route is usually strewn with legal obstacles, lengthy procedures, and expensive legal bills. Rare is the person who picks her nationality. And it is impossible to give up nationality altogether.

Nationality is a central criterion for promotion in the Commission, and this is likely to make it a critical resource – or handicap – for top officials. Rational-calculating top officials are likely to have different preferences on EU governance depending on whether their nationality does well or badly under current rules.

Recruitment – utility or socialization?

Several variables are not easily categorized as capturing utility maximization or socialization. Rather than forcing these into one or the other mold, I take a cautious methodological path and define them at this stage as hybrids of socialization and utility maximization. The arrows in figure 1.1 register my guess as to which of the two logics they lean to. The two hybrid variables pertain to distinct recruitment paths to top positions in the Commission.

Parachutage. Officials who are recruited from outside the Commission to take up a top position are called parachutists. The key difference from recruitment-through-the-ranks is that national governments are more intimately involved in the recruitment of parachutists. It seems likely therefore that parachuted appointees would be inclined to adjust their preferences to the wishes of their career master – their national government.

Delors factor. Officials who were recruited into a top position during the Delors years (1985–94) are sometimes referred to as the "Delors mafia." Former Commission president Jacques Delors and his cabinet took a keen interest in nominating the right people to key positions. Delors demanded from his employees extraordinary efforts to achieve the internal market and its flanking policies by the 1992 deadline. It is likely that work for Delors has shaped top officials' preferences in distinctive ways.

Chapter 2 introduces the data, the methodology, and the people at the center of this inquiry. Chapter 3 examines where Commission officials stand on basic issues of governance; that is, whether the EU should promote regulated capitalism or market liberalism, whether it should have supranational or intergovernmental institutions, whether decision-making should be democratic or technocratic, and whether top officials should defend the general European interest or be responsive to national interests. I establish the relevance of these four dimensions with the help of factor analysis, which I complement by introducing the reader to in-depth interviews with 137 top officials.

Chapters 4–7 take up these four dimensions one by one. Chapter 4 examines where top officials stand on a supranational versus an intergovernmental polity. Chapter 5 explains why some top officials support regulated capitalism whereas others favor market liberalism. Chapter 6 analyzes top officials' preferences on the role of the Commission in the European polity – should it be an administrative agent or a government-like principal? Chapter 7 examines preferences on how supranational authorities should accommodate multinationality.

2   Men (and women) at Europe's helm

Between June 1995 and February 1997 I conversed with 137 directors-general, deputy directors-general, directors, and senior advisors of the European Commission in semi-structured interviews lasting on average 79 minutes.[1] I also asked them to mail back a structured questionnaire containing behavioral and attitudinal questions. By May 1997, I had received 106 mail questionnaires. These interviews and mail questionnaires provide the empirical basis for this book. I elaborate below five important elements in this research: the context, the organization, sampling, interviewing, and the people.

The context

The European Union is at a crossroads between 1995 and 1997. Its future is deeply contested and uncertain, and yet Europe's elites, if not its citizens, seem determined to integrate deeper and faster. Three major issues dominate the headlines and structure the daily dealings of top Commission officials: economic and monetary union (EMU) – at first, the plan's survival, and, later, the conditions of implementation; the ban from the European internal market of British beef infected by BSE (bovine spongiform encephalopathy – "mad cow disease"); and preparations for the 1996–7 intergovernmental conference, which would culminate in the 1999 Amsterdam Treaty. Two deeper concerns cloud EU politics during that period. Public opinion polls register a rapid rise in public dissatisfaction with European integration, and, on the economic front, most European countries suffer from persistently high unemployment whereas the US economy is booming. This is the political background against which I probe top Commission officials' basic preferences on EU governance.

---

[1] The length of the interviews ranged from 30 to 180 minutes. Two officials insisted on talking off the record, so I made extensive notes. The transcripts for the 137 interviews amount to over 3,500 single-spaced pages of text.

Summer 1995

A bleak mood hangs over the Commission when I begin my first major round of interviews in June 1995. Economic and monetary union, the centerpiece of the Maastricht Treaty due to start by January 1997, appears in jeopardy. According to the latest forecasts, the annual public deficits in Europe's key economies, France and Germany, are set to overshoot by a long way the maximum target of 3 percent of gross domestic product (GDP). It does not seem likely that the European economies will recover in time to meet EMU deadlines. Economic growth in 1995 is sluggish – around 2 percent. Only Ireland, Sweden, and Finland are doing well. Most economists forecast worse growth figures for 1996, and unemployment in the EU as a whole is already above 11 percent. In June 1995, the ministers of finance agree, over the objections of the Commission, that the initial starting date for the third and final stage of EMU – January 1, 1997 – is "not realistic." At the European Council of Cannes in June, the heads of state and government in effect abandon the 1997 starting date (Cameron 1997). Proponents of deeper European integration lose heart. Their despair deepens when Europe's government leaders renew their promise of EU membership to the new democracies of Central and Eastern Europe over the heads of a skeptical public opinion, while paying minimal heed to warnings that, without institutional reforms, enlargement will bring EU decision-making grinding to a halt.[2] And, on top of that, an uncooperative British Conservative government besieged by its nationalist wing frustrates day-to-day EU politics. The heady Euro-optimism under Jacques Delors' Commission presidency seems light-years away.

Since 1990, public opinion polls have shown a steady erosion of public support for European integration. The Eurobarometer poll data for 1995 and 1996 are particularly ominous for proponents of European integration. In the summer of 1995 – for the first time since 1981 – the

---

[2] The Cannes European Council accepts the Commission's white paper on enlargement, which lays out how Central and East European countries can adopt EU single market regulations. It stresses that, to qualify for EU membership, prospective members need to reform their legal and administrative infrastructure, and not just "transpose" EU legislation into their domestic systems. Yet the white paper says little about requirements in social, environmental, or other areas outside the internal market, and it is silent on how EU institutions and policies should adapt to make enlargement feasible.

The first official endorsement of EU membership as a goal for Central and East European countries – in delicately crafted words – dates from the Copenhagen European Council in June 1993. So mid-1995, the consensus among Europe's elite in favor of enlargement is still fresh and fragile. For a discussion of the evolution of elite opinion, and the Commission's critical agenda-setting role in this, see Sedelmeier and Wallace (2000).

percentage of respondents who believe that "EU membership is a good thing" drops to 51 percent, and it will dip to 48 percent in early 1996. Support for EU membership is not only on the decline in the traditionally skeptical countries, such as the United Kingdom, Denmark, and, since its entrance in 1995, Sweden. It also drops precipitously among publics that used to be staunch supporters: Spanish (from 80 percent in 1990 to 51 percent mid-1995), Belgians (72 percent to 52 percent), and Germans (72 percent to 47 percent) (European Commission 1997).

These trends sting against the backdrop of a winter of discontent, when public sector unions in several European countries go on strike against privatization plans, and cuts in public sector jobs and welfare programs. French protests against the plans of the conservative Juppé government are soon labeled "strikes against Maastricht" (de Boissieu and Pisani-Ferry 1998: 56). These protests are estimated to have shaven 1 percent off French GDP (Cameron 1997, 1998). The reason one national government after another tries to impose budgetary austerity in the 1990s has little to do with EU membership. Yet the EMU convergence criteria add urgency to – and provide a convenient justification for – national governments' austerity efforts.[3] It is not a huge leap for ordinary citizens, then, to blame EMU for their hard times (Dalton and Eichenberg 1998).

The economic downturn in Europe and the corroding consensus for European integration do not bode well for the European Commission. It is charged with the implementation of the Maastricht Treaty, and this requires it to develop policies in newly integrated areas, to lay the groundwork for EMU, and to prepare for enlargement to Central and Eastern Europe. This is a tall order for the newly appointed Commission team, led by former Luxembourg prime minister Jacques Santer. The new Commission started inauspiciously. Santer was the member states' second choice to succeed Jacques Delors as Commission president, after the UK government vetoed the Belgian prime minister Dehaene, and the European Parliament confirmed his appointment with a very small margin (Cini 1996: 204). Six months into his term, Santer appears to lack authority and vision. The College of Commissioners is riven by national, partisan, and personal rivalries (Peterson 1999).

These circumstances weigh on top Commission officials in 1995. Few are satisfied with the state of the European Union, and hardly any expect

---

[3] The main causes are (a) an aging population, which puts pressure on public pension and health systems; (b) more open economies competing for mobile capital, which leads to calls for greater flexibility in the labor markets; (c) and an ideological turn to the right, which induces politicians to apply market principles to government functions. There is a considerable scholarly literature examining these sources and their implications for West European societies. For overviews of this literature and analysis, see, among others, Kitschelt et al. (1999), Scharpf (2000), and Huber and Stephens (2001).

rapid improvement. Yet many officials emphasize that the European Union has weathered such crises before. Rather than becoming despondent, they prefer to focus their energies on the challenges ahead: streamlining EU decision-making, enlargement, preparing for EMU, unemployment, and winning the loyalty of Europe's citizens.

Spring 1996

At the time I am preparing for my second major round of interviews in spring 1996, the skies start to clear. Against economic odds – and notwithstanding reluctant public opinion – Europe's political leaders reaffirm their commitment to EMU at the European summit of Madrid in December 1995, "confirming unequivocally that stage three of economic and monetary union will commence on January 1, 1999." They also agree to name the new currency the "Euro," and they plan the actual changeover to occur between January 1, 1999 and July 1, 2002 (Cameron 1997). In subsequent months, national governments tackle the remaining thorny issues one by one. They reach an agreement on sanctions for EMU members with high public deficits (the Growth and Stability Pact), and work out future relations between the Euro and the currencies from EU countries outside EMU ("ins" and "outs"). These agreements go hand in hand with a firm promise to open accession negotiations with Central and East European countries soon after the start of EMU.

Over the past year, the Commission's practical groundwork has helped to digest EMU and enlargement. The Commission has quietly refined EU mechanisms for economic surveillance and deeper monetary coordination to help national governments achieve lower public debt, privatization, and cuts in the public sector. It has also begun to formalize cooperation with Central and Eastern Europe through programs such as Phare (Poland and Hungary: Action for the Restructuring of the Economy), Tempus (Trans-European Mobility Programme for University Studies), and TACIS (Technical Assistance for the CIS Countries). It has prepared initial reports on the likely impact of enlargement on the European Union's institutions and policies. It has outlined "necessary" adjustments for potential applicants, and it has suggested timetables that de facto put off enlargement until well into the first decade of the twenty-first century.

However, the headlines in spring 1996 are dominated by the BSE crisis. In March, the British government announces that scientists have established that a link might exist between the disease BSE in cattle and a new variant of Creutzfeld-Jakob disease, a degenerative and ultimately fatal neural disease in humans (Peterson and Bomberg 1999;

Grant 1997). This sends a wave of panic through Europe. In response, several governments on the continent threaten unilaterally to bar British beef from their markets. Under the gun, the European Commission bans certain British beef products likely to be contaminated with BSE, and soon thereafter all British cattle from the European market. The ban will be lifted only in December 1998. British public opinion, whipped up by the British Conservative government, fiercely criticizes the measures, singling out "Eurocrats" as the villains. When the UK government announces its intention to veto all EU decisions until the ban is lifted, the conflict threatens to throw the EU into an institutional crisis reminiscent of the "empty chair crisis" in 1965–6, when French president de Gaulle ordered French officials to stay away from EU negotiations. But the UK's principled veto ultimately fails to bring EU decision-making to a halt, because member state governments agree to overrule British opposition whenever possible.[4] Paradoxically, the BSE crisis creates a more propitious political environment for EU reform by relegating the British Conservatives to the sidelines and reviving the traditional Franco-German axis. In this climate, the European Union embarks on another round of intergovernmental negotiations about institutional reform, which will culminate in a new treaty in Amsterdam in June 1997.[5]

The tide has turned. Most top officials exude a quiet, cautious confidence on EMU and enlargement. They are less certain about the outcome of the intergovernmental conference, which is supposed to adjust the European institutions to these challenges. And they realize public opinion has not turned around. They worry about public discontent and they are aware of the Commission's precarious role in a contentious EU polity.

Spring 1997

By the time I set off for my third and final major round of interviews in February 1997, EMU is a near-certainty. Certainly, support among Europe's publics is still lukewarm: slightly more than half of all Europeans support the introduction of a single currency, but one-third does not. Enthusiasm is tepid among the French, with 55 percent for and 30 percent

---

[4] Most day-to-day decisions now fall under the qualified majority rule, which makes it possible to overrule national vetoes. This is a critical difference from the mid-1960s, when the decision rule was unanimity.

[5] The heads of government reach agreement in Amsterdam in June 1997 and sign the treaty in October 1997, and the agreement comes into force in 1999 as the Amsterdam Treaty after ratification in all member states.

against their country's participation in EMU; it is strikingly low in Germany and Austria, where strong relative majorities oppose giving up their national currency, and in Finland, where an absolute majority is against (European Commission 1997). However, it appears that much of this opposition is soft rather than hard-nosed. To the extent that EMU is sold as a tool to bring non-inflationary growth, or as a mechanism for reducing the costs and uncertainties of the single market, or as a buffer against American economic policies – three European goals with widespread public support – the Euro may yet receive a warm welcome (Dalton and Eichenberg 1998). National government leaders will decide in June 1998 which countries qualify for EMU, set to start on January 1, 1999. Yet, by early 1997, eleven countries appear on track.

Politicians and policy makers are gradually shifting their attention to the implications of EMU for Europe's economy and society. European economic growth has by now picked up modestly, but unemployment levels refuse to budge. That is bad news, because EMU will deprive national governments of monetary instruments and it will severely constrain the use of fiscal policy to achieve macroeconomic policy goals. The result is intense dissension about whether or not the European Union should develop some kind of fiscal policy to deal with asymmetrical shocks under EMU. The debate about unemployment is fueled by the fact that left or center–left parties are now in government in most EU countries. The change of government in the UK, in May 1997, reinforces this trend. Of the remaining four conservative governments (France, Germany, Ireland, and Spain), the French conservatives give way to the socialists a few weeks later, and, in the fall of 1997, a social democratic/green cabinet replaces the CDU–FDP coalition in Germany.

Many top officials argue that the Commission should highlight general problems of growth and employment in Europe, and suggest how the European Union can provide common solutions. They remind themselves proudly of the 1993 white paper on *Growth, Competitiveness and Employment*, a concerted effort by all directorates-general, led by a driven Jacques Delors, to kick-start Europe's economy. It sought to show how market liberalization and social democratic concerns for equity and employment could combine to build a competitive European economy. The white paper received wide praise, though it remained largely unimplemented. Perhaps it is time, these top officials argue, for a sequel. And yet not all share this view. Some top officials are reluctant to drag the Commission into these ideological debates; they are more concerned with getting the Commission's management of its own resources and its existing policies in better shape. The ground is shifting in-house from creation to management.

The organization

Top officials often refer to the Commission as "the House." What is this House like? What type of bureaucracy is the Commission? In his monograph on the Commission, Edward Page applies four models to analyze the role of the Commission in the European Union (Page 1997: 4–21). Page argues that none of the models fits the Commission like a glove. Yet each highlights different features of the EU administration and, in combination, they shed light on the daily work environment within which the subjects of this study, top Commission officials, form preferences on EU governance.

The first model conceives of the EU administration through the eyes of the Commission's founding father – Jean Monnet.[6] Monnet's vision was to recreate at European level a sort of Planning Commission (Commissariat de plan). Set up after World War II in France as a high-level team of civil servants and experts outside the normal bureaucratic hierarchy, the Planning Commission wrote the first five-year national economic plan. Jean Monnet led that team. In the same vein, he saw the Commission as a small, organizationally flexible and adaptive, multinational nucleus of individuals. It was their role to develop ideas and to stimulate and persuade others, but to leave bureaucracy and implementation to national administrations. As François Duchêne, a long-time collaborator of Jean Monnet and author of a wonderful biography of Monnet, put it, there was "a comic incompatibility of humor between Monnet and routine administration" (Duchêne 1994: 240). Monnet did not want a permanent core of civil servants. The tasks at hand should determine who should work for Europe, and so he conceived of the Commission as an ever-changing body where experts from diverse backgrounds would come and go as needs change.

As Page points out, the Monnet spirit is still palpable. Commission officials rely on national or regional administrations to implement most EU legislation; they are an exceptionally diverse and multinational lot, and though "proper" Commission officials now have career tenure – something Monnet would have found quite unnecessary – the Commission is far more inclined than national administrations to attract temporary experts from outside.[7] Yet precisely these Monnet features, such as the

---

[6] Technically speaking, Jean Monnet was the founder only of the Commission's predecessor, the High Authority (for the European Coal and Steel Community). Jean Monnet retired as president of the High Authority in 1955. The Commission was created in 1958.

[7] This happens primarily through secondment, that is, the practice by which outsiders, usually national or regional civil servants but occasionally experts affiliated to interest groups or research institutes, take up a job in the Commission. Secondment is in principle limited to three years, but there have been many exceptions.

Commission's bias in favor of policy initiation and its relatively unorthodox recruitment for top positions, have come under criticism.[8]

The Commission also echoes features of an international bureaucracy. After all, the League of Nations secretariat and the United Nations secretariat stood model for the High Authority, the predecessor to the Commission (Page 1997). Like international civil servants, Commission officials enjoy some immunity against prosecution, as well as tax privileges. More importantly, like many international organizations, the Commission struggles with the problems of "efficient administration" (reconciling efficiency with the need to represent all nationalities), "dual allegiance" (balancing supranationality with national identity), and "political initiative" (maintaining equilibrium between political entrepreneurship and deference to elected politicians).[9]

Yet, here too, several recent developments rebel against this heritage. In the heat of the Commission crisis in 1999 and subsequent criminal investigations by the Belgian police, the Commission lifted the immunity of some commissioners and officials, and it agreed to define Commission officials' rights to immunity more strictly. Commission officials' taxation exemptions have also come under attack. When the Prodi Commission took up office in September 1999, it voluntarily renounced several tax-exempt provisions.[10] But the criticism of this model goes deeper. The main purpose of the latest reform plans by commissioner Neil Kinnock is to make the organization more efficient and managerial – more like a modern national bureaucracy and less like an international organization.

The Commission also has much in common with the national bureaucracies of continental Europe. As in the grand bureaucracies of Germany, Austria, and France, work conditions in the Commission are designed to help officials resist financial or other pressures, hence the high pay and secure status. In return, a Commission official (including each commissioner) must pledge neither to seek nor to receive instructions from his home state. And, as in those Weberian continental bureaucracies, Commission procedures are strongly hierarchical. Reports are supposed to travel up the ladder from one immediate superior to the next. The chain of command is usually lengthy.

The organizational structure and the terminology in the Commission are imported from France: *directions générals* and *directions*, and *cabinets* to

---

[8] Chapters 6 and 7 touch upon this.

[9] On international organizations, see Claude (1956); Cox and Jacobson (1973); Cox (1996); Kille and Scully (1997).

[10] European Commission, "Press Release – 29 September 1999. By Neil Kinnock, Vice President of the European Commission." *http://europa.eu.int/comm/commissioners/kinnock/pr290999_en.htm* (accessed on September 29, 1999.)

assist the minister/commissioner. Like the French bureaucracy, the Commission bureaucracy is divided into four categories: A for those conducting conceptual work and providing leadership (*fonctionnaire de conception et de direction*); B for executive work (*fonctionnaire d'application*); C for secretarial work (*fonctionnaire d'exécution spécialisée*); and D for basic custodial or menial jobs (*fonctionnaire d'exécution simple*).[11] And the terms for the top positions are borrowed from the French: *directeur-général, directeur-général-adjoint, directeur, conseiller, chef de cabinet* (on France, see Safran 1995, ch. 8).

The organizational structure and the formal hierarchic rules are still very French. However, these hierarchical provisions are much criticized inside and outside the organization, and some top officials encourage their people to undercut formal hierarchy with informal horizontal practices. The extent to which hierarchical rules are implemented varies considerably across the Commission.

The fourth model is the US bureaucracy. As in the United States, the Commission is part of a system where power is dispersed among various branches of government and across different territorial levels. Neither the American political system nor the EU has a focal point for authority equivalent to the ministerial cabinet in West European countries. Interests are aggregated and authority established within narrower policy terrains – "issue networks" or "iron triangles" in Hugh Heclo's terms, and "subgovernments" in Richard Rose's language. This system fragments the bureaucracy into relatively autonomous parts. Laura Cram has coined an EU-specific label: the Commission as a multi-organization, where parts function as relatively autonomous bureaucratic organizations with their own goals and operational style (Cram 1994). The most telling indicator of this type of bureaucratic tradition in the European Union is comitology. Most Commission work takes place in a dense web of committees, each of which brings together specialized stakeholders to make decisions.

Comitology and bureaucratic fragmentation are unintended outcomes of a particular political-bureaucratic system. As far as I know, nobody has ever put forward the American model of subgovernment as a blueprint for the Commission. In fact, report after report on Commission reforms, including the most recent round led by commissioner Kinnock, has recommended strengthening central political control over "local fiefdoms" or cozy networks. Coordination across units and directorate-generals is perceived to be an endemic problem in the Commission.

---

[11] On February 28, 2001, commissioner for personnel policy Neil Kinnock announced plans to replace this four-tiered letter system with a more linear career structure (Press Release, "Commission proposes a new staff policy from recruitment to retirement," IP/01/283, *http://europa.eu.int/rapid/start/cgi/*, accessed on March 8, 2001.)

The Commission is an amalgam of diverse bureaucratic agendas and traditions: Monnet's vision of a European vanguard, a powerful international organization, a Weberian civil service in continental European tradition, and a US-style bureaucracy. There are palpable tensions among these traditions, and these impose contradictory and, from time to time, incompatible demands on top officials. And so the men (and women) at the helm of the Commission must steer an unpredictable vessel in an increasingly choppy political sea.

Sampling

The Commission is a small civil service. It has just over 4,000 A-level employees, of whom 200 are top officials.[12] I did not spend much time worrying about sampling; I simply tried to interview *all* A1 and A2 officials, that is, every director-general, deputy director-general, director, and senior advisor based in Brussels. For practical reasons, my inquiry excludes services in Luxembourg (mainly the directorate-general XVIII for credit and investments, and the statistical office).[13] It also does not include the translation and conference services or the centers for research and development because they do not engage in policy-making. This brings the universe of top officials to 204.[14] Overall, 67 percent of this group granted me an interview ($n = 137$), and, of these, 77 percent filled out the mail-back questionnaire ($n = 106$). Given their rank and time constraints, this response rate is high. The willingness of top officials to accommodate the curiosity of an academic is remarkable.

One does well to regard samples with a healthy dose of skepticism. Why did not all 204 agree to be interviewed? Who dropped out? And were the reasons for non-response ad hoc or systematic?

---

[12] I refer here to the policy-making A grades in the Commission. In 1999 the Commission employed just over 20,000 staff. Of these, just over 14,000 were employed in administration, including 4,000 in the A grades, 3,900 in research and technological development, and 1,900 in translation and interpretation work. This is less than one official per 10,000 inhabitants, against on average 322 national civil servants per 10,000 inhabitants (Nugent 1999: 108–9).

[13] These posts are predominantly inherited from the European Atomic Energy Community, which was set up in 1957 along with the European Economic Community. They concern mainly "hard" scientists.

[14] Of these 204 positions, 189 are "line positions," that is, their holders have authority over personnel and budgets. These important top positions are held by directors-general, deputy directors-general, and directors. Principal advisors or chief advisors make up the remaining 15 positions. The Commission also employs a sizeable number of advisors (close to 70) at this top level, but I do not include them in my analysis because their responsibilities and status vary dramatically. Some are surrogate directors or principal advisors, while others have subordinate roles or participate only marginally in policy making. Their formal rank varies as well: a few are A2 (top management), but most are A3 or A4 (middle management).

Time constraints appear to have played a part, though I did my best to minimize this as a factor. The typical top Commission official has a busy schedule, but I spread the interviews over five stays in Brussels, and these visits amounted to roughly 180 days of interviewing. So I was able to repeat interview requests visit after visit, from June 1995 through February 1997. This strategy made it harder for top officials to claim they did not have time to see me.[15] I would simply try again – next time.

Yet I suspect that, notwithstanding my persistence, time constraints are the single most important reason for non-response. The Commission experienced an unusual turnover in top personnel between 1995 and 1997, because it was making space for people from the new member states and it was bringing its organizational structure in line with the Maastricht Treaty. This was not a good time to organize interviews! I caught many officials in the middle of a move – on their way out, finding their feet in a new organization, moving sideways to a different position or another service, or shooting up the hierarchical ladder. Between 35 and 45 percent were on the move. Some movers undoubtedly moved off my radar screen. Others chose not to devote scarce time to an interview. Typically, they (or their secretaries) agreed in principle, but put off making an iron-cast appointment. As I fired off phone calls and faxes with increasing frequency at the end of each stay in Brussels, they promised to meet me during my next sojourn. Some meetings never materialized. By far the most common ground for my failure to interview every single official was job pressure.

Outright rebuttal was rare; fewer than 15 officials flatly refused to be interviewed. One made a point of calling me to explain why he considered my research futile. After twenty minutes discussion on the phone, we cordially agreed to disagree. That was not the general pattern though; officials who refused to cooperate usually instructed their secretary to convey the message to me. To the extent that an explanation was given, it was often because the official considered it against the civil service ethos to grant interviews to outsiders, or because she did not think the research project was interesting.

It is difficult to test sample bias conclusively because systematic socio-demographic data on top officials are not available. However, it is possible to approximate such a test for the distribution across directorates-general (DGs) and across nationalities. To assess whether the interviews are evenly spread across the various departments in the Commission, I use

---

[15] Some top officials have a punishing schedule year in year out. One director-general, with whom I had been trying to arrange a meeting since my first visit in July 1995, finally invited me for lunch in February 1997, my final sojourn in Brussels, "because that was the only window he had." The solid two-hour interview, with clattering plates and humming voices in the background, was a delightfully frank and informative encounter.

as a benchmark the 1997 *EU Information Handbook*, annually updated and published by the EU Committee of the American Chamber of Commerce in Belgium.[16] To test bias I use the chi-square statistic, which tests the null hypothesis that the distribution in sample and population is the same. If the significance level of the chi-square statistic is below .05, then there is a 95 percent chance that sample and population have a different distribution. When I apply this statistic to distribution by DG, I find no evidence of systematic bias, though energy (DG XVII) and to a lesser extent research (DG XII) are slightly underrepresented (see table A.1 in the Appendix). The chi-square statistic is well above the .05 level (alpha = .61 for interviews, alpha = .49 for questionnaires).

Chi-square tests become less sensitive to bias as the number of categories increases. That is why I also run the test for subgroups of DGs. I group the 27 DGs into six categories: market-oriented services, administration, external affairs, supply-side-oriented services, social regulatory services, and redistributive/provision services. Table 2.1 compares distribution across these types among population, interview sample, and questionnaire sample.

In the interview sample, officials from provision services are somewhat overrepresented, whereas those from supply-side services and, to a lesser extent, market-oriented services are underrepresented. Yet these differences are not significant. The trends are similar for the questionnaire sample, where supply-side and market-oriented services are somewhat underrepresented, but external relations overrepresented. Again, these differences are not significant.

To test sample bias for nationality, my point of departure is the Commission's informal norm to seek a "geographical balance" in the top layers of the administration. The Commission does not like to publicize the rule for calculating geographical balance, though it is fairly well known that the distribution holds the middle ground between being proportionate to member state votes in the Council of Ministers – which benefits smaller countries – and being proportionate to population strength – which helps larger countries. I construct a yardstick that gives equal weight to population strength and votes in the Council. French, British, Danish, and, to some extent, Dutch officials are overrepresented, whereas my samples have too few Germans and Spanish (table A.2 in the Appendix). However, for neither sample are these biases statistically significant (interview sample: chi-square = 20.39, alpha =.12; questionnaires: chi-square = 16.51, alpha = .28).

---

[16] This private publication is usually more accurate and more up to date than the Commission's own *Directory of the Commission of the European Communities*.

Table 2.1 *Officials by DG grouping*

DG grouping	All top officials		Interviews		Questionnaires	
	%	No.	%	No.	%	No.
Administration	13.7	28	15.3	21	16.0	17
External affairs	13.2	27	15.3	21	17.0	18
Market-oriented	18.1	37	15.3	21	14.2	15
Supply-side	21.6	44	16.1	22	17.0	18
Provision & redistribution	19.6	40	23.4	32	19.8	21
Social regulation	13.7	28	14.6	20	16.0	17
Total	100.0	204	100.0	137	100.0	106
Chi-square			4.338		3.970	
Degrees of freedom			5		5	
Alpha			.502		.554	

Administration = Secretariat-General, Spokesperson service, IX, XIX, XX
External affairs = I, Ia, Ib
Market-oriented = II, III, IV, XV
Supply-side = VII, XII, XIII, XVII, XXI, XXIII
Provision = VI, VIII, XIV, XVI
Social regulation = V, X, XI, XXII, XXIV

The results change somewhat when I group nationalities into four categories: the original Six members, the first enlargement (Danish, Irish, and British), the second enlargement (Greeks, Portuguese, and Spanish), and the third enlargement (Austrians, Finns, and Swedes). The second enlargement is underrepresented in the questionnaire sample, and this bias is just significant at the .05 level (chi-square = 7.86, alpha = .05). The interview sample, however, is statistically unbiased.

Let us now turn to a comparison between the interview and questionnaire samples. The one serious (that is, statistically significant) discrepancy concerns the representation of DG VIII (development); fewer than half the interviewees returned the questionnaire. A smaller proportion of Greek, Portuguese, Spanish, and French officials than average mailed back the questionnaire, but this difference is not significant (see the Appendix). So the two samples are for all practical purposes interchangeable.

I expect the effect of these DG and nationality biases on the analysis to be limited. To explain top officials' preferences, the analysis uses not proper nouns, but theoretically relevant categorizations. I do not engage "DG VIII" as an independent variable; instead, I examine whether or not

Table 2.2 *Officials by nationality grouping*

Nationality grouping	All top officials		Interviews		Questionnaires	
	%	No.	%	No.	%	No.
First Six	52.9	108	56.2	77	55.7	59
First enlargement	18.8	38	21.9	30	26.4	28
Second enlargement	18.8	38	14.6	20	10.4	11
Third enlargement	9.5	20	7.3	10	7.5	8
Total	100.0	204	100.0	137	100.0	106
Chi-square			2.961		7.864	
Degrees of freedom			3		3	
Alpha			.398		.049	

officials in redistributive DGs, such as development aid, have different preferences from those in market-oriented DGs. For these broader categories, the samples are not statistically different. Similarly, I do not use "Spain" or "Greece" as causal variables; instead, I analyze whether, for example, officials from major beneficiaries of EU cohesion funds (Spain, Portugal, Greece, and Ireland) have significantly different preferences on EU governance than those from contributors to the EU budget.[17]

Table A.3 in the Appendix goes several steps further in testing whether or not the interview and questionnaire sample are interchangeable. It compares respondents from the two samples on a range of personal and professional characteristics: position, seniority, gender, education, transnational education, prior career, prior service in the national civil service, Commission cabinet experience, and parachutage. I will discuss the most striking substantive findings later in this chapter; here it is sufficient to notice that, using non-parametric chi-square tests, I do not find systematic differences between the two samples.

Interviewing

Each top official received a letter explaining the study in general terms, stressing its scholarly and confidential character, and requesting an appointment for 45 to 60 minutes. I offered a choice between English and

---

[17] But underrepresentation may cause other problems. It is possible that the analysis runs into a small-n problem, that is, there are too few cases to conduct the necessary statistical controls. The small number of Spanish, Portuguese, and Greek officials in my sample may restrict my capacity to test hypotheses that juxtapose these officials against their colleagues. I will indicate to the reader where this small-n factor may hamper analysis.

French as the language of communication, and I made it plain that I would need to have the interview taped. I deliberately did not seek approval from the Commission hierarchy, because I was anxious to avoid constraints on the questions I could ask. I reckoned that I was more likely to have sincere and frank exchanges with officials who cooperated in their personal capacity.

My one concern was that, because the interviewing made inroads in the Commission's top layers, the hierarchy might at some point intervene. To minimize the chance of this happening, I wrote first to all directors-general and to their *primus inter pares*, the secretary general of the Commission. And I held my breath. On the very last day of my first summer in Brussels, July 1995, I was able to extract a promise of a half-hour interview from the secretary-general, who was then Mr. David Williamson. Our conversation lasted an hour and a half. I relaxed; the research was on track!

All but two interviews took place in Commission offices. Most officials asked their secretary to put through only urgent calls, so that we could converse without major interruptions. My interviewees were generally willing, attentive subjects. No doubt this interest was deepened by the fact that I was asking them primarily about themselves – their beliefs, their motivations, their plans. No topic is more fascinating for political actors, as several officials admitted chuckling. In a few cases, the interview was extended over two visits. Almost always, we found another time to continue the interview.

I conducted all 137 interviews myself.[18] Before I contacted officials, I collected basic personal characteristics, such as nationality, date of birth, education, and career path, available from published sources. The reader will find this form, and other documents related to interviewing, in the Appendix.

Questions

The purpose of the interviews was to capture preferences and role perceptions that exist in the minds of the officials, not in the mind of the researcher. In their study of foreign policy makers, Martin Hollis and Steve Smith make a strong case for taking accounts by elite actors seriously: "Our actors *interpret* information, *monitor* their performance, *reassess* their goals. The leading idea is that of reasoned judgment, not of manipulation" (1986: 283 emphasis in original; quoted in Searing 1991, fn 17.)

---

[18] Except for two interviews conducted jointly with a colleague, Dr. Hussein Kassim.

I used in-depth interviews that contain primarily open-ended questions on three broad topics: motivations, preferences on EU governance, and preferences on EU policy problems. The interview started with motivational questions close to the official's life and work. What are the reasons for his initial interest in European affairs? What motivates him today? How does he conceive of his role as senior official? What does she consider her main accomplishments, and what are her greatest disappointments? I used these motivational questions to jump-start a discussion about issues of EU governance. A second set of questions probed cognitive and evaluative orientations on EU governance and the EU policy process more directly. In the third part of the interview, the respondent reflected upon future challenges for the European Union, possible solutions, his (or, more rarely, her) role, and the Commission's role in general. My aim was to assess how respondents approach problems, solutions, and the actors involved. Finally, the interview came full circle by taking the respondent back to his motivational core. What influenced his views? And were his professional plans in or outside the Commission? Sometimes I did not have the time to pose every question, but I made sure to put key questions on the motivational core (parts one and four), EU governance (parts one and two), and preferences about the policy process (part two).

At the end of the interview, each interviewee received a five-page questionnaire consisting of a range of behavioral questions, alongside thirty-two scale items on issues of EU governance and the relationship between politics and public administration. For each statement, the interviewee indicates whether (a) he agrees without reservations, (b) agrees with reservations, (c) disagrees with reservations, or (d) disagrees without reservations. The interview questionnaire and the mail-back questionnaire are in the Appendix.

Responses

Hardly anyone disputed the use of a tape recorder. Of the 137 respondents, 2 refused to be taped. One discussed topics in an open, informative, and frank fashion, whereas the other person remained very reserved even after I had tucked away the tape recorder. At any time during the interview, interviewees could use the *pause* button if they felt uncomfortable about recording, but only two officials took advantage of this.

It is difficult to assess the impact of tape recording on a respondent's frankness and the quality of the interview, though I have reasons to believe it to be minimal. From the viewpoint of the respondent, few questions, if any, were sensitive. I was interested in respondents' fundamental beliefs about the future of Europe, not their views on contested policy cases, such as the BSE affair (mad cow disease). I did not ask them to go out on a limb on particular persons or events, and yet this did not stop many from volunteering opinions.

My pledge to preserve anonymity was appreciated. I stand by this promise, and I will attribute quotes not to proper names but instead to numbers. I will further disguise the identity of the respondent by blanking or altering nationality or DG.[19]

Officials realized that this interview was a one-off encounter. I was unlikely to call upon them again any time soon. And finally, at this stage in their career, the potential costs of impolitic public statements are relatively low. I know of only one recent instance where a senior Commission official was reprimanded for public statements. In 1996, the freshly appointed Swedish deputy director-general for industry was censured for an interview in a Swedish newspaper in which he was highly critical of the internal workings of the Commission. I had interviewed the same person a few months earlier, and I had been struck by his openly critical account.[20]

---

[19] No doubt my credentials as an academic scholar helped persuade my interviewees that I was not going to break my promise. One should also not discount that one out of seven interviewees had been academics themselves before joining the Commission. Some officials openly envied my freedom to pose probing questions, while others had a keen sociological interest in the research findings.

It is sometimes argued that outsiders find it easier to build trust with public officials because they are unlikely to become an interested party. The fact that I have lived in North America since 1994 makes me an outsider of a sort. Yet I have the impression that it was as often my status as an "insider" – a multinational European, albeit an "expatriate" – that helped me to establish a personal connection. I am a Belgian/European citizen who was educated in Belgium and lived for several years in Britain and Italy. I found it frequently helpful to draw upon one or the other biographical facet to facilitate trust.

All this may have played to my advantage. However, the most important creator of goodwill was my decision to let respondents choose the language of communication (English or French). This indicated to Commission officials that I understood, and respected, the strong norm of multilingualism in the Commission. Several respondents told me how much they liked this gesture, and a few playfully switched back and forth between English and French . . . much to the despair of the transcribers of these tapes!

[20] Very few officials seemed to self-censure themselves. This may be surprising, given that there have been several well-publicized incidents in which Commission officials' freedom of speech clashed with their duty to be discreet professionals. One incident concerned the Danish commissioner, Ritt Bjerregaard. She was forced to cancel a contract with a Danish newspaper, which ran her satirical column on life in Brussels. Bjerregaard is a politician, though, not a permanent official. Another, more serious scandal erupted in 1996 around the publication of a book forecasting the disastrous consequences of EMU for Europe, including possibly war. The British-born author, Bernard Connolly, was head of division in DG II (economics and finance), the directorate-general that handles EMU. He was fired. The fact that he was directly responsible for EMU preparation made the episode highly embarrassing for the Commission. However, even this case hardly seemed to persuade my top officials to mince their words. This incident might have made it more difficult for me to meet top officials from DG II, including Connolly's immediate superior, all of whom I contacted after the incident. With the exception of

Of those who agreed to an interview, 77 percent filled out the questionnaire. Were the rest simply forgetful? Mere oversight is highly unlikely – I sent up to three reminders. Time constraint is also a weak excuse: it took at most 10 minutes to fill out the questionnaire, but it took on average 80 minutes for the oral interview. Several factors may explain why some officials failed to fill out the mail-back questionnaire.

Commission officials may be reluctant to stake out positions on sensitive items. Do they support more power for the European Parliament? Should the Commission become the actual government of Europe? Should more power move back to the member states? What should be the role of the Commission president? Do they support an extensive EU cohesion policy? Do they consider the Commission vulnerable to national favoritism? One official sent back the questionnaire blank, with a note stating that these questions were too intrusive. Another considered the questionnaire offensive. Others disagreed with the way certain items were phrased. One official scribbled dense comments next to virtually every item, but he did not take a position on a single one of them. A few respondents abstained on certain items.[21]

Politically sophisticated actors tend to dislike closed-ended questions. Likert scales force respondents to condense complex beliefs in blunt agree/disagree statements, whereas an interview allows them to qualify their position by expanding on pros and cons.[22] Some officials may have refused to fill out the questionnaire for these reasons, as the following incident illustrates. I sent a friendly reminder to a director-general who had shown genuine interest in the project during the interview but had failed

one respondent who was anxious to have complete anonymity in light of that case, I did not find them more reserved.

[21] I deliberately omitted a neutral position to give officials the strongest possible incentive to take a stance. Rather than having their hand forced, some officials preferred to abstain on sensitive items. On two items, 5.6 percent abstained (6 respondents). The more sensitive of the two summarizes former Commission president Jacques Delors' "European model of society" (Ross 1995b: 109): "Europe has developed a unique model of society, and the Commission should help to preserve it: extensive social services, civilized industrial relations, negotiated transfers among groups to sustain solidarity, and steer economic activity for the general welfare." Yet, the highest non-response rate concerns an item that is formulated ambiguously. "A Commission which tolerates this much infighting among its staff will eventually destroy itself" produced an abstention rate of 9.4 percent (10 individuals). This item conflates cognitive ("whether there is infighting") and evaluative ("whether infighting is a bad thing") components, and this may have deterred some officials. On all other items, abstentions are below 5 percent: 4.7 percent (one item); 3.7 percent (three items); 2.8 percent (two items); 1.8 percent (two items); and no abstentions (twenty items).

[22] Other students of elite preferences have noticed this as well. Robert Putnam reprints part of a letter with a British parliamentarian, who makes this point eloquently (1973: 19). See also Donald Searing (1994: 408).

to send back the questionnaire. His secretary promptly contacted me by email, confirming that the official was willing to do the questionnaire if I could clarify the closed-ended statements. I wrote back in some detail to explain why I could not possibly give more background information. I never received the questionnaire.

I had great difficulty getting Greek, Spanish, and Portuguese officials to send the mail questionnaire back: only 55 percent did. Although it was much easier to set up interviews with French officials, only 68 percent mailed back the questionnaire. In contrast, the response rate for officials from "northern" countries ranges between 79 percent for Scandinavians, 82 percent for Germans, 83 percent for Beneluxers, and 100 percent for UK and Irish citizens. Italians rank in between, with a 75 percent response rate.

EU scholars have noted before that political actors from Mediterranean countries tend to be less cooperative in scholarly endeavors. This appears true of members of parliaments, representatives in the Council of Ministers, party officials, regional officials, and interest group representatives, and also of top Commission officials. There are plausible cultural reasons for this. Mediterranean political cultures tend to put less value on responsiveness to citizens and more on serving the general public interest; less on openness of government and more on preserving state unity; less on personal initiative and responsibility of civil servants and more on hierarchical relations. Yet these characteristics were not palpable during the face-to-face interviews. It is likely that the real reason for Mediterranean reluctance is linguistic discomfort. Whereas officials could choose between French and English for the oral interview, this was not so with the mail questionnaire, which was in English only. Many older Southern European officials use French as primary working language, not English, and so it is possible that they felt uncomfortable. This would also explain the below-average response rate on the mail questionnaires among French officials. It is likely that my linguistic oversight in designing the mail questionnaire depressed the response rate.

Responses and non-responses are randomly distributed across DGs, with the exception of DG VIII (development policies). Of the ten interviewees in DG VIII, only four filled out the mail-back questionnaire (a response rate of 40 percent against a 77 percent average for the whole Commission). All four arrived within a few days after the interview. A fifth one was delivered around the same time, but it contained strenuous objections. (This is the questionnaire with extensive scribbling in the margins.) This meager response rate for the second part of the inquiry is odd, given that officials in DG VIII were extremely generous with their time during the interview and frank in their responses. After the protests by the fifth person, no other official returned the questionnaire, notwith-standing several reminders.[23]

Having said all that, 106 questionnaires out of a maximum of 137 came back duly completed. Quite a few respondents wrote they were satisfied with the selection and wording of the items. Overall, positive comments outweigh negative comments. Top Commission officials are savvy participants and experienced witnesses of EU governance, and it should be no surprise that they hold strong personal opinions on how one should examine the European Union.

Coding

This book uses two streams of evidence. The first consists of in-depth, taped interviews. Such interviews allow politically sophisticated indivi-duals to make realistic qualifications while conveying complex opinions (Putnam 1973; Searing 1994). One challenge that confronts the re-searcher is *data reduction*, that is, to distil a respondent's basic preferences from the rich particularities of a personal account. A further challenge is that of *data aggregation*, that is, to summarize individual data into a lim-ited number of dimensions that capture relevant variation in respondents' preferences.

In order to facilitate comparison, I kept the interview questionnaire similar across respondents. I also singled out key open-ended questions on motivations and EU governance, which I presented to each respon-dent in a standardized way. I allowed more flexibility with questions that invite the official to speculate about Europe's future. Furthermore, I paid close attention to the sequencing of questions. For certain themes, I fol-lowed open-ended with closed-ended questions. This forced respondents to conclude a freewheeling discussion with a definitive statement. Re-sponses to closed-ended questions work as a reality check for answers to open-ended questions.[24]

The second stream of evidence flows from the closed-ended ques-tionnaires. A chief virtue is that closed-ended questions produce easily

---

[23] At one point, one more person appeared willing to fax the questionnaire, but I received only the first page (out of five). I informed his secretary about the incomplete transmis-sion, but never received the rest of the questionnaire.

[24] I took a great deal of care in coding the responses to open-ended questions. For each topic, I identified key questions that would form the input for a coding schema. I then developed a coding schema based on my reading of a subset of the interview transcripts. Next, the schema became the blueprint for trained coders to assess and categorize the responses of top officials. By having two coders evaluate each interview transcript I was able to assess inter-coder reliability.

quantifiable data. The quantitative analysis of preferences in chapters 4–7 is primarily based on these data.[25]

The actors

Who are the people at the center of this inquiry? Where do they come from, why are they in the Commission, and how did they get here?

A mission for Europe – with moderation

Only out-of-the-ordinary people choose to go to Brussels. More than 80 percent of top officials were interested in European politics well before they joined the Commission (table 2.3). Of these, 41 percent became attentive to European issues through previous jobs. Others were deeply influenced by courses on European integration at school or university. A sizeable minority were born into a multinational family; some started one; many lived abroad previously (30 percent).

Almost one out of four regards European integration as a guarantor of important ideals. The older generation frequently mentions the desire for peace, particularly between France and Germany: "I am a child of the war. People of my generation would do anything to avoid a third world war. We did not have a sophisticated notion of an institutionalized Europe as we know it now, but we were deeply European because we never wanted to repeat that experience" (official #70). Respondents from Spain, Portugal, and Greece are often motivated by different ideals. For them, European integration consolidates democracy at home.

For 7 percent of Commission officials, interest in European politics was an outgrowth of their work in the Commission: "When I passed the exam and started working here a long time ago, I was not at all interested in the European Community itself. I came here simply because I had graduated as an economist, and I was looking for a job as an economist. . . . It was only after immersing myself in the particular aspects of my job that, by necessity, I became interested in European questions" (official #103). Finally, 8 percent of Commission officials were drawn to Europe because they thought Europe was essential for the economic well-being or security of their country, region, or class.

These figures suggest that self-selection is common among Commission officials. Strong, often personal, factors lead them to perceive

---

[25] One may also match data collected through coding schemata with those from the questionnaire. This is possible for questionnaire items that overlap with interview questions. If the two instruments capture basic preferences effectively, there should be a high association between these data streams.

Table 2.3 *Interest in European politics*

Why did you become interested in European affairs?[a]	First choice	Second choice	Total	Percent[b] $n = 137$	Median year of birth
Because of my previous occupation	41	15	56	40.9	1940
Because of my studies at school/ university	15	7	22	16.1	1945
Because of the ideals it embodies: peace, democracy, order, good governance	29	5	34	24.8	1940
Because of my personal life: lived abroad, multinational family	29	11	40	29.2	1940
Because I developed interest on the job (through work in the Commission)	3	7	10	7.3	1935
Because it benefits my nationality or group (economic benefit)	7	4	11	8.0	1945
Not asked/not acknowledged	13	0	13	9.5	1937

[a] Question: "What was the most important reason for your interest in European affairs? What is your earliest recollection of being interested?" (Open question)
[b] Total is higher than 100 percent because several individuals have two codings.

European integration as a momentous and positive development, and this attracts them to the Commission. Yet self-selection goes well beyond idealism. By 1970, David Coombes discerned (and regretted) that the original generation, who had joined the Commission out of a sense of mission, was giving way to a bright, ambitious, more instrumentally oriented, younger crowd who considered the Commission a convenient outlet for their professional ambitions (Coombes 1970). At the turn of the century, I detect a similar tension between idealism and instrumentalism among top Commission officials. Older officials mention peace or democracy as motivating influences more often than their younger colleagues, who are more likely to cite instrumental reasons. Still, the generational divide is not as sharp as described by Coombes.

A male, highly educated, cosmopolitan crowd

The promotion of equal opportunity for men and women in the workplace has been a European Union success (Leibfried and Pierson 1995). But not in the Commission. Until 1995, political and bureaucratic leadership of the Commission was almost exclusively male. That changed with the arrival of five female political commissioners in the Jacques Santer Commission. Under their pressure, the Commission has adopted a policy

Table 2.4 *Men and women interviewees*

DG grouping	Men		Women	
	%	No.	%	No.
Administration	14.8	19	22.2	2[a]
External affairs	15.6	20	11.1	1[b]
Market-oriented	16.4	21	–	
Supply-side	17.2	22	–	
Provision & redistribution	24.2	31	11.1	1[c]
Social regulation	11.7	15	55.6	5[d]
Total	100.0	128	100.0	9

[a] One woman was appointed in 1989, and a second person in 1995.
[b] Appointed in 1995.
[c] Appointed in 1995.
[d] One woman was appointed in 1990, one in 1995, and three in 1996.

to promote more women. I caught the Commission at the beginning of this policy change. Less than 7 percent of interviewed top officials are female, and seven of the nine were appointed in 1995 or later (table 2.4).

Contemporary top civil servants without university degrees are a rare species (Dogan 1975; Page 1997; Page and Wright 1999a; Suleiman and Mendras 1995). It is no different in the Commission. A university degree is a formal entry requirement for all policy and management positions in the Commission (A-level in Commission jargon). Only two of my interviewees did not meet this criterion when they were hired. One worked his way up from proofreading and layout in the Commission's publication department; another started as a journalist posted in Brussels, but later acquired a university degree. Yet, whereas top civil servants in national bureaucracies often have similar degrees and are recruited from a core of elite schools, top Commission officials have diverse educational experiences. In this respect, the Commission is closer to the bureaucracy in the United States than to the caste-like civil services in Western Europe or Japan. The preponderance of legal training nurtures unity of purpose and style among German or Austrian civil servants (Derlien 1994; Liegl and Müller 1999). Most British civil servants are products of generalist philosophy, politics, and economics (PPE) programs at Oxford and Cambridge (Dargie and Locke 1999). In France, the prestigious *grandes écoles* (ENA – *école nationale d'administration*, and the *polytechniques*) monopolize the supply of top civil servants (Rouban 1999). And most Japanese civil servants are trained in special programs at Tokyo University (Page 1985; Page and Wright 1999a; Ross Schneider 1993; Suleiman 1975;

Table 2.5 *Study abroad for top officials*

Percentage who studied abroad as part of formal education	
No foreign education	61.2
In other European countries	23.1
In North America	13.4
In Europe & North America	2.2

Suleiman and Mendras 1995). The Commission is, in contrast, an amalgam of people from diverse cultural and educational systems, and this is not conducive to forming a homogeneous, single-purposive service (Page 1997).

Most top Commission officials are cosmopolitan. Nearly 40 percent studied abroad, about two-thirds of them in other European countries and one-third in North America (table 2.5). Some take advantage of a Commission visiting scholar program that allows officials to spend up to a year at a major research university, usually in the United States; many more express interest in the program. In my own university, the University of North Carolina at Chapel Hill, the Center for European Studies hosts a Commission fellow every other year.

Many top officials have a keen interest in academic life. Close to a fifth of the interviewees held academic positions prior to joining the Commission. Quite a few, including several directors-general, combine their Commission job with some university teaching, usually one or two courses. A substantial minority regularly participate and present papers at academic conferences. One interview took place during such a conference at the European University Institute (EUI) – an evening conversation at the end of a day during which the official had presented one paper and commented on another. Several publish in academic journals, some write books in law or economics, or occasionally in political science. One has been editor of a leading EU law journal, *Revue du Marché Commun*, for years. And quite a few dream of retiring to a teaching or research position in a European university. During my stay at the EUI in 1996–7, I discussed drafts of this project with two ex-Commission officials, whom I had interviewed in 1995. Claus-Dieter Ehlermann, formerly director-general for competition policy, was at that time a permanent fellow at the Robert Schuman Centre; Eberhard Rhein, who was director in external political affairs (DG Ib) until his retirement, was a regular visitor to the Centre. One year later, another interviewee, Horst Krenzler, retired from his post as director-general for external economic relations (DG I) and joined the multinational EUI.

Continuity and mobility

Personnel turnover in the Commission was high during my fieldwork. When I compare the personnel list of early 1997 with that of June 1995, almost one out of five top officials are new. Of these, slightly more than 8 percent entered the Commission between 1995 and 1997, largely in response to the latest round of EU enlargement, and 11 percent were recently promoted to a top job from a middle-management position. In addition, 16 percent rotated positions at the top – sideways from one director post to another, or upwards to the highest level. These figures suggest that one needs to refine the common belief that there is little mobility in the Commission (Bourtembourg 1987). Although the percentage of new recruits is modest (19 percent), job changeover has been high: no fewer than 35 percent are new on the job. And by May 1999, 18 percent of those in top positions in 1997 had retired or resigned, while another 16 percent had changed jobs.

So much job changeover between 1995 and 1997 – and again between 1997 and 1999 – might create the impression that the top administrative layer in the Commission is relatively inexperienced. On the contrary, the typical top official is an old hat. He has worked in the Commission for eighteen years on average (the median is twenty-one years). He has been in a senior position for seven to eight years, and in his current position for between four and five years. Moreover, mobility between directorates-general of the Commission is relatively low. A typical top official has worked in only two services during his entire career in the Commission. Of course, the longer an official has been in the Commission, the more he has had a chance to move around. However, 24 percent of those who have served the Commission for a quarter of a century or more have never set foot in another DG, and 30 percent have worked in two DGs only (table 2.6).[26]

These figures lend some support to the oft-heard thesis that departmental divisions and distinctive organizational cultures are more pronounced in the Commission than in most national bureaucracies (Abélès, Bellier, and McDonald 1993; Cini 1996; Peterson 1999; Richardson 1996). Yet mobility in the Commission is no less than, say, in the German, Dutch, or Swedish civil services (van der Meer and Raadschelders 1999; Page 1997; Pierre and Ehn 1999).

An early student of the European Commission once described it as a collection of "feudal fiefdoms" (Coombes 1970). These accusations

---

[26] Overall, 57 percent have worked in two DGs or more. This figure is commensurate with Edward Page's finding that 61 percent of senior Commission officials have worked in another directorate-general. According to Page, this figure suggests "a significant degree of mobility at the senior levels" (1997: 35).

Table 2.6 *DG experience by seniority (%)*

Number of DGs served	Seniority in the Commission				
	Less than 5 years	5 to 15 years	16 to 25 years	More than 25 years	All ($n = 137$)
1	13.1	18.3	5.8	5.8	43.0
2	–	7.3	13.1	7.3	27.7
3	–	3.6	8.1	6.6	18.3
>3	–	–	6.6	4.4	11.0
All	13.1	29.2	33.6	24.1	100.0

emerged anew after the Commission crisis in 1999. In September 1999, the fresh commissioner for personnel, Neil Kinnock, pledged to end feudalism by requiring top officials to change posts at "reasonable regular intervals," that is, every five to seven years.[27] Yet average interdepartmental mobility at the top level is already below five years. Contrary to what is commonly believed, only a minority of officials are entrenched in a departmental world.

Leaders with diverse professional experiences

Civil services in most western democracies have been under pressure to introduce private management techniques and greater customer-friendliness (Hood 1998a; Morris 1998; Rhodes 1992; Rockman and Peters 1996; Wright 1994a). In Europe, these demands have been strongest in the United Kingdom, where Conservative governments under Margaret Thatcher and John Major tried to achieve this by privatizing

---

[27] Kinnock made these measures public in a press statement on September 29, 1999. The broad general principles pertaining to mobility read as following:

1.1. A1s and A2s will be expected to rotate between functions at regular intervals. Once a post holder has occupied a post for five years, s/he should be interviewed by the Commissioner for Personnel and Administration (for A1s) or the Secretary General (for A2s) to consider career moves. This should be repeated annually until rotation occurs.

1.2. By 2002, no Director General will have been in post for more than seven years. (European Commission, "Press Release – 29 September 1999. By Neil Kinnock, Vice President of the European Commission," *http://europa.eu.int/comm/commissioners/kinnock/pr290999_en.htm* (accessed on September 29, 1999). Strictly speaking, the new rules make rotation mandatory only for the current group of directors-general. It is less clear whether directors, and directors-general after 2002, could be forced to rotate against their will, though the interview procedures are sure to put considerable pressure on reluctant officials.

Table 2.7 *Top officials' prior work experience (%)*

Most important occupation before entering the Commission	
Commission was first job	18.0
Elected political mandate	6.0
Civil service:	37.6
National (includes diplomacy)	25.6
EU (includes permanent representation)	12.0
Expertise:	38.4
International organizations	4.5
Central bank/courts	5.3
University, research, journalism	16.5
Business, banking, professions	11.3
Trade unions, public interest groups	0.8

certain public services. Where privatization was impracticable or politically infeasible, they brought in private sector people, particularly from industry and banking, to head public services (Richards 1997; Rhodes 1992).

Some voice these demands for the European Commission (Laffan 1996; Metcalfe 1992, 2000; Peterson 1999). The Prodi Commission, which took office in September 1999, has embarked on a modernization program that takes a leaf out of the New Public Management book – a shorthand for reforms applying market principles to public service.[28]

Yet the Commission's starting point is different from that in most member states. Commission top officials are more familiar with private sector techniques than are national senior civil servants. Close to 45 percent of top officials have extensive experience outside the public sector: university, culture, and media (16.5 percent); private business and banking (11.3 percent); politics (6.0 percent); semi-independent, specialized public jobs in central banks or courts (5.3 percent), and international organizations such as the IMF and the World Bank (4.5 percent) (table 2.7). Though a majority of top Commission officials served at some point in a traditional line ministry or diplomatic post, nearly four out of ten have no prior experience with public administrations.

This is very different from top officials in the United Kingdom, where the civil service provides few openings for outsiders. Nearly all civil servants enter Whitehall almost directly from university. Civil service reforms under the Thatcher and Major governments opened up more top positions to outsiders in an attempt to attract private sector managers.

---

[28] See chapters 6 and 7 for detailed discussion.

Yet the reforms have so far met limited success. Recruitment for central line posts is still mainly internal and, to the extent that there are external recruits, they tend to be specialist appointments – lawyers, statisticians, and economists – rather than officials in general managerial posts (Dargie and Locke 1999). In the French and German bureaucracies, top positions have traditionally been more open to outsiders. The French mechanism of *pantouflage* allows ambitious officials to switch back and forth between the public and private sectors – and in the latter they usually assume various managerial responsibilities in business or, more often, in a public enterprise. But one has to keep in mind that virtually every top civil servant emerges from the same narrow set of educational institutions (Rouban 1999). Whereas British and French recruits typically enter the civil service straight from graduate school, recruitment in Germany gives priority to candidates with working experience in the private sector, universities, or the *Länder* administrations. So German practice is not very different from Commission practice, with the one telling difference that most German civil servants are lawyers, whereas Commission officials have more diverse educational backgrounds. Another difference is that the German bureaucracy brings in fresh faces with each change of government in Berlin. An incoming government is entitled to appoint outsiders, usually with party-political connections, to key top posts (*Seiteneinsteiger*), and these people keep their status as civil servants even after "their" government makes space for a new one. Yet only a small proportion of all top positions are allocated that way (Götz 1999).

Commission officials are not simply more nationally diverse than civil servants in a member state. They are also far more diverse in their disciplinary background (law, economics, or generalist), their educational institutional background, and their work experience.

Not political appointees, but nonetheless political

In the United States, top bureaucratic posts are allocated through a spoils system, which means that, when the president moves on, so do a substantial proportion of senior administrative personnel. They usually take up private sector jobs. Most top bureaucrats, then, do not have tenure. This is how, in the US system, politicians ultimately exercise control over the bureaucracy.

The absence of career tenure for top officials in the United States contrasts sharply with practice in Western Europe, including the European Commission. How is political control exercised, then, in Europe? And how does it work in the Commission?

The furthest away from the US system are the British, Danish, and, to a lesser extent, the Dutch civil services. In these systems, top officials are expected to be *neutral executors* of government policy, irrespective of the government of the day. Professional top bureaucrats have the right to express pragmatic reservations about a particular policy but, if the policy is adopted against their advice, they must implement it. In most European countries, though, like in the United States, partisanship among top officials is widely accepted, but, unlike the USA and like in the neutral civil services, this combines with career tenure. In France, Germany, and Sweden, a system of rotation of partisan appointees guarantees governments political control. Party appointees staff the "commanding heights," that is, the key administrative positions. When the party complexion of the government changes, these people rotate to less sensitive bureaucratic positions. In the *Proporz* systems of Belgium and Austria, partisanship has a more wide-ranging impact on promotion in the bureaucracy. One usually needs a party card to get promoted – even at middle-level management. The difference with the French–German system is that governments exert control not by rotating top appointments, but rather by filling vacant or newly created top positions with their own supporters to reflect their relative party strength. So, at any time, the party color of the top bureaucracy is expected to reflect the relative strength of parties in the parliament (Page and Wright 1999b).

The European Commission is a mixture. Its baseline takes after the British–Danish system: top officials are expected to be neutral; there is no rotation of top officials, except to avoid that a director-general has the same nationality as his commissioner; and officials have career tenure. Yet this is interspersed with characteristics that evoke the Belgian–Austrian *Proporz* system. Though recruitment and promotion should be based on merit only, there is a strong norm to ensure proportionate representation of nationalities at the top. These national quotas roughly reflect the distribution of member state votes in the Council of Ministers (more on this in chapter 7). Moreover, like the French, German, and, recently, British bureaucracies, the Commission may attract external candidates for top bureaucratic positions if no suitable internal candidate can be found – 43 percent of senior appointments are recruited through *parachutage*, that is, from outside the Commission (table 2.8). Also like the French and German systems, every commissioner has a cabinet of temporary political appointees, which assists in designing policy.

Top Commission officials tend to view political control of the Commission bureaucracy through national spectacles. British or Danish officials stress officials' neutrality; Belgian and Austrian officials assume that top

Table 2.8 *Recruitment into the Commission (%)*

Recruitment through ranks	57.0
Before 1965[a]	14.6
Competitive examinations	27.7
Fast-track (entry at middle-level management)	14.6
Recruitment through parachutage	43.0
Enlargement parachutage[b]	15.3
Ordinary parachutage	19.7
Entry from Commission cabinet	8.0
All	100.0

[a] The Commission set up a central system of competitive examinations in 1965 ("*concours*").

[b] With each enlargement, a proportion of top posts are set aside for nationals from the new member states. All these positions have to be filled by external candidates, because there are no nationals to be promoted from the Commission's middle management. This type of parachutage is by necessity, not by choice, contrary to "ordinary parachutage" or "parachutage from cabinets."

appointments are parceled out according to nationality and party affiliation; and many French or Germans emphasize the role of cabinets – the epitome of political appointment and rotation. Each view has some truth; the Commission does all of the above.

Parachutage, partisan recruitment, and national quotas are not the only channels for political engagement. Many top officials join the political fray in some way or another. One of four top officials has served in a Commission cabinet. And many top Commission officials nurture extensive political connections with European and national parties. Around 60 percent of officials have been active in politics at some point in their life, and most continue some activity after they enter the Commission; 34 percent report a fairly high level of involvement as party member, activist, or candidate for elections. Table 2.9 shows the extent of political involvement by party-political identification.

Generalist managers and busy networkers

Top officials work within a highly structured technocratic and bureaucratic environment. They spend on average more than 80 percent of their professional time in Brussels, and the remainder on the road.

Table 2.9 *Party identification and political activity (%)*

Party identification	Political activity				
	None/not known	Low (interest in politics)	Medium (party member)	High (party activist, candidate for election)	All
Communist	–	0.9	–	0.9	1.9
Socialist/social democratic	0.9	4.8	5.7	10.4	21.7
Christian democratic	0.9	2.8	3.8	4.8	12.3
Centrist	–	3.8	–	0.9	4.7
Liberal	1.8	6.6	2.8	1.8	13.2
Conservative	0.9	0.9	0.9	–	2.8
Radical right	–	–	–	0.9	0.9
Refused to disclose	23.5	5.7	0.9	–	30.2
Not known/not asked	11.3	0.9	–	–	12.2
All	39.6	26.4	14.2	19.8	100.0

Note: Cell figures may not add up to row or column totals because of rounding.

Almost 60 percent of total time is taken up by internal Commission affairs, of which more than two-thirds involves administrative and organizational tasks, such as coordinating activities with other DGs, planning work in the directorate, or solving staff problems (table 2.10). Many top officials are unhappy with the red tape that comes with the job. On my interview rounds, I saw many a desk laden with infamous *circulaires*, folders containing anything from draft policy papers, spending accounts worth tens (or hundreds) of millions of Euros, reports on missions, to permissions for a one-day leave for a junior official. Many of these folders travel up (and sometimes down and up again) the hierarchical ladder, amassing *paraphes* (signatures) until they reach the director-general (or the secretary general). Top officials have very little spare time to make policy. By their own reckoning, they spend only 15 percent of their time on drafting and defending new proposals. Monnet would have frowned.

However, they set aside considerable time for external contacts. On average, 38 percent of time is spent on policy-related activities with actors outside the Commission. This usually involves public relations and advertising new policies. Top officials also travel occasionally to the European Parliament in Strasbourg to negotiate legislative acts (7 percent). And they may be called upon to solve implementation problems (8 percent).

Table 2.10 *Time budget of a typical top Commission official (%)*

Total administrative activities in-house	42
Supervision, organization, coordination in DG (including personnel)	34
Coordination with other DGs	8
Total policy activities in-house	15
Preparation of documents for higher authority	10
Promotion of policies in-house	5
Total outside activities	38
Promotion of new policies	9
Public relations	14
Negotiation of legislative acts	7
Solving implementation problems	8
Various other	5
Total	100

This Janus-type mix of internal/external focus is reflected in officials' interactions with a range of actors. I asked top officials to estimate how often they meet *in person* with a variety of actors (the results are in tables 2.11 and 2.12). It is not difficult to distinguish three concentric circles of actors. Top officials meet most frequently with actors directly relevant to their policy area: more than once a week with officials in their own DG, weekly with their own commissioner or her cabinet, and nearly as often with administrative equals in other DGs.[29]

The second circle, at some distance, consists of most EU institutions, but it also contains some governmental and societal actors. Top officials meet once a month or so with the Commission president or his

[29] After they vacated the Berlaymont building in the early 1990s, the political Commission and the DGs were no longer housed in the same building. The political Commission resided in the Breydel building, a stone's throw away from the European Parliament and the Council of Ministers. The various DGs were scattered throughout Brussels. This physical separation, often regretted by older officials, made it more difficult for permanent top officials to interact with their political bosses and it also impeded contacts among DGs. When the Prodi Commission took office in September 1999, the commissioners decided to move out of the Breydel and set up shop with their respective services. The various Commission departments are still scattered across Brussels, but the political and bureaucratic leaderships of each department are now again under the same roof. The Prodi Commission decided to take this step to restore political control over its departments. However, our data indicate that the bureaucratic and political leaderships had relatively regular contact, notwithstanding the physical separation; to the extent that political control faltered under the Santer Commission, it was not for want of communication opportunities between commissioners and their departments.

Table 2.11 *Frequency of contact with actors inside the Commission*

How often do you meet this position holder in a typical month?[a]	Mean
Inside your DG	3.3
Middle-level manager (head of unit)	3.9
Administrative equal or superior (director, deputy DG)	3.8
Junior administrator	3.6
Collective meeting with bureaucratic equals	3.1
Collective meeting with middle-level managers	2.4
Other DGs	2.3
Administrative equal outside your DG	2.6
Collectively with administrative equals outside your DG	2.0
Your commissioner	2.7
Cabinet of your commissioner	3.2
Your commissioner	2.3

[a] Question: "We would like to know how often you meet in person the following positions in a *typical month* of your work year: daily (5), several times a week (4), weekly (3), 1–2 times a month (2), less than once a month (1), never (0).

cabinet, the European Parliament, Coreper (Committee of Permanent Representatives), Council working groups, and the Council of Ministers. Strikingly, Commission officials meet equally often with the European Parliament – directly elected politicians – as with the Council working groups – national diplomats or civil servants. This reflects mutual interlocking among the three European institutions in EU decision-making (Marks, Hooghe, and Blank 1996). Three governmental and societal actors belong to this second circle as well. Top officials meet national civil servants on average about once a month, mainly in advisory committees convened by the Commission to assist drafting proposals. Of societal actors, only lobbyists representing industry enjoy regular access to top officials. Top officials typically meet the media once a month.

The third circle is an amalgam of weaker governmental actors (regional civil servants), weaker societal interests (organized labor, environmentalists, consumers, and regions), and weaker institutional actors (Committee of the Regions). Top officials meet each of these at most a few times a year.

Note the low profile of elected actors, with one exception – the European Parliament! Top Commission officials have less personal contact with elected politicians than with certain societal or bureaucratic actors. They meet less frequently with the Commission president or his

Table 2.12 *Frequency of contact with EU institutional actors and governmental and societal actors*

How often do you meet this position holder in a typical month?[a]	Mean
EU institutional actors	1.1
Commission president or cabinet	1.2
European Parliament	1.3
Coreper/Council working groups	1.3
Council of Ministers	1.2
Committee of Regions/ECOSOC	0.7
Ministers (elected executives)	0.8
(Individual) national minister	0.9
(Individual) regional minister	0.7
Civil servants	1.4
National civil servants	2.0
Regional civil servants	0.9
Societal actors	1.1
Industry	1.4
Press	1.3
Trade unions	0.9
Regional offices	0.9
Environmental and consumer groups	0.8

[a] Question: "We would like to know how often you meet in person the following positions in a *typical month* of your work year: daily (5), several times a week (4), weekly (3), 1–2 times a month (2), less than once a month (1), never (0).

cabinet, responsible for the Commission's political agenda, or with the Council of Ministers, the main EU legislator, than with industrial interests and the media. And they meet more often with the Council working groups and national civil servants. Other elected actors, notably national and regional ministers and the Committee of the Regions, also trail societal and bureaucratic actors.

This preponderance of unelected actors among officials' interlocutors is not unusual – most national top bureaucrats also deal primarily with other bureaucracies, interest groups, and other levels of government. Yet top Commission officials stand out in that their immediate political superior, the commissioner, is not herself an elected politician, whereas the immediate political boss of a national top bureaucrat almost always is.

Industry enjoys considerably better access to the Commission than do trade unions, environmental groups, or regional interests. Comparative

Table 2.13 *Frequency of contact between societal groups by DG grouping*

DG grouping	Industry	Trade unions	Environmental and consumer groups	Regional offices
Administration	0.7	0.4	0.3	0.8
External affairs	1.3	0.8	0.7	0.4
Market-oriented	2.1	0.8	0.7	0.8
Supply-side	1.7	1.0	0.9	1.0
Provision & redistribution	1.1	1.1	0.9	1.0
Social regulation	1.7	1.4	1.3	1.1
Total	1.4	0.9	0.8	0.9

analysis indicates that this is, again, not surprising. Mobile capital and industry generally have better access to the civil service, as has been well documented for the United States, Britain, or France. Only civil services in corporatist societies tend to provide more access to trade unions – though not necessarily equal access; and they usually score considerably worse for consumer or environmental interests.

The picture of uneven societal access is more nuanced when one examines access by type of DG (table 2.13). I use the same six-type categorization of DGs, in expected descending order of openness to societal interests: social regulation, supply-side policies, market-oriented DGs, provision, external relations, and administration. Industry's contacts are strongest in market-oriented DGs, followed at some distance by DGs for supply-side policies and for social regulation, and by external relations; industrial interests are least likely to meet officials in DGs for provision or in administrative DGs. Access for trade unions is concentrated in DGs dealing with social regulation, provision, and supply-side services; trade unions rarely interact with officials from market-oriented DGs or external relations; contacts with administrative DGs are virtually non-existent. It is indicative of the asymmetry between societal actors that even the DGs that are most open to trade unions – those dealing with social regulation – talk more with industrial interests than with labor interests. Environmental and consumer groups deal most often with DGs for social regulation, though the intensity of contact is low; top officials from other Commission services rarely meet environmental or consumer advocates. Finally, regional interests have consistently very low access across the Commission.

Introductions made, let us get down to business. What kind of European Union do top Commission officials desire? In the following chapter, I examine Commission officials' preferences on basic issues of governance. Should the EU promote regulated capitalism or market liberalism? Should it have federal or confederal institutions? Should the Commission be an initiating principal or an administrative–managerial agent? And should the Commission defend the general European interest or be responsive to sectional interests?

3   Images of Europe

It is a sticky, hot July afternoon in Brussels. My interview with the Commission director was scheduled for four o'clock, but it is now well past five. At last, the door swings open and four people leave, talking animatedly. I am waved into the room, and I switch on the tape recorder. Towards the end of the interview, I accidentally find out what kept me waiting for so long. When I ask my interviewee to define the European Union's greatest challenges, he recounts the following story:[1]

The reason why this little meeting before the interview went on and on is that we were talking about Town X [a depressed town in Northern Europe], where we try to actually do things to help development in disadvantaged communities. I have difficulty talking about this without sounding like a twentieth-century saint – which I am not – or like a sociologist – which I am not trained to be. But I have asked a colleague to work and live there for three weeks among voluntary organizations, and this is unusual for a civil servant. She has just come back, and she paints a picture of a world in which crime, which we would all condemn, is in a certain sense the only manifestation of initiative. In fact, you can almost say that the potential for economic development of a depressed region could be expressed by its crime rate: high crime rates suggest that people still have spirit! The society is in a way flipped over; it is upside down!

One day, a television team goes to Town X, and parks its van loaded with expensive filming equipment in a quiet spot. When they return from a filming trip, the van is empty. The equipment is stolen. They get ready to drive away, when boys aged eleven or twelve – children! – jump forward and shout at the crew: "What do you pay to get your kit back?" These kids have the initiative to steal all the stuff, take it around the corner, hide it, and, not wanting to deprive the crew of the equipment, extort a price for their "protective services." This is kidnap of the gear, not theft. Apparently the television team paid an excessive Euro 500 [approx. US$500] to get these thousands Euro worth of equipment back. I do not know whether to condemn these children or admire their sense of enterprise. It sounds to me like capitalism is alive and well in this deprived area!

The world is upside-down. We would be able to employ hundreds of people like those kids if we could think of a way of flipping society back onto its proper position. We are talking about these great disparities in wealth as a major challenge

---

[1] I have altered details to disguise the identity of the interviewee.

to the Community. But these wealth disparities are not, it seems to me, the most important problem. It is the fact that, in large segments of our cities and regions, people have been out of society for so long that they do not believe in society any more. They are no longer able to see how it has anything to do with them. So that is my challenge. (Official #57)

Diagnosing Europe's problems and advising on possible solutions is second nature for top Commission officials. That flows naturally from the Commission's constitutional duty to "formulate recommendations or deliver opinions on matters dealt with in this Treaty, if it expressly so provides or if the Commission considers it necessary" (Article 211 of the

Table 3.1 *Indicators for factor analysis*

1. The member states, not the Commission nor the European Parliament, ought to remain the central pillars of the European Union.
2. The strength of Europe lies not in more power for Brussels, but in effective government at the lowest possible level.
3. It is imperative that the European Commission become the true government of the European Union.
4. The Commission acts too much as an administration, and not enough as the government of Europe.
5. Europe should be more than a common market.
6. Europe has developed a unique model of society, and the Commission should help to preserve it: extensive social services, civilized industrial relations, negotiated transfers among groups to sustain solidarity, and steer economic activity for the general welfare.
7. No united Europe without a mature European cohesion policy.
8. European Union policy is too much influenced by big business.
9. The Commission cannot function properly without a vision, a set of great priorities, a blueprint for the future.
10. The Commission should support the European Parliament's bid for full legislative powers, even if the price would be to lose its monopoly of initiative.
11. The Commission should concentrate on maintaining the internal market.
12. The Commission should concentrate on administering things efficiently.
13. Pressure groups and special interests, like trade unions, farmers' organizations, industry, environmental lobbyists, and so on, disturb the proper working of European government.
14. The egoistic behavior of some member states threatens the very survival of the European project.
15. Too many Commission civil servants let their nationality interfere in their professional judgments.
16. It hurts the Commission's legitimacy that certain DGs tend to be dominated by particular nationalities, such as agriculture by the French, competition by the Germans, regional policy by the Spanish, environment by the north ...
17. The best advice on a proposed policy usually comes from the interests directly affected.

new Treaty on European Union). But the above story is a compelling illustration of how this apparently impartial duty may jolt top officials into taking a stance on the future of Europe – and to act accordingly.

The quoted official desires a fairer, more egalitarian European society. He wants a European Union with the instruments to redistribute opportunities and income and, above all, to restore social cohesion. Yet not all his colleagues think that way. There is no unique blueprint for the European Union. There are a variety of institutional options – images of Europe – from which Commission officials may choose.

Dimensions

Like other European elite actors, top officials consider the eternal questions of politics: Who governs, how, and over whom? How should authority be structured across territorial layers of government? What should be the role of European authority in the economy? Should European policy making be democratically accountable? What role(s) should interest groups play?

I search for answers to these questions in the reasoning and words of these people. But how does one know whether my understanding of officials' preferences is accurate? Validation is difficult when one limits oneself to qualitative methods of interpretation. Quantitative analysis and causal analysis are needed to help one choose among contrasting interpretations (Searing 1994; Strauss 1987). Causal analysis – explaining variation in top officials' preferences by testing competing hypotheses – is the focus of chapters 4 through 7. In this chapter, I use exploratory factor analysis to characterize Commission officials' preferences on four dimensions of EU governance. Factor analysis assesses the degree to which particular questions or items tap the same concept. If individuals respond in similar ways to two questions, then we may assume that these questions are conceptually related. Table 3.1 lists seventeen items that canvass officials' preferences on EU governance.[2] To minimize the risk of acquiescent responses, I distributed these political items randomly over a list of thirty-two items (see appendix III). Let us begin by outlining

[2] Respondents indicate whether they agree without reservations (4), agree with reservations (3), disagree with reservations (2), or disagree without reservations (1). I allocate a value of 2.5 to respondents who indicate neutrality or abstain.

It is possible that the manner in which I treat neutral positions influences the results. To test for this, I reran the factor analysis for three alternatives: (a) neutral positions as missing values, (b) recalculation of the four-point scale to a five-point scale, with a value of 3.0 for neutral positions, (c) neutral positions equal to the mean value of each item (instead of a uniform 2.5). These factor analyses produce the same four dimensions, and the same variables load high on these dimensions. The results are for all purposes identical to the ones reported in table 3.2.

my expectations on how specific items relate to the larger issues of EU governance.

Expectations

A fundamental question for EU players is where authority should rest in the European Union. Should authority be devolved back to member states and the Council of Ministers, or should supranational institutions be strengthened? Four items speak directly to the tension between *intergovernmental* and *supranational* images of Europe. Item 1 states that ultimate authority should remain vested in the member states, while item 2 takes on the issue of subsidiarity, arguing that the strength of Europe lies not in more power for Brussels but in effective government at the lowest possible level.[3] These items represent the intergovernmental pole. Items 3 and 4 exemplify a supranational alternative. They argue that the Commission should be the true government of the European Union, and that it should act less as an administration and more as the government of Europe.

What should be the scope of authoritative regulation in the European economy? Should the European Union promote *market liberal capitalism*, based on the Anglo-Saxon model, or should it support *regulated capitalism* that builds on the continental European Rhine model? Regulated capitalism promises more generous welfare state services, more redistribution and thus less income inequality, greater regulation of labor markets, a larger role for trade unions in economic decision making, and lower unemployment (Kitschelt et al. 1999). Item 5 evokes general opposition to pure market liberalism in the European Union by stating "Europe should be more than a common market." Item 6 summarizes former Commission president Jacques Delors' definition of European regulated capitalism, which calls for a unique model of society in which the Commission helps preserve extensive social services, civilized industrial relations, negotiated transfers among groups to sustain solidarity, and steers economic activity for the general welfare. Item 7 brings to the

[3] The item on subsidiarity in my survey is different from the one used in Eurobarometer surveys of public opinion and the special 1996 elite survey. The question in Eurobarometer reads: "The European Union should be responsible for matters that cannot be effectively handled by national, regional or local governments." This is a studiously depoliticized statement that avoids the contentious issue of the distribution of competencies between the various territorial levels. It is no surprise, then, that Europe's elites find it difficult to disagree with the statement (81 percent in favor). The fact that support is equally high among generally Euro-cautious British and normally Euro-enthusiastic Italian elites (87 percent each) patently demonstrates that this item is ill suited to differentiate European elites (or public, for that matter) according to their supranational or intergovernmental preferences (European Commission n.d.).

fore EU cohesion policy, the bedrock of anti market-liberalism. The goal of the policy, which currently absorbs 35 percent of the EU budget, is to reduce regional inequalities in the European Union through structural programming.

My expectations on the relationship between the next two items and this dimension are less definite. Item 8 invites top officials to take a stance on big business's influence on European policy. The conventional view among the European left has been that "big business" (especially multinational corporations) supports European integration only to the extent that it helps consolidate neoliberalism in Europe (for overviews see Christensen 1996; Lankowski 1997). According to that view, proponents of European regulated capitalism should be wary of big business's influence. Yet Maria Cowles' studies of the European Round Table of Industrialists – Europe's major lobby for big business – demonstrate considerable support for European regulated capitalism among big business (Cowles-Green 1995). If proponents of regulated capitalism find this support credible, they may not be so hostile to big business. Predictions are equally difficult for item 9, which tests views on whether or not the Commission should have a blueprint for the future. Proponents of regulated capitalism usually want a more ambitious role for the Commission, and so they are likely to be most keen on a Commission with a blueprint, and the resources to carry it out, whereas market liberals are likely to prefer a slimmed-down organization that restricts itself to managerial tasks. Yet market liberals may also want a strong, effective, and strategic Commission, albeit to achieve more selective goals having to do with deepening market intergration.

The European Parliament has been a consistent supporter of European regulated capitalism, including regional policy, environmental policy, social policy, and R&D, and so one may expect proponents of European regulated capitalism to support a strengthening of the European Parliament (item 10). Item 11 is the last item on this dimension, and it voices the market-liberal alternative, suggesting that the Commission confine itself to policing the internal market.

The third dimension pits proponents of greater *democratic accountability* in the European Union against defenders of a *technocratic,* expert-based form of governance. Item 10 is the litmus test for "democrats." Do they support a European Parliament with full legislative powers (as one would expect in a modern democracy), even if this costs the Commission its exclusive right to propose legislation? For Jean Monnet and many advocates of deeper European integration, the Commission's monopoly of initiative is the single most important source for the European Union's resilience (Monnet 1962, 1978; Tsebelis and Kreppel 1998). A top official willing to give up this power in exchange for full parliamentary powers unambiguously favors a democratic Europe. Contrast this with items 11 and 12, which evoke a technocratic Europe. Whereas item 12 casts the Commission in the role of efficient administrator, item 11 states that the Commission should concentrate on maintaining the internal market.

Finally, how should the public interest be reconciled with sectional pressures? Should Commission officials consider themselves *guardians of a common European interest* that transcends national, cultural, social, and territorial particularities? Or should the EU authorities be *responsive to sectional interests*? Proponents of a common European interest want to keep at bay any type of interest – whether it concerns the distorting influence of functional interests, such as trade unions, farmers' organizations, industry, or environmental lobbyists (item 13), or whether it involves egoistic member states (item 14). Furthermore, they are more likely to disapprove of national favoritism by their own colleagues in the Commission. Item 15 solicits their views on whether individuals let their decisions be unduly influenced by nationality concerns, and item 16 does the same for whole units or DGs. I expect officials skeptical of an overarching European public interest to be more positively oriented towards sectional interests, whether these are functional or national. This preference is worded in item 17, which argues that the best policy advice usually comes from affected interests.

Results

Factor analysis substantiates that top Commission officials' preferences on European governance can be conceptualized along these four dimensions.[4] The results in table 3.2 include all factor loadings of .30 or higher. To make it easier for the reader to compare expectations and results, I rank factors and variables in the same way as in table 3.1. The four factors explain 47.4 percent of the variance. Let us take a closer look at the results.

Intergovernmentalism vs. supranationalism. The first factor captures the traditional conception of European integration as a contest between intergovernmentalism and supranationalism. The two intergovernmental

---

[4] Each factor has an eigenvalue of more than 1.5. The standard Kaiser's criterion requires a minimum eigenvalue of 1.0, which would have withheld six factors for seventeen variables (with 61 percent of variance explained). A scree plot demonstrates a downward kick in the curve of variance explained after the fourth factor. The results I report here are based on the principal component method and varimax rotation, though the findings are robust across alternative methodologies. Oblique rotation produces the same four factors, and the correlation between the factors is very weak (see note 5).

Table 3.2 *Factor analysis of attitude indicators for Commission officials*

	Factor			
Indicators	I[a]	II[b]	III[c]	IV[d]
1. Member states should remain central pillars of EU	.47		.51	
2. Subsidiarity – more power at the lowest level, not for Brussels	.72			
3. The Commission should become the true government of the European Union	−.59			.31
4. The Commission is too much administration, not enough the government of Europe	−.49			.55
5. Europe should be more than a common market	−.37	.55		
6. The Commission should preserve unique model of European society		.62		
7. No united Europe without mature EU cohesion policy		.77		
8. Too much influence of big business	.44	.34		.32
9. The Commission needs vision, blueprint for future		.65		
10. The Commission should support full legislative powers for the European Parliament		.35	−.43	
11. The Commission should concentrate on maintaining the internal market			.73	
12. The Commission should concentrate on administering efficiently			.70	
13. Special interests disturb the proper working of European government				.63
14. Some egoistic member states threaten the European project			−.37	.39
15. Too often nationality interferes in official's judgment				.77
16. Certain DGs are dominated by nationalities, and this hurts the Commission legitimacy				.68
17. The best advice usually comes from directly affected interests			.41	
Eigenvalues	1.72	2.18	1.92	2.23
Variance explained (%)	10.1	12.8	11.3	13.1

[a] Intergovernmentalism: Intergovernmentalists vs. Supranationalists
[b] Regulated Capitalism: Regulated Capitalists vs. Market Liberals
[c] Technocracy: Technocrats vs. Democrats
[d] European Interest: Eurofonctionnaires vs. Responsive Euroservants

items – one on member states as central pillars (item 1), and one on subsidiarity (item 2) – boast very high scores. The supranational counterparts – the Commission as the true government (item 3), and the Commission acting too much as an administration (item 4) – load negatively, and powerfully so, on this dimension. And so does item 5, which says that Europe should be more than a common market.

It is noteworthy that item 8 – big business has too much influence on European policy-making – finds much support among proponents of intergovernmentalism. Its high score on this dimension corroborates neofunctionalist arguments, which have conceived of transnational business as a key supporter of deeper European integration (Cowles-Green 1995; Cram 1997; Haas 1958; Sandholtz and Zysman 1989). Officials who favor intergovernmentalism may be aware of this neofunctionalist dynamic, and they may wish to avoid it. This first factor explains 10.1 percent of the variance.

European regulated capitalism vs. market liberalism. The second factor pits regulated capitalism against market liberalism. This factor is most powerfully identified with officials' stance on EU cohesion policy (item 7), on Delors' conception of a European societal model (item 6), and on the broad statement that Europe should be more than a common market (item 5). Proponents of regulated capitalism are also inclined to consider big business too influential (item 8), and to favor a Commission with a political vision (item 9). They also support more powers for the European Parliament (item 10).

Note that the internal market item fails to load on this dimension, which is consistent with the view that the internal market program was never a bone of contention between market liberals and regulated capitalists (Bornschier 2000; Hooghe and Marks 1999). As we will see, Commission officials associate this item with a different choice on Europe: whether Europe should be technocratic or democratic. This factor explains 12.8 percent of total variance.

Technocracy vs. democracy. Five items score high on the factor capturing the tension between a democratic and a technocratic European Union. The leading items on this dimension are item 11 ("the Commission should concentrate on maintaining the internal market") and item 12 ("the Commission should concentrate on administering things efficiently").

Top Commission officials generally believe in a trade-off between policy efficiency and democracy. Subjecting EU decision-making to more democratic control, they fear, will make policy outcomes less efficient. Those who want to safeguard the internal market realize the need for efficient management, and they prefer to de-politicize EU decision-making as much as possible. They distrust the European Parliament (item 10), and they put their faith in conventional participants in technocratic governance: professional experts from member state bureaucracies (items 1 and 14) or from affected private interest groups (item 17). Proponents of greater parliamentary powers do not see things that way; they do not want the Commission to be primarily a managerial organization concerned with the "core functions" of market integration. This third factor explains 11.3 percent of the variance.

European interest vs. sectional interest. Five items load strongly on the last factor, summarizing the conflict about whether Commission officials should speak for the general European interest or be responsive to sectional interests. Two results are worth highlighting.

First of all, officials do not make a strong conceptual distinction between national (items 15 and 16) and functional (items 8 and 13) interests. What matters are contending preferences about how to deal with sectional interests, not whether particularistic preferences are advanced by national governments or by societal interest groups. Second, top officials entertain sophisticated views on the role of nationality in EU politics. As the high loadings on items 15 and 16 on this dimension demonstrate, some top officials are critical of national bias in recruitment, allocation of funds, and policy-making, whereas others feel more comfortable with national quotas. Yet their opinion on this issue does not prejudge their views on an intergovernmental or supranational European Union. In other words, a critic of national quota may very well be an intergovernmentalist – or she may not be. That is why the correlation between *Intergovernmentalism* (factor I) and *European interest* (factor IV) is statistically insignificant.[5] This factor explains 13.1 percent of the variance.

---

[5] Oblique rotation demonstrates that the four factors can be considered orthogonal. The one significant deviation from orthogonality concerns factors II and IV, which suggests that those favoring regulated capitalism are also more likely to believe in the common European interest (sign .04, one-tailed). The correlation matrix with oblimin procedure gives the following results:

	Factor I	Factor II	Factor III
Factor I – Intergovernmentalism	1.000		
Factor II – Regulated capitalism	−.071	1.000	
Factor III – Technocracy	.092	−.133*	1.000
Factor IV – European interest	.050	.169**	.013

$**p < .05$, $*p < .1$ (one-tailed significance)

Table 3.3 *Images of Europe – where Commission officials stand*

	Intergovernmentalism	Technocracy	Regulated capitalism	European interest
Max. value	3.8	3.4	4.0	3.4
75 percentile	2.8	2.6	4.0	2.5
50 percentile	2.4	2.4	3.3	2.3
25 percentile	2.2	2.0	3.0	1.8
Min. value	1.2	1.2	2.0	1.0
Mean[a]	2.4	2.4	3.4	2.2
Standard deviation	0.50	0.44	0.55	0.59
Skewness	−0.23	−0.18	−0.67	0.11

[a] Values range between 1.0 (unconditional disapproval) and 4.0 (unconditional approval). $N = 105$.

Factor analysis helps one to make sense of a complex social reality by identifying underlying patterns, but it does so at a cost. It does not tell one where Commission officials stand within each dimension. To examine variation in preferences one needs to disaggregate the four dimensions into the individual items that constitute them, and examine where top officials stand. Are most officials on the whole supranationalist and Euro-socialist – as is often claimed in public discourse? To what extent do they resist greater democratic accountability? How many feel strongly about defending a common European interest?

Images of Europe

These four dimensions form the backbone of coherent images of Europe that are clearly articulated by Commission officials. I employ two methodologies to explicate more systematically the various ideal Europes of top officials.

As a first step, I construct scales for each dimension.[6] Table 3.3 reports minimum and maximum values, quartile values, mean, standard deviation, and skewness of the distribution. I use as labels for these scales the

---

[6] The items I use for each scale are the items with a factor loading of .4 or more in the factor analysis. I then calculate the average value for each interviewee on each dimension. Each scale meets the standard criterion of scaling reliability (Cronbach's alpha). The Intergovernmentalism scale consists of items 1, 2, 3, 4, and 11 (Cronbach's alpha = .54). The Regulated Capitalism scale is composed of items 10, 12, and 8 (Cronbach's alpha = .59). Item 7 is excluded because there is virtually no variation and the distribution is highly skewed (mean = 3.9). The Technocracy scale consists of items 9, 5, 1, 6, and 15 (Cronbach's alpha = .55). And, finally, the European Interest scale consists of items 16, 17, 13, and 4 (Cronbach's alpha = .66).

high end of the continuum. For example, scores on the Intergovernmentalism scale vary from 1.0 (supranationalist) to 4.0 (intergovernmentalist). So the higher a person's score, the more he supports an intergovernmental Union; a score below 2.5 suggests that he leans to supranationalism. Similarly, values on the Technocracy scale read as the extent to which individuals value technocratic decision-making above democratic accountability; values between 2.5 and 4.0 indicate support for technocratic governance, while lower values express support for greater democratic control. Even a cursory glance at table 3.3 makes plain that there is extensive dissension among top Commission officials. In a next step, I hope to add flesh, life, and nuance to these numbers by means of focused interpretative reading of the interview transcripts. This technique enables me to construct Weberian ideal-types – stylized images, and yet firmly rooted in the conscious understanding that Commission officials themselves have about thier political world.[7]

Intergovernmentalism or supranationalism?

The Commission's top officials rule out a Europe of sovereign nation-states. The following response is as far as "Euro-skeptical" officials go:

It is obvious that nation-states should retain a very great role in the European construction. The problem is to find an efficient institutional form – I am not only thinking of economic efficiency, but also of political efficacy. We know very well that, politically, in one or the other way, we need to go somewhat beyond the nation-state. But the construction must ultimately rest on relationships between states. Our public opinions [sic] are not ready to accept federalism in the classical sense of the word. We must therefore find a different form. (Official #27)

Top Commission officials wish to create a common structure of authoritative decision-making in Europe. No interviewee flirts with Euro-skeptical nationalism by arguing for a loose confederation of European states. European collaboration in areas where governments hang onto their veto is considered suboptimal. Nearly all, intergovernmentalists included, are willing to trade the national veto for majority rule on market regulation.

Yet intergovernmentalists and supranationalists disagree on where the main locus of authoritative decision-making should lie – with the Council (intergovernmental) or the Commission (supranational) – and to what extent competencies should be pooled – minimally (intergovernmental) or more extensively (supranational).

---

[7] Donald Searing (1994) makes use of this methodology to unpack British MPs' understanding of their political roles. See Anselm Strauss (1987) for a detailed manual on qualitative data analysis.

As a group, Commission officials tend slightly to the supranational pole; mean and median dip just below the neutral value of 2.5. However, 25 percent of the interviewees lean strongly to intergovernmentalism (table 3.3, column two, 75 percent quartile); 46 percent of the interviewees reject the view that the Commission should become the government of the European Union, almost 23 percent categorically and 24 percent with some reservations (item 3); 32 percent support the radical intergovernmentalist statement that member states should remain the central pillars of the European Union, not the European Parliament or the European Commission (item 1). Note that this item echoes former French president de Gaulle, a committed nationalist and confederalist, who during a historical press conference in September 1960 exclaimed: "What are the realities of Europe? What are the pillars on which it can be built? The truth is that those pillars are the states of Europe... states each of which, indeed, has its own genius, history and language, its own sorrows, glories and ambitions; but states that are the only entities with the right to give orders and the power to be obeyed" (quoted in Nelsen and Stubb 1998: 43).

Most top officials are wary of shifting further competencies to Brussels: 13 percent unconditionally support subsidiarity and 49 percent underwrite it with reservations (item 2). To some degree, this high level of support may be tactical; after the Maastricht referendums, popular resistance to further EU expansion has induced many political actors, including Commission officials, to embrace subsidiarity. However, the strong association between this item and other items on this dimension suggests that support for subsidiarity is rooted in deeper intergovernmental convictions. Support for subsidiarity is solid among intergovernmentalists.[8]

Among the leadership of the most visible supranational institution in the European Union, largely intergovernmental designs find considerable backing. What, then, are key conceptual differences between Supranationalists and Intergovernmentalists?

Europe as end or means. For a Supranationalist, the dominant issue in the European Union is the future of European integration. "I am

---

[8] Subsidiarity became a buzzword in the European Union after Maastricht. It was used by both intergovernmentalists and supranationalists. In her 1988 address to the College of Europe in Bruges, British prime minister Margaret Thatcher advocated the intergovernmentalist view: "Working more closely together does not require power to be centralized in Brussels or decisions to be taken by an appointed bureaucracy" (Nelsen and Stubb 1998: 52). Jacques Delors responded in his 1989 address to the College of Europe in Bruges with a definition that focuses on reconciling "a united Europe and loyalty to one's homeland. The need for a European power capable of tackling the problems of our age and the absolute necessity to preserve our roots in the shape of our nations and regions" (Nelsen and Stubb 1998: 56). My survey shows that top officials associate subsidiarity with intergovernmentalism.

not in the business of right-wing or left-wing policies.... Whether we promote *European integration* is what counts.... [Ideology] is the wrong axis. We are most divided on another axis: pro-integration or anti-integration" (official #58, his emphasis). An Intergovernmentalist does not share this zest to build Europe: "For me, it is something realistic, concrete, and inevitable" (official #120). A Supranationalist fears and fuels the debate between supranationalism and intergovernmentalism, whereas an Intergovernmentalist waits for the constitutional storm to subside so that he can get on with the job. A Supranationalist rejoices talking about the Commission's role in the EU; an Intergovernmentalist turns to his policy dossier.

Activism or mediation? A Supranationalist loves a good institutional fight, in which he invariably comes down on the Commission's side: "I love everything having to do with defending the prerogatives of the Commission vis-à-vis Council and Parliament" (official #70). An Intergovernmentalist finds this institutional tug of war a waste of time and energy: "I am interested in better policies – *that* is important. The part played by the Commission – minor problem.... Fighting for the Commission's prerogatives is counterproductive and ridiculous" (official #120, his emphasis). "Defend the prerogatives of the Commission? Frankly, that is not my problem. This is a false issue. Either the Commission is useful, or it is not. If it is useful, it does not need to be defended! The Commission must be recognized and respected – and that is the best defense. And by the way, to provoke an institutional tug of war on this issue – I do not have the temperament to be a syndicalist for the Commission!" (official #27). An Intergovernmentalist believes that the Commission should not confront member states but act as "an independent, balanced clearing house for ideas, a springboard for ideas." When national governments overlook their partners' interests and sensitivities, the Commission should step in to remind them of the common ground: "You need to consolidate consensus and, as it is written into the treaties, the Commission can and often does play this role" (official #217).

Political leader or agent to national principals? A Supranationalist is convinced that only the Commission's political leadership can advance European integration. That makes the role of a Commission official very different from that of a civil servant in an international secretariat or in the Commission's intergovernmental alter ego, the Council secretariat:

[A Commission official] is there to formulate European policies and to get fifteen member-states behind a certain policy line. The Council itself is incapable of doing the work. And our colleagues in the Council secretariat are *not* policy-makers; they finalize compromises; they are a secretariat. They do not have the mentality of coming up with policy proposals. As a Commission official, on the other hand, one has to learn very early on that there must be a *political* drive, and one must exchange views, and then one has to *decide*. And this is what the people in the Council [secretariat] never learn: to decide. Commission people have to decide. They have to say: "This is the line I propose, and this is my price." Next, they have to go to the member states, and fight for it. (Official #182, his emphasis)

For an Intergovernmentalist, the political objectives should be set elsewhere:

I am an official servant of the European construction. I have tried to make Europe as relevant as I could in the various policy areas I have been responsible for. Yet I am convinced that this construction must remain very attentive to national sensitivities.... We know very well that the national states must retain a very important place in the [European] construction. (Official #27)

Regulated capitalism or liberal market economy?

The institutional design of the European Union has always privileged market liberalization (negative integration) over market-correcting regulation (positive integration). Regulating markets requires legislation and, thus, Commission initiative and political agreement among the Council and the European Parliament. In contrast, the basic principles of liberalization are laid down in the Treaties. The European Court of Justice and the European Commission can extend them under the guise of rule application or adjudication. With strong competencies in competition policy, external trade, and customs, the Commission has been instrumental in deepening the asymmetry between market-making and market-correcting policies (Leibfried and Pierson 1995; Scharpf 1996, 1999; Streeck 1996).

Notwithstanding this powerful institutional bias, no top official wants Europe to be a mere free trade area. Very few would describe themselves as neoliberals. On the scale for Regulated Capitalism, the distribution is heavily skewed to regulation. Mean and median scores are well above 3.0 (table 3.3). More than one out of four officials score the maximum value of 4.0.

Nearly half the officials (47 percent) give unconditional support to Delors' unique European model, which entails an extensive welfare state, social dialogue between both sides of industry, a redistributive regional policy, and industrial policy (item 6). For 46 percent, extensive redistribution through cohesion policy deserves full support, and another 31 percent give qualified support (item 7). Notwithstanding the fact that top officials generally look kindly upon European political regulation, there is real disagreement on how and to what extent Europe should regulate capitalism. One out of five officials distance themselves from the majority view: 20 percent reject cohesion policy, and 2 percent abstain; 14 percent do not agree with Delors' European model, and another 5 percent abstain or remain neutral. How does the Europe of a Regulated Capitalist differ from that of a Market Liberal?

European social model or liberal market? Disagreements between Regulated Capitalists and Market Liberals are rooted in distinct preferences about the future European society. A Regulated Capitalist believes that the European Union should champion different values from the United States or Japan:

I am proud that I have participated with Jacques Delors, as one of his lieutenants, in constructing a certain model for the European Union, where the values are solidarity, cohesion, local empowerment, empowering the citizen in regions and localities.... This is not a free trade area, not simply the creation of a market for 400 million inhabitants.... We are defending a cultural model, neither the Japanese model nor the American model, but the social market economy, the Rhine model. And that idea is shared from the south of Spain to the north of Sweden. (Official #25)

This is not how a Market Liberal sees the European Union: "I have combated public interventionism, protectionism, and overregulation. That has been my mission to date, that has been my ambition" (official #114). A Market Liberal fights Olsonian rent-seeking and protectionism (Olson 1982), because only a liberalized market is able to provide conditions for economic growth and greater welfare.

Center–left or moderate-right? Top officials differ on how state, market, and society should relate, but they do so within fairly narrow ideological parameters. There is no revolutionary language, little trace of conventional class politics.

A Regulated Capitalist has doubts about the market as a self-correcting mechanism. Public authority is indispensable to reduce benefits for winners and costs for losers: "We should operate in those parts of the European economy that the market does not reach or that the market has let down. I would get into a wild argument with the right about the market. Maybe the market would be so long coming [to save these deprived areas] that by the time it gets there, there would not be any people left to save" (official #57). For a Market Liberal, on the other hand, the priority is to stimulate growth through private initiative: "The benefits are in the greater market as such, and in the opportunities we can create [through a liberalized] market" (official #55).

Few Regulated Capitalists reject the market as a primary allocative mechanism, and they appear uncomfortable with a language of class struggle. Rare is the official who criticizes the influence of big business. Only 28 percent do, and most of them only mildly (item 8), though a Regulated Capitalist is significantly more likely to do so than a Market Liberal.[9] Moderation reigns also with Market Liberals, who are reluctant to insulate market-making policies from social policies: "How can you take that view [i.e. to separate economic liberalization from social policies]? The fact is that whatever you do has implications and repercussions in other areas" (official #10). Neoliberal views on state and market are hard to find in the Commission. A Market Liberal, commenting on the neoliberal preferences of the British Conservative government in 1995, draws the line: "The UK government has a problem. The House [i.e. the Commission] continues to work as if that viewpoint does not exist, because it is not part of the history [of Europe]" (official #10).

Political mobilization or exploiting institutional asymmetry? A Regulated Capitalist mobilizes politically by necessity. He fights against a liberal bias in the policies and institutional set-up, and so he must mobilize support for regulated capitalism wherever he can find it – inside *and* outside the Commission. A Regulated Capitalist pays special attention to the European Parliament. Unlike a Democrat, who supports the institution as an integral component of a democratic polity, a Regulated Capitalist has pragmatic reasons for wanting greater parliamentary powers. The European Parliament has traditionally supported environmental regulation, redistribution, and social policy. "We have the European Parliament, which helps us a lot.... [The European parliamentarians] are our objective allies, even though they are often not very comfortable allies" (official #47). A Market Liberal, on the other hand, exploits current rules and policies, and takes advantage of the ideological turn to the right: "There is no question that the balance has changed [in the European Union], that there is much greater emphasis on creating greater opportunities [through liberalization] rather than giving out money [to support industries]. Some people are pushing more than others in that direction, and I am one of them" (official #10). A Market Liberal is less likely than a Regulated Capitalist to support further powers for the European Parliament.[10]

---

[9] The difference in means for this item between the highest and lowest quartile of the Regulated Capitalism scale is significant (Bonferroni, significant at .05 level).

[10] The difference in means for this item between the highest and lowest quartile of the Regulated Capitalism scale comes close to passing the Bonferroni test ($p = .13$).

Technocratic governance or democracy?

Most Commission officials believe that the era of benevolent technocracy in the tradition of Jean Monnet has come to a close. Mean and median scores are well below the neutral point (table 3.3). The standard deviation is lower than for the three other dimensions, which indicates that there is less disagreement among top officials.

However, this consensus is not unequivocally in favor of a democratic European Union. The litmus test for top officials is their attitude towards the European Parliament, the key symbol of a democratic Europe. Item 10 forces them to weigh positional interests against democratic conviction because it states that the Commission should support the European Parliament's bid for full legislative powers even if the Commission would lose its monopoly of initiative as a result: 36 percent think the Commission should support the Parliament, though less than 8 percent without reservations; 61 percent disagree. Many officials fear that greater parliamentary democracy would make European policy-making less effective. That is why opposition against trading the Commission's initiative for greater parliamentary powers is quite strongly associated with support for primary attention to the internal market and sound administrative management (items 11 and 12). When it comes to the crunch, however, only a small minority want unconditional priority for these two policy objectives: 11 percent for the internal market, and 17 percent for sound management. Most officials would like somehow to balance democratic principles and functional imperatives. What are the central bones of contention between Democrats and Technocrats?

Promote a polity or build a functional organization? In the eyes of a Democrat, the Commission should first and foremost encourage Europeans to become citizens: "I believe *that* is our task: to make of *subjects* [sic] active members of the European Union. My role is to introduce the citizen in Europe" (official #70, his emphasis). A Technocrat believes that the Commission's role is to deliver good policy and to implement it efficiently. European integration can be built only on sound functional results: "Let us concentrate on the essential, first of all, which is making sure that [the internal market] operates properly. And if you can get it to operate properly, *then* you can demonstrate the superiority of a European solution, and new political perspectives may open up. Unfortunately, the history of the Community over the last twenty years has been a *fuite-en-avant*" (official #16, his emphasis). Opening up the policy process to public, parties, and politicians should be done with due reticence.

Representative democracy or benevolent elitism? A Democrat has a positive view of politics:

We officials stand on expertise and we think we are great, but the person who goes out and faces the electorate to get elected and defends [her voters'] views in a democratic process on a continuing basis, deserves admiration. Where would democracy be without the people who are willing to face the choice of their fellow citizens? . . . I love going to the [European] Parliament and exchanging views with parliamentarians. [Official #30]

A Technocrat feels ambivalent about the political process, because political conflict greatly complicates expert-based problem-solving.

[I would accept greater democratic input] *provided* you can do it in a way which retains the capacity to take important decisions effectively. The problem is that the institutional debate [about greater parliamentary powers] gets in the way of the substantive debate we try to engage in. We often get institutional results that, in the name of democracy, actually make it harder to achieve what the Community needs to achieve. This is false democracy. (Official #16, his emphasis)

A common interest or sectional interests?

Top Commission officials must balance the overarching European good with sectional demands. As a group, they emphasize that all participants in EU decision-making depend on one another, and they prefer to reach decisions through partnership and persuasion rather than command and control. They are significantly closer to the responsiveness side of the European Interest scale: mean and median are well below 2.5 (see table 3.3). For Responsive Euroservants, networking, partnership, and openness to a variety of opinions and forms of governance are essential.

However, there is considerable variation among officials, evident from the relatively high standard deviation – the highest of the four scales. One out of four Commission officials, whom I term "Eurofonctionnaires," lean to a European civil service at arm's length from sectional interests.[11] Commission officials are understandably concerned most of all about national interests. More than 29 percent regret the influence of national considerations on colleagues' judgment, and 39 percent disapprove of national influence on particular Commission services. They fear that too

---

[11] "Eurofonctionnaires" is the term I choose to describe officials defending an autonomous European interest. European Commission officials usually describe themselves as *fonctionnaires*. The fact that this is a French term is no coincidence. Jean Monnet himself, as well as the first secretary general of the Commission, Emile Noël, consciously modeled the European civil servant after the French top civil servant *(fonctionnaire)*, groomed in France's *grandes écoles* to interpret, articulate, and defend the overarching French public interest.

much networking with national civil servants could make the Commission dependent on its "partners." For a Eurofonctionnaire, insulation may protect the Commission against capture. What are the key conceptual differences between the ideal Europe of a Eurofonctionnaire and that of his counterpart, the Responsive Euroservant?

European identity or national sensibilities? A genuine Eurofonctionnaire steps out of his nationality to become transnational: "It is of course wrong to say that one does not have anymore a passport, a nationality... But it is also true that one should try to lose one's national identity – no, not to lose it, but to make abstraction of it. I have many links with [my country], but my thinking is not anymore like a [countryman]" (official #70). Out of the mélange of different national cultures a new identity emerges. The contrast is great with a Responsive Euroservant, who highlights the different ingredients of the mélange: "I like my service to be a microcosm of the Community. I like my colleagues to reflect the diversity within the Community... There is some wonderment in that. There is a certain mystery as to how people with such different backgrounds can work together" (official #30).

Commission cohesion or independent mind? Creating the true European in spirit and mind is not sufficient for a Eurofonctionnaire. An official should give priority to the unity of the European civil service, not to his own ideas. "I find very often that people have their *own* agenda, and they push it through regardless of what the Commission thinks. If the *Commission* wants to work as a whole, it should be much more coherent than it is now" (official #55, his emphasis). A Eurofonctionnaire abhors the infighting in the Commission: 46 percent of top officials find that the current level of infighting hurts the Commission's legitimacy, but 70 percent of Eurofonctionnaires regret infighting against 27 percent of Responsive Euroservants.[12] For a Responsive Euroservant, on the other hand, the Commission is an arena where priorities can be pursued, not a purposeful actor in its own right with whom one should invariably identify. Unity and team spirit are at most secondary virtues. Innovation comes from small groups of creative people. "If you put together a few people who are *visionnaires*, ... you can get things done" (official #22).

Making or taking cues? A Eurofonctionnaire does not simply act upon requests, but is in the business of identifying priorities from a

---

[12] The item reads: "A Commission which tolerates this much infighting among its staff will eventually destroy itself." Percentages refer to those who agree or agree with reservations.

European vantage point. "What is relevant is the image one has about oneself, and about the policy one is making. That is where a commissioner and a director-general must lead, and you can give the staff the opportunity to contribute to that. That is what public interest is. Outside influences do not weigh" (official #58). A Responsive Euroservant finds it hard to believe in a separate European viewpoint. He takes cues from people and interests around him.

Role definitions and images of Europe

How robust are these findings? Is this really what motivates top officials? Let us examine whether these findings are consistent with a second stream of data that tap into top officials' job motivations. During the interview, I handed each official a card with nine possible motivations, and I asked him to prioritize these. It was made clear to the individual that I was interested not in what he *actually* does, but in what he *wants* to do as top official.

Table 3.4 ranks the motivations from high to low priority. It lists preferences having to do with inter-institutional relations (items 4 and 5),

Table 3.4 *Role definitions of top officials*

Here is a list with tasks a number of senior officials may set themselves. Could you rank them in order of your priorities?	Mean[a]	First priority (%)[b]	Low priority[c] (%)	Not ranked (%)
1. Identify new policy problems and devise new policies	8.4	64	0	2
2. Promote a positive working environment in the DG	6.7	24	6	13
3. Provide expertise in a specific policy area	6.3	7	6	18
4. Mediate conflicts in the Council, and between Council and Parliament	6.2	8	7	26
5. Defend the Commission's prerogatives vis-à-vis Council and Parliament	5.9	8	10	24
6. Respect divergent national interests	5.3	2	17	21
7. Fight public interventionism and overregulation	5.2	4	14	41
8. Combat pure market ideology and promote social values	5.0	2	17	44
9. Be accessible for fellow nationals	3.0	1	34	46

[a] Mean value for those who prioritize this objective, with 9 as highest priority and 1 as lowest priority.
[b] Proportion of officials who give this objective highest priority.
[c] Priority of 1, 2, or 3.

policy (items 1 and 3), ideology (items 7 and 8), accommodating national diversity (items 6 and 9), and the quality of the work environment (item 2). Some descriptions recall roles ascribed to national bureaucrats (Aberbach and Rockman 1988, 1995; Aberbach, Rockman, and Putnam 1981; Brewer and Maranto 1998; Derlien 1998; Dogan 1975; Downs 1967; Posner and Schmidt 1994; Suleiman and Mendras 1995), or to national or European politicians (Katz 1997; Searing 1994; Wessels 1998). I have also taken cues from earlier studies of the European Commission (Coombes 1970; Michelmann 1978a,b; Neunreither 1972) and more recent work (Abélès, Bellier, McDonald 1993; Page 1997; Ross 1995a,b).[13]

Top officials' self-placement on these nine potential motivations enables us critically to examine my findings from a different angle. If top officials hold consistently divergent images of Europe, this should be reflected in how they prioritize these motivations. If top officials are divided along the supranational/intergovernmental dimension, they can be expected to rank the two institutional motivations differently. Defending the Commission's prerogatives should be a high priority for Supranationalists, but of little importance for Intergovernmentalists. Similarly, one would expect significant variation on the two ideological motivations. So whereas Market Liberals should give the market-liberal ideological statement of fighting public interventionism high priority, Regulated Capitalists should rank it low. Finally, one would anticipate that top officials give very different weight to the two nationality-related motivations. Responsive Euroservants should find it important to listen carefully to national interests, and possibly to fellow nationals; Eurofonctionnaires should give this objective low priority.

Table 3.4 reports average ranking, and the percentage of officials allocating the motivation highest priority, low priority, and not ranking this motivation. A value of 9 indicates highest priority and a value of 1 lowest priority. Officials who choose not to rank a motivation usually do

---

[13] I discussed this list with a retired top Commission official. Our conversations induced me to make some alterations to the original version. The one difficulty in the final list that neither of us had foreseen concerns the choices on national diversity. I had originally combined items 6 and 9 in one statement, but an important subset of officials insisted on making a sharp distinction between "to respect divergent interests" and "to be accessible for fellow nationals." So, about a quarter of the way through the interviews, I decided systematically to probe respondents for their ranking on each item separately. It is possible that my failure to separate out these items in the first forty interviews may exaggerate the association between items 6 and 9. To test for this, I have run separate analyses (rank orderings, correlations, factor analysis) for the subset of cases where top officials were explicitly offered the opportunity to distinguish between the two items. The results are virtually identical to the ones for the whole sample. For example, the correlation between item 6 (respect divergent national interests) and item 9 (be accessible to fellow nationals) is .35 ($p = .000$) for the whole sample, and .34 ($p = .001$) for the ninety-seven interviews where these items were separate.

so because they find it irrelevant or harmful to their job or they firmly oppose it. So the last column contains explicit opposition to a particular motivation.

Overall, top officials rank these motivations very differently. The one exception concerns the highest-ranked motivation – "to identify (new) policy problems and devise (new) policies." This motivation is unambiguously rooted in the Commission's exclusive right to legislative initiative, and its high ranking demonstrates how vital this authority is for Commission officials. If there is one expectation that top officials share, it is to be proactive, that is, to anticipate problems and to come up with solutions. They think of themselves as professionals who do not shy away from big, politically contested policy issues – albeit within their area of expertise and with due respect to given policy objectives. A top official in budgetary and financial matters characterizes this role aptly:

We should solve problems that are obstacles to European cooperation. We should identify where certain things are going wrong, or where there may be missing links in regulating problems. So I dare not say that we necessarily need to define *new* policy problems. We should identify blockages in the smooth working of the Community. Once one has identified problems relating to the objective of good administrative management, one should devise, perhaps not new policy, but new instruments to eliminate obstacles to a satisfactory working of Community financing. Indeed, that is the task of this Directorate. So the key is to identify where problems are and try to find the most appropriate solution – be it through regulation, common action, or bilateral action with a member state. And that may go as far as proposing a new system of financing for the Community, if we think that the present one is not suited for the future development of the Union. So I would rank this as my first priority. It is, ultimately, a political role, though of course we do not play at this political level all the time, especially in the field of financing. But we are going to have to be prepared to do this with respect to enlargement. (Official #103)

Beyond this broad policy-oriented motivation, top officials differ on what they find important. That is most explicit for ideological objectives: 41 percent refuse to rank the market-liberal motivation, and 44 percent decline to rank the left-wing motivation. These naysayers fall into two almost equally large groups. Both motivations are rejected by 30 percent of all officials. They argue that civil servants should not let their own ideological predispositions interfere with their job. As one top official put it: "You can read me off these rankings because I am interested in the things that are seen more as *the duty* of a civil servant and not so much *the ideals* of a civil servant. We all have our own ideals of course, but we do not always put them on the table. Let me word it like that" (official #1, his emphasis). These "non-ideologues" are counterbalanced by "ideologues," representing 26 percent, who firmly reject one ideological motivation but endorse the other.[14] Overall, among the 70 percent of top officials who rank ideological motivations, the association between rankings for leftist and rightist objectives is strongly negative ($R = -.41$). An official who gives high priority to market-liberal ideals is very likely to give low priority to social democratic objectives, and vice versa.

Even "non-ideologues" do not believe that policy advice is value free, but they are convinced that their personal values should be subordinate to impartial professional service. Yet they are willing to discuss values and – if they have to – draw a line beyond which they refuse to serve values they do not support. A top official characterizes the delicate relationship between professional service and personal ideological integrity in these words:

Official: These ideological objectives seem to have a distinctly different quality. They depend on who my political boss is. This is not really for me. I have my private opinion, and I advise my bosses, but my personal ideological motivations are low priority.

Interviewer: So you have a sense that it is not up to you – at all – to let your political opinions play into your role?

O: No, I would not say that at all. It is important that I have a view but, as a top official, that is not what is in any sense primary. To put it in caricature terms: if I have a commissioner who wants to intervene in what I personally think is an excessive manner, or vice versa, I will test his opinion for him. I will put before him matters he should have in mind before he launches himself. However, ultimately, it is not up to me to decide.

I: Would you do this irrespective of whether it concerned left-wing or right-wing positions?

O: No, there are limits [for me]. I was interviewed once for the job of *chef de cabinet*. The question put to me was a canny question: "Sometimes we need to take difficult decisions. What would you do if I asked you to do something you disagree with?" I answered: "Under normal circumstances, I would fully discuss with you the reasons for why you wanted to do it and I would tell you why I thought it was wrong. Under normal circumstances, if you did not change your mind, I would do it. But there would be some circumstances in which I would say that you had better find somebody else." ... This is what this job is about. I believe it is our job to say to our bosses: "If you do that, this will occur." (Official #16)

Officials also differ systematically on the two inter-institutional motivations. Naysayers on whether officials should defend the Commission's

---

[14] One might expect to find these "non-ideologues" disproportionately among officials from countries where ideological neutrality among top bureaucrats is a strong norm – the United Kingdom, Denmark, or the Netherlands – but the reverse is true. Belgians, Italians, Spanish, Portuguese, and Greek – nationals from bureaucratic traditions characterized by *Proporz* and extensive partisanship – are more likely to refuse to express an ideological stance than are the British, Danes, or Dutch. Officials from "commanding heights" traditions, such as the French, Germans, or Swedes, are quite comfortable expressing ideological preferences.

prerogatives (supranationalist) or whether they should mediate in Council or between Council and Parliament (intergovernmentalist) fall again in two groups. Some officials (17 percent) have no patience for these institutional issues, and they reject both motivations. But 20 percent give high priority to inter-institutional relations. Some find it important to defend the Commission and firmly reject that they should simply mediate in the Council. Others emphasize the need to mediate, communicate, and build bridges, and they refuse to pay attention to the defense of Commission priorities. In the words of a committed mediator:

Official: [The emphasis on] defending the Commission's prerogatives is one of those things that has amazed and annoyed me. The Commission is far too much preoccupied with legal and competence considerations. This is highly inefficient when one seeks to solve problems, and, of course, I am very often forced to take stands on competence because this is general policy in the Commission. You play the game – but it is not very fruitful. This is early twentieth-century politics and I cannot see how we can create modern-style governance this way in the next century.

Interviewer: How would you explain that?

O: It has to do with the way in which the institutions have evolved. Institutional evolution has been shaped by a perpetual debate between Commission competence and national competence: is the European Union intergovernmental or is it Community based? And now the Parliament has joined the debate. Part of [this ongoing institutional struggle] is due to the way in which the Treaty is organized. But I think we could find new ways to deal with one another. I am a firm supporter of those who want to achieve results, not through formal means that require adherence to Treaty procedures, but by establishing networks or other ways of cooperation within the European Union, and between member states and the Commission. This world is changing. It is not any longer working only according to legislative rules. The key is networking. (Official #20)

More than 80 percent prioritize at least one of these inter-institutional motivations, but they tend to prefer one above the other. Those who rank defense of Commission prerogatives highly tend to think less favorably of mediation in the Council, and vice versa ($R = -.19$, significant at the .05 level).

Concerns about national diversity too provoke divergent reactions among top officials. More than 21 percent refuse to rank the motivation "respect divergent national interests." So one-fifth feel strongly about the need to keep their distance from national interests: "It is not *my* job to respect divergent national interests. That is for other institutions!" (official #61). They almost always firmly oppose special attention to country nationals as well. But an almost equally high proportion (19 percent) give it high priority (rankings of 7, 8, or 9 out of a maximum of 9).

Almost 80 percent of officials are prepared to pay at least some attention to divergent national interests, but many make a clear distinction between sensitivity for national diversity on the one hand, and defending one's own nationality on the other. A British top official explains:

Interviewer: "Respect of national interests, and be accessible for fellow nationals." Do you feel it part of your duty to be more accessible for British than for Spanish or Finnish nationals?

Official: In a sense, you have to be naturally more accessible for other nationalities than for your own. You can take it for granted that you have *some* comprehension of the values and interests of your own member state because you *come* from there. And you presumably obtained your job because you understood your country rather well. Some of my compatriots say: "I do not have any contact with the UK anymore." I sometimes meet Danish officials saying: "I do not want to go back to Denmark. I do not want to think about Denmark." But in fact, if *they* do not know their country, they are *less* valuable to this institution. They *have* to reflect; they are *here* to reflect their national cultures and values. But at the same time, they have to *listen* very carefully to what people are telling them about other countries. Let us say someone was telling me – a Brit – about the specific conditions at Frankfurt airport. Well, perhaps I know that all airports in Germany are privately run, but I may not know that they are private monopolies. If one is concerned with breaking monopolies, such a regime requires a different approach than if one were to deal with public monopolies. These *local* conditions are often not known except by nationals. (Official #39, his emphasis)

For many officials, there are good functional reasons to be sensitive to national diversity. "If we did not have a policy of openness to national diversity, it would be impossible to keep information networks feeding into the Commission. The Commission is only as good as the latest information it received" (official #39). Some Commission officials go one step further, and emphasize that one cannot ignore political reality; in fact, it would be illegitimate to do so. "Contrary to some of my colleagues, I believe that the Union is made of member states, whether you like it or not, of country nationals who are very attached to their nationality. We have to respect and work with this reality" (official #150).

Conclusion

What are top Commission officials' preferences on basic issues of governance in the European Union? How do they think about the organization of political authority in Europe, the scope of European authoritative regulation in the economy, and the role of national and societal interests in European decision-making?

In this chapter I shed light on these questions through quantitative and qualitative analysis. A factor analysis of 106 officials' responses to items on political preferences has identified four dimensions, which correspond to coherent images of Europe as articulated by Commission officials during in-depth interviews.

Should the European Union be supranational – with powerful, autonomous supranational institutions such as the Commission, the European Parliament, and the European Court of Justice? Or should it be intergovernmental – with authority primarily vested in the member states? As a group, top Commission officials tend slightly to supranationalism, but one out of four support an intergovernmental design.

To what extent should market activity be regulated at the European level? Commission officials overwhelmingly prefer regulated capitalism to market liberalism. However, at least 20 percent oppose the majority view.

Should decision-making be technocratic – as in most international organizations, and as during much of the European Union's history? Or should it become democratic – as in the EU's member states? Half seek to keep democratic principles and functional – technocratic imperatives in balance. Yet one quarter would like to strengthen EU democracy, even at the expense of the Commission's exclusive powers of legislative initiative. Another quarter defend technocratic principles for pragmatic reasons; they fear that unbridled democratic input would make European policy-making less effective.

How should top Commission officials balance the European public good with sectional interests? As a group, Commission officials are most comfortable with an approach that emphasizes responsiveness to national and sectoral interests. But there is considerable variation – more so than on previous dimensions. Though very few ardently advocate primacy for the common European good, about one out of four give it more weight than national interests.

The question is then how Commission officials come to think the way they do. What makes some officials support supranationalism and others intergovernmentalism? Why are there so few market liberals? Why do some want more democratic decision-making in the European Union, whereas others defend technocratic principles? When one applies the analytical framework of chapter 1, what does it tell us with respect to top officials' preference formation on each of these dimensions? Is the Commission environment more important in shaping preferences than institutional contexts outside the Commission? Are top officials motivated by values internalized in earlier walks of life, or are their preferences informed by rational utility calculation in current institutional constraints? Do values trump interests, or vice versa? I now turn to these questions.

4   Beyond supranational interest

In search of supranationalists

Interviewing in the Commission's most powerful directorates-general is carefully regulated, perhaps because the prey is much in demand, highly prized, and occasionally somewhat threatening to the hunter. Visitors to the directorate-general (DG) for competition policy are chaperoned from the security guards' reception desk to the interviewee's office and back, to prevent them from roaming through secret competition files. Security guards also man access to the DG for agriculture – as they do for virtually all Commission buildings. They collect passports and information on profession and address, and they phone the contact person. The guards in the DG for agriculture allow one to make the journey up to floor five, seven or eight all by oneself. Yet the headquarters of this DG are intimidating: the floor plan is labyrinthine, the silent windowless corridors with closed doors are endless, and the building's lopsided structure with multiple exits is confusing as it plunges from the hilltop on Wetstraat onto Joseph II Straat approximately 70 feet lower. Maybe because of this architecture – incomprehensible to the outsider – the ethos of discipline, power, and confidence is all the more palpable.

A visitor may be forgiven for perceiving these fortress-like features as telling symbols of the Commission's preference for supranationalism. Reality is more complicated. Top officials in these strongholds vary appreciably in the degree to which they support a supranational or an intergovernmental Union. Barriers to entry (and exit) in the DGs for competition policy and agriculture do not keep out intergovernmentalism.

Committed supranationalists exist in the Commission's top ranks – sometimes in unexpected locations and under surprising guises. And so, in between interviews in power-exuding Commission buildings, I meet a passionate supranationalist. He serves in one of the socially oriented DGs. Perhaps because I had been targeting directors-general and leading officials from the Commission's powerhouses, I had come to associate effectiveness among top officials with strong opinions and a direct, combative, somewhat brisk style – softened by worldly charm. This soft-spoken, silver-gray, slightly hesitant director in education does not fit the stereotype. And yet this person turns out to personify Jean Monnet's neo-functionalist strategy in which the European fonctionnaire puts to use his technical expertise to deepen European integration.

Interviewer: What would you miss most if you were to leave the European Commission?

Official: What would I miss? I would miss that I could no longer contribute to the well-being of European citizens in general. I have been instrumental in creating Erasmus, Comett, Lingua, Socrates.[1] . . . I believe that these are on balance good programs. [If I were to leave] I would no longer have the opportunity, then, to bring Europe to the citizens – to create European citizens. I would miss that. Unfortunately, there are too many anti-European morons. And I mean by these not the convinced anti-Europeans, whom I respect. I mean those who turn anti-European when things go badly, to conceal party disunity, or to score cheap political points. I am dead set against such behavior. As long as I am here, my aim is to make citizens aware so that they do not act like those anti-European morons who place self-interest above the interest of Europe.

I: What are for you the most important challenges to the future of the European Union?

O: The most important task is to create some form of European Union, that is, a European society with opportunities for everyone. Nothing is more important. . . . While the twentieth century was the century of the muscle, the twenty-first century will be the era of intelligence, of the brain. So in an information society it is paramount to provide everyone with an excellent educational base. This will be the foundation upon which a good society can be built.

I: Does the Commission have sufficient competencies to achieve this, or does it require more competencies, more resources?

O: We always need more competencies and resources.

I: But is it wise to ask for these?

O: We must ask for them, because the day we no longer make demands signifies the end of the dynamic process of European integration. So, sure, I could be happy with my Socrates program, and live a simple life. That may be "wise," but it also means this dynamic process would falter. I would, for example, not be responding anymore to what we currently define as the challenges for education in the twenty-first century. . . . I believe that a society must adapt continually.

I: You know very well that you will probably have to fight the member states or fight the idea of subsidiarity.

O: That is not a problem. It would be a mistake to centralize all of [education policy]. Only someone who does not understand Europe could think along those lines; Europe means diversity. We *need* decentralization. We *need* subsidiarity. The problem is that one should not resort to decentralization and

[1] These are the names of student exchange programs co-funded by the Commission.

subsidiarity as a means to oppose European policy. Those who do not want European collaboration often resort to subsidiarity so as to do nothing. No, I am in favor of subsidiarity because I believe that the citizen wants policy making as close as possible to him or her. And our role in the Commission is to take initiatives, and to persuade member states that a young adult without knowledge of new technologies and computer science will be marginalized. And thus it is not our role to impose all these changes, but rather to develop clear arguments and make the fifteen member states realize that they need to prepare their educational systems in that direction. And they must especially be made aware that if the German government prepares [for the twenty-first century] but the Portuguese government does not, there will be discrimination because there will be nothing left to protect the poor Portuguese [from competition in the single market]. That is our role. We have the opportunity to transcend [national interests], to be independent from the constraints that states and regions experience. We are free from constraints in that sense. And moreover, we can have a forward-looking vision, which is precisely our unique contribution.

I: What can you do when persuasion does not work?

O: Even if one is not legally competent, one should not abandon ideas lightly but continue to explain and persuade. I am convinced that, in a union, member states need to demonstrate a certain discipline. One member cannot simply say: "I do not like this, so I do not want it." In that sense, I am the ayatollah of the institutions. As much as I am in favor of subsidiarity, as much as I support decentralization and respect diversity, I am very much opposed to self-interested behavior. I say *no* to that, because this is what differentiates the European Union from other forms of regional integration. That was the fundamental choice between two destinies: the supranational route and the intergovernmental route. (Official #70)

Since Ernst Haas' *The Uniting of Europe* (1958), the history of European integration has been perceived as a contest between two fundamentally different strategies for collaboration in Europe: intergovernmentalism and supranationalism.[2] Should political authority be vested in the member states and the Council of Ministers, or should supranational institutions such as the European Commission and the European Parliament be strengthened? The protagonists in this ongoing play have long since been identified: the member states defending national sovereignty on the one

[2] As Haas points out, supranationality is an elusive concept – too often defined ad hoc by politicians, legal scholars, or occasional observers. He prefers a definition that emphasizes the hybrid character of supranationality as a state of integration that holds the middle ground between federalism and intergovernmentalism (1958: 526). More (independent) power is given to the new central agency than is customary for conventional international organizations, but less than is generally yielded to an emergent federal government (Haas 1958: 34; see also Lindberg and Scheingold 1970: 14–21). The central feature of supranationalism is that decisions can be taken at a supranational level that bind member states. The degree of supranationalism increases – and approaches federalism – to the extent that these binding decisions are taken by independent European organizations, such as the European Court, European Parliament, or an autonomous European Commission.

hand, and the European Commission guarding the common European interest on the other. On two occasions, this conflict between member states and the Commission hit the headlines when powerful politicians of conviction took up the banner for one side. French president Charles de Gaulle collided with Commission president Walter Hallstein in the 1960s, and in the 1980s British prime minister Margaret Thatcher took Commission president Jacques Delors to task for overzealous integration.

Perceptions of these titanic struggles have marked the study of European integration. Much of the debate has evolved around the consequences of European integration for the autonomy and authority of the state in Europe. Almost invariably, the assumption that has underpinned this work is that the Commission has an institutional interest in advancing supranational empowerment. That is a major assumption. It presumes that the Commission as an institution is best served by increasing its own governmental capacity at the expense of member states. However, in certain circumstances, the Commission's institutional interest may be better served by the status quo than by deeper supranational integration.

Even if the Commission's institutional interest were invariably in favor of supranationalism, very little is known about how people with leadership positions in this institution conceive of authority in the European Union. In this chapter I explain why some officials advocate supranational governance whereas others want to keep authority vested in the member states.

Discord in the monolith

Studies of European integration have rarely paid systematic attention to the preferences of Commission officials with respect to European integration. Throughout the European Union's history, scholars have provided glimpses of discord in the institution.

In his study of the European Coal and Steel Community, Ernst Haas (1958) devoted a chapter to the ideology and activities of the members of the High Authority, the precursor of the European Commission. His analysis focused on the commissioners rather than on the bureaucracy, but his insights are illuminating nevertheless. He contrasted the activist, pro-federalist objectives of Jean Monnet (the first president of the High Authority) with the restrained, passive/consensual, and decisively non-federalist preferences of most other members. Haas did not systematically examine why commissioners held particular views, though he hinted that economic ideology (whether one was for or against planning) and party-political and interest group connections might explain preferences.

A decade later, in *Politics and Bureaucracy in the European Community* (1970), a study of the European Commission, David Coombes stressed that only a minority of officials were committed supporters of supranationalism. Whereas Haas discerned seeds of discord in the early days of the European Coal and Steel Community, Coombes diagnosed it ten years later. According to Coombes, two different kinds of officials, neither of them necessarily wedded to the European idea, began to supplant supranationalists from the late 1960s. The first consisted of "technicians" seconded from national administrations, who were respected for their expertise but suspected of being highly conscious of their national background. A second, rapidly growing group consisted of young, highly specialized, and talented officials, whose main motivation was to take up challenges in difficult circumstances and beat the odds. So, alongside the pro-integration old-timers, Coombes recognized one group of likely intergovernmentalists and another group of entrepreneurs who were indifferent between supranationalism and intergovernmentalism. Like Haas, Coombes did not examine the sources of this variation systematically, though his analysis suggests that preferences may be associated with timing of recruitment (whether one was a pioneer or joined in later years), type of recruitment (whether one was seconded from the national government or recruited directly by the Commission), and perhaps age.

In the early 1990s, Marc Abélès, Irène Bellier, and Maryon McDonald found that Commission officials themselves are fully aware of less-than-complete supranational support among their colleagues. One official bitterly remarked, "to proclaim one's attachment to the European idea in the Commission inevitably leads to disaster" (quoted in Abélès, Bellier, and McDonald 1993: 46). Though the purpose of the authors' anthropological study is neither to chart nor to explain these sentiments systematically, their thick description conveys widespread discord – even lack of trust – among Commission officials. They illustrate how Commission officials point time and again to national stereotypes to explain their differences. Several officials singled out the first enlargement of 1973 as having a detrimental impact on unity in the Commission. British officials, in particular, were accused of introducing the intergovernmental practice of turning to their national networks and national ministries for advice and support.

A seasoned top official in external relations, who entered the Commission in 1958, ponders on the fading European commitment among his colleagues. He echoes concerns raised by Coombes and reported by Abélès and his collaborators, and he adds material goals – money and career advancement – to the list of possible distractions from supranationalism:

Official: The question is what are we here for. I think we are here to continue this patient and difficult job of making Europe tick. To make it work in all its variety and richness, while at the same time building a system that makes it impossible for people to get into each other's hair again. The political message of making peace is certainly very central. My basic motivation is the fact that I was just old enough to experience the war. I think that plays a very big role. It is a gut feeling. It was traumatic for all those who lived through it. I think I have always felt a very strong stimulus to make peace. Similarly, I have rather strong feelings about nationalism. I frankly hate British nationalism because it is destroying what I strongly believe in.

Interviewer: Do you feel this is difficult to explain to your younger colleagues here?

O: No, it is not difficult. The younger generation consists of excellent people. They are taking over now. I have always worked with great pleasure with young people. I also have very good relations with *stagiaires* [interns] and I think the young people are to a certain extent accessible for this so-called ideal. But not all of them are, because many are attracted by quick money and by career prospects. They may not have the conviction that this is the only way to [make Europe tick].

I: Because this is an exciting environment, and you can do things, and there seems to be more space than in national administrations?

O: Yes, whatever its finality. And of course, then you get the intellectual jet set. When they are so imbibed with the pleasure of the mechanics, they forget what they are doing it for. So, it does not even need to be only money, it can also be the sheer pleasure of making the machine work well.

I: So when you said [earlier] "I enjoy diplomacy," you mean you do because, for you, there is always something there that drives you.

O: Yes, and I am probably a bad diplomat because I always have a certain *engagement*. You have to do it for some good reason. And of course, for me, the reason is the same: to make Europe tick. (Official #170)

The notion that top officials defend the Commission's institutional interest hinges on the Commission being an insulated institution capable of instilling within its employees a uniform set of norms. But is the Commission sufficiently shielded from the outside world to convince its employees that there is a single institutional interest for which they must all strive? For Haas, Coombes, and Abélès and his collaborators the answer to this question is clearly no. In the post-Maastricht European Union, pressures on Commission officials have multiplied, as one official testifies:

You have to realize that the Commission is a kind of filter. It is bombarded with one-and-a-hundred ideas and proposals by way of resolutions from the European Parliament. It is confronted with all kinds of suggestions from member states, from representatives of vested interests – quite legitimately, because the Commission needs lobbies and organizations. The Commission is a clearing-house, a springboard of ideas. And this leads it to be in itself a first-stage compromise of so many influences. (Official #217)

Such openness to diverse influences, susceptibility to outside ideas, and dependence on internal compromise is hardly what one would expect from a unitary, pro-integration actor. The Commission falls short of being a monolithic bureaucracy for several reasons. Top officials are culturally and professionally diverse; the Commission has only loose control over recruitment and promotion; decision-making inside the Commission is fragmented; and the Commission depends on external actors to achieve its goals.

Haas, Coombes, and Abélès and his collaborators suggest that the preferences of some top officials may diverge from the Commission's institutional interest. Recent contributions to public administration have sought to specify the conditions under which employees defend their organization's institutional interests (Bawn 1995; Pollack 1997; Ringquist 1995; Wood and Waterman 1993). This chapter builds on this literature to explain why some Commission officials advocate intergovernmentalism whereas others are supranationalist.

Why top officials may diverge

In chapter 1, I introduced a model of preference formation that rests on two principles. First of all, I have shown how top officials live and work in multiple institutional contexts, and one must therefore examine how contexts inside and outside the Commission shape their preferences on supranationalism or intergovernmentalism. I have also argued that there are two basic causal pathways for institutions to shape human motivation. One emphasizes utility maximization – interests – as a mechanism for preference formation, and the other stresses socialization – values. To understand what drives top officials to favor supranationalism or intergovernmentalism, one must study the relative impact of both influences.

The socialization logic predicts that Commission officials who spend time in institutions supporting supranational or intergovernmental principles are likely to internalize these values, and hold on to them even if they move to another environment. Supranational or intergovernmental preferences may be learned in a variety of institutional settings: at work in the Commission, through previous job experiences in a national administration, in a particular political system, or in a political party. According to the utility maximization paradigm, rational actors may bring their preferences in line with the institutional opportunities available to them. There are different ways of conceptualizing this. In a world where the Commission is insulated, top officials would adopt the supranational interest of the institution to enhance their career prospects. But, as I have argued, the Commission is embedded in a system of multi-level

Logic of influence (causal mechanism)	Source of influence (type of institutional context)	
	Type I Inside the Commission	Type II Outside the Commission
Socialization	Length of service in Commission	Experience in national administration Experience in political system (federalism, country size) Political party identification
Hybrid category		Parachutage ↓
Utility maximization	Position in Power-DG	National economic interest Character of national network

Figure 4.1 Hypotheses on top officials' preferences for supranationalism.

governance, and institutions smaller than the Commission as well as institutions beyond the Commission itself shape officials' incentives. First and foremost among the latter are national governments; central among the former are directorates-general in charge of supranational competencies. These influences are amenable to testing because their presence varies across top officials.

Figure 4.1 gives a visual presentation of where these hypotheses fit into the broader model of preference formation. Let us now turn first to socialization variables, and then to utility explanations. I start each time with institutional contexts inside the Commission and move on to institutions beyond the Commission. In the next section, I examine how these hypotheses fare with the data.

Commission socialization

The most common assumption in European integration studies is that the European Commission has an interest in supranational empowerment, whereas member states have an interest in retaining maximal national sovereignty. Perhaps the most obvious expectation about the preferences of Commission officials is, then, that the longer they have served in the Commission, the more supranationalist they will be. This hypothesis refines the common notion that "you stand where you sit" with the assumption that it takes time for institutions to shape individual prefer-ences. The longer an individual has worked in a particular institution, the more he or she will identify with it (Rohrschneider 1994; Ross Schneider 1993; Searing 1994).

H_1: *The longer an official has worked in the Commission, the more he or she is likely to support supranationalism.*

The indicator for *Commission Socialization* is the number of years served in the Commission prior to the interview. Note that top officials have spent on average eighteen years in the Commission, ranging from a few months to thirty-seven years.

Experience in national administration

I have stressed time and again that the Commission is ill equipped to monopolize its employees' preferences. So here is an argument to extend the above logic to prior work experiences outside the Commission – first and foremost in national administrations.

It is the role of national civil servants to serve their nation. This suggests that officials whose careers were established in a national civil service may have internalized the value of preserving national sovereignty, and that this value still guides them in the Commission. There are several reasons this may be so. A national civil servant may have been socialized to place the highest value on public service to the nation. Moreover, as we saw in chapter 2, Europe's national civil services have distinctive bureaucratic traditions, and it seems plausible that a national civil servant who has internalized his national bureaucratic values wants to preserve them. Former national civil servants may also still be keyed into national networks of mutual support in the EU.

H_2: *The longer an official worked for a national administration, the more he or she is likely to support intergovernmentalism.*

My indicator for *National Administration* is the number of years served as a national civil servant prior to joining the Commission. Values range from zero to twenty-eight years, with an average of six years and a me-dian of three years; 58 percent of officials worked in the national state sector.

National system: multi-level governance

Socialization theory points out that the national political system shapes how individuals think about political objects, and that individuals carry over these learned dispositions to different political contexts (Rohr-schneider 1994, 1996). It therefore seems reasonable to expect top officials to transfer their dispositions on territorial authority from their own country to the European Union. There are strong affinities between *national* debates on whether authority should be centralized or decentralized across multiple territorial levels and the relatively new *European* question of whether the European Union should be supranational or intergovernmental. Top officials are sophisticated political observers; they are likely to recognize these similarities.

Federalism. Experience with federalism is likely to dispose individuals favorably to territorial dispersion of authority. Federalism is multi-level governance – the sharing of authority across multiple territorial levels of government – within national borders. Officials from federal countries may be less likely to view relations between constituent states and European institutions in zero-sum terms and more likely to support sharing of sovereignty across different territorial levels.

H_{3a}: *Officials from federal countries are more likely to be supranationalist.*

My indicator for *Federalism* is an index of regional governance developed by Gary Marks and myself (Hooghe and Marks 2001, appendix 2). This index ranges from 0 (centralized authority) to 12 (dispersed authority), and it combines measures for the extent of constitutional federalism, autonomy for special territories in the national state, the role of regions in central government, and the presence or absence of direct regional elections.

Country size. Growing up in small countries may also predispose individuals to favor dispersing authority over centralizing authority. International borders constrain life most patently in small countries. To grow economically, they must trade. To feel secure, they must cooperate internationally. As Peter Katzenstein has shown, the smaller democracies of Western Europe have learned that it is better to open borders than to shield their society from the outside; in contrast, larger states search more readily for national solutions (Katzenstein 1985). Sovereignty is worth less for small countries; a system of multi-level governance in Europe allows them to participate in decisions that would otherwise be beyond their control.

H_{3b}: *Officials from smaller countries are more likely to be supranationalist.*

For *Country Size,* I use population size in the country of origin of each top Commission official. Values are expressed in millions.

Political party identification

For the final socialization variable, let us examine how parties – key framers of political contention in Europe – may shape top officials' preferences on supranationalism.

Ideology and party identification have remained very strong predictors of political attitudes in West European societies. They are more stable than other dispositions (Sears 1993; Weisberg 1998). Yet there are different scholarly views on the relationship between party identification and preferences on supranationalism in the European Union. Some point out that extreme Euro-skepticism is concentrated among small extremist parties on the left as well as the right, and this weakens a general relationship between left/right ideology and supranationalism (Taggart 1998). Europe's mainstream party families – social democrats, Christian democrats, liberals, and conservatives – have long taken largely similar positions on the broad constitutional issue of whether the European Union should be supranational or intergovernmental (Hix 1999). Yet, several scholars show that this mainstream consensus began to unravel in the mid-1980s (Gabel and Hix 2000; Hooghe, Marks, and Wilson 2000; Marks and Wilson 2000). Supranationalism has grown among social democrats while, as Christian democratic and conservative parties have become more nationalist, they have turned more intergovernmentalist. One would therefore expect ideology to have the largest influence among officials who entered public life at the time when mainstream parties began to diverge on European integration. That is, the preferences of younger officials should reflect current party preferences more closely than those of older officials socialized when mainstream parties held largely similar views.

H_4: *For officials with a party identification, those who place themselves on the ideological left are more in favor of supranationalism than are their colleagues on the ideological right.*

The variable *Party Identification* is a set of dummies for the main party families: *Socialist* (socialists or social democrats), *Christian Democrat, Conservative,* and *Liberal.*[3] To model the generational effect, I add interaction terms consisting of a generation dummy to each party family dummy. I report only three of the four potential dummies (*Young_Socialist, Young_Christ Democrat,* and *Young_Liberal*).[4] My reference category

---

[3] Only 2 of the 137 officials indicate support for extreme parties – one for a radical left and one for a radical right party. I can therefore dispense with the party dummies for extreme party families.

[4] There are only six conservatives in the dataset. This is too small a group to distinguish young from old conservatives.

consists of non-partisans, that is, officials who did not disclose their party allegiance. So the party dummies reflect, in standardized form, the difference between the means for these party families and the means for non-partisans; the interaction terms reflect the difference between the means of young and old socialists, young and old Christian democrats, and young and old liberals, respectively. I collected data on party identification for each top official during interviewing. Of 105 officials, 61 disclosed party identification; the others described themselves as non-partisan.

Maximizing utility in power-DGs

Rational actors are likely to bring their preferences in line with concrete institutional opportunities in their immediate work environment. This makes directorates-general in the Commission the first institutional context that needs to be examined from the viewpoint of utility maximization.

The conventional wisdom in studies of bureaucracies is that bureaucrats want to expand their power (Downs 1967; Niskanen 1971). But what this means depends on the particular demands of the job. Officials in policy areas with strong EU competencies – e.g. competition, external trade, or agriculture – need maximum regulatory and financial authority to buttress their position, and this should lead to them to support supranationalism. Officials with weak EU competencies may achieve more professional success by serving as honest brokers for national governments, or by providing them with information. These are resources that can be supplied in an intergovernmental European Union. So officials seeking to maximize their utility face very different incentives depending on whether they sit on strong or weak EU competencies.

H_5: *Officials from directorates-general with strong EU competencies support supranationalism.*

I combine formal and reputational measures of Commission power in a composite index. I draw formal indicators from figures compiled by Edward Page, who collected data on secondary legislative activity by the Commission (Page 1997). In addition, I use a reputational question that I posed to my interviewees. I asked them to name the three or four most powerful directorates-general at the time of the interview. *Power-DG* ranges from 1 (weak DG) to 9 (powerful DG).

National economic interest

If countries are powerful reference groups for EU actors, then it is plausible that national economic interest shapes Commission officials' preferences on supranationalism. There is a reasonably transparent and stable pattern of national contributions to and receipts from the EU budget, and one might expect net beneficiaries to favor supranationalism and net contributors to be intergovernmentalist. Although the Commission is formally independent of national interests, it often gets embroiled in national conflicts. To the extent that it does, those who work in the Commission can be conceived as agents who work for member state principals.

H_6: *The greater the net economic benefits of EU membership for an official's country of origin, the more supranationalist that official is likely to be.*

I use subjective and objective indicators to estimate who benefits from European policies. To measure perceptions, I employ data from an elite survey by the European Union's official polling agency, Eurobarometer (European Commission 1997), which asked whether the respondent's country had benefited from EU membership. *Perceived Benefit* is the proportion of respondents who replied "benefited" (the alternatives were "not benefited" and "don't know"). I allocate scores to Commission officials by nationality. Yet it is possible that support for European regulation and redistribution is linked more directly to financial benefits. *National Economic Benefit* is a measure of EU structural intervention, the EU's largest redistributive instrument, by member state for the 1994–9 programming period. I allocate country scores to Commission officials by nationality.

Utility and national networks

The extent to which Commission officials defend national economic interests is one way in which citizenship may matter. Yet in an organization that takes after the Belgian/Austrian *Proporz* system – except that nationality substitutes for party membership – nationality is a critical resource for top officials motivated to secure professional success.

A promotion system in which nationality takes priority over merit gives a head start to nationalities with social networks among compatriots in Brussels that stretch across the various European institutions and interest groups. Such networks allow them to exchange information on upcoming job opportunities and muster support for their candidature. Extensive networking turns nationality into an asset to officials competing for professional success.

Some nationalities have a strong reputation for networking – "clubness" – while others have not. Clubness has several sources. Nationalities with a strong identity, such as the Irish, the Danes, or the Spanish, are more likely to develop clubness, because their national consciousness induces them to seek each other out in a foreign environment. They meet at golf courses, in bars, or at literary evenings, and these occasions are invaluable for nurturing professional contacts (Abélès, Bellier, and McDonald 1993). Clubness also depends on the availability of organizational and financial resources. Larger nationalities have more resources, and as a result they are better able to monitor and lobby Commission personnel policy.[5] Thirdly, some national governments consciously strengthen networks among expatriates in Brussels. And finally, some Commission cabinets invest more resources in personnel affairs for the commissioner's compatriots than others.

Officials with high clubness should excel in an intergovernmental system in which governments take decisions – including career decisions. Strong national networks also make it easier for governments to keep tabs on "their" top Commission officials, and that should induce officials to be more attentive to national interests. Either way, nationalities with high clubness have rational reasons to favor intergovernmentalism.

H_7: Officials from strongly networked nationalities support intergovernmentalism.

I combine the effects of cultural cohesion, financial and organizational resources, intentional government policy, and intentional Commission cabinet policy into a composite index, *National Clubness,* which varies between 0 (weak) and 2 (strong). For this I draw from a range of sources – descriptive accounts (Christoph 1993; Cini 1996; Grant 1994; Ross 1995a,b), anthropological studies (Abélès, Bellier, and McDonald 1993; Bellier 1995; McDonald 1997), primary sources (including personnel data on Commission cabinets), and my interviews.

Parachutage

Finally, rational actors seeking to maximize professional success should pay keen attention to career rules. Rational top officials should bring their preferences on supranationalism in line with the power that hires and fires them. Under the Commission's system of "parachutage," by which almost half of top officials are appointed, national governments appear to call the shots. "Parachutists" usually owe their selection to fervent lobbying by their own national government, and it is widely thought that this guarantees the appointment of national faithfuls to top positions. One interviewee described parachutists as "Trojan horses" brought in to undermine Commission independence. All this leads one to expect parachutists to support their government's wishes.

---

[5] This argument echoes research on the presence, cohesion, and effectiveness of state delegations. Analyses have found strong associations with population size, size of state bureaucracy, and professionalism (Morrisroe 1998).

Table 4.1 *Top officials on supranationalism*

Item	Yes	Yes, but	Neutral	No, but	No	Mean[a]
1. The member states, not the Commission or the European Parliament, ought to remain the central pillars of the European Union.	7.6%	24.8%	4.8%	34.3%	28.6%	2.1
2. It is imperative that the European Commission becomes the true government of the European Union.	13.3%	24.8%	4.8%	46.7%	10.5%	2.4
3. The Commission acts too much as an administration, and not enough as the government of Europe.	12.4%	36.3%	3.8%	24.8%	22.9%	2.4

[a] Values range from 1.0 (No) to 4.0 (Yes); neutral = 2.5. A high value on item 1 is consistent with intergovernmentalism, whereas high values on items 2 and 3 indicate supranationalism.

H_8: *Parachuted officials are more likely to be intergovernmentalist.*

Parachutage is a dummy variable with a value equal to 1 if an official was appointed from outside the Commission to a top position.

I use multivariate linear regression (OLS) to examine the relative validity of these hypotheses. I measure supranationalism through a composite index of Commission officials' responses to three statements that contrast supranational and intergovernmental preferences (table 4.1). The first item represents the intergovernmentalist view, which says that ultimate authority should rest with member states, not with Europe. The following two items tap supranationalism. On a scale of 1.0 (intergovernmental) to 4.0 (supranational), the mean score of Commission officials is 2.6 and the median is 2.3. So, as a group, top officials are about evenly divided between supranationalists and intergovernmentalists on the index I have created.[6]

[6] The neutral value is 2.5 for mean and median. The standard deviation is 0.68. More than 12 percent are radical intergovernmentalists and 18 percent are moderate intergovernmentalists, against 17 percent radical and 16 percent moderate supranationalists; the remaining 36 percent balance the two principles (calculated by dividing the index into five categories).

Explaining supranationalism

A quick glance at table 4.2 reveals that top officials' preferences regarding authority in the European Union are mainly formed outside the Commission – in national bureaucracies, nationality-based networks in Brussels, and domestic territorial institutions. These are the variables that jump out in the multivariate analysis. The findings cast doubt on the presumption that working for the Commission encourages supranationalism – an assumption readily made by practitioners. According to one top official, "it is not the man that makes the job, but the job that makes the man. So when you are working in this environment, after a certain time, you become *pro-communautaire*" (official #58). Yet my data do not lend much support to such beliefs. Let us now examine the hypotheses one by one.

National administration trumps Commission socialization

Many studies of European integration start from the assumption that the Commission has an institutional interest in deepening supranationalism, and that states prefer intergovernmentalism. They also expect individuals who work in these institutions to share these interests; more precisely, the longer they have worked for the Commission, the more they are supranationalist, and the longer they have served in a national administration, the more they are intergovernmentalist. The fact that many Commission officials spent extended periods in a national administration earlier in their career makes it possible to compare the relative strength of Commission and national socialization.

As table 4.2 shows, national administration is strongly associated with intergovernmentalism, but Commission socialization is only weakly associated with supranationalism. The longer former national civil servants, diplomats, or government ministers have "served their country," the more likely they are to be intergovernmentalist.[7] But, contrary to conventional wisdom, Commission officials do not become significantly more supranationalist over time. State institutions appear to be more effective socializing agents than the Commission. When one controls for other variables, as in model 2, national administration remains a powerful predictor, but Commission socialization drops out.

---

[7] The most intergovernmentalist individuals among former state officials are diplomats who were previously posted to the European institutions. At first sight, this appears to go against the "going native" argument: that people who work in and around EU institutions become more susceptible to EU values and norms (Beyers and Dierickx 1997; Christoph 1993; Cram 1997; Lewis 1998; Schneider 1997). But the reason these ex-diplomats are more intergovernmentalist is that they spent more years in state service: fifteen years on average, against nine-and-one-half years for domestic civil servants.

Table 4.2 *Explaining supranationalism: multivariate OLS regression*

Variable	Correlation coefficient	Model 1[a]	Model 2[a]	Model 2 (standardized)
		Regression coefficients		
Commission Socialization	.13	.001 (.010)	–	–
National Administration	−.29***	−.018 (.011)	−.024*** (.009)	−.252***
National System				
Federalism	.25***	.081*** (.023)	.081*** (.021)	.349***
Size	−.18**	−.009** (.003)	−.008*** (.003)	−.320**
Party Identification				
Socialist	.07	.160 (.197)	–	–
Christian Democrat	.09	.275 (.307)	–	–
Conservative	−.06	.159 (.259)	–	–
Liberal	−.04	.116 (.268)	–	–
Young_Socialist	.04	−.088 (.256)	–	–
Young_Christ Democrat	−.10	−.867** (.368)	−.631*** (.238)	−.234***
Young_Liberal	−.05	−.138 (.295)	–	–
Power-DG	.14*	.061** (.029)	.057** (.027)	.173**
National Economic Benefit	.15*	.131** (.064)	.119* (.060)	.181*
National Clubness	−.37***	−.143* (.082)	−.145* (.077)	−.177*
Parachutage	−.10	−.117 (.177)	–	–
R^2		.38	.35	.35
Adj. R^2		.27	.31	.31
Durbin–Watson		1.79	1.76	1.76

Note: $N = 105$.
[a] Unstandardized regression coefficients, with standard errors in parentheses.
Significance levels (one-tailed): *** $p < .01$ ** $p < .05$ * $p < .10$.

In addition to the conventional unstandardized coefficients, I also report standardized coefficients, because they provide reliable estimates of the relative strength of causal effects. They are in the last column of table 4.2. National administration has the third-largest effect on top officials' preferences. How well do other socialization hypotheses fare?

The powerful pull of multi-level governance

Federalism is a powerful predictor of top officials' position on supranationalism. Austrian, Belgian, German, and Spanish officials are considerably more likely to support supranationalism than are officials from unitary countries such as Denmark, France, Ireland, the Netherlands, or Portugal.

Country size is also strongly significant, especially in the presence of controls. Controlling for federalism strengthens the influence of country size because federalism picks up supranationalism in large, but federal, countries such as Germany and Spain. Country size is strongly significant for unitary countries: $R = -.45$ (significant at the .01 level).

The smaller the effective territorial unit of political and social life in their home country, the more likely are Commission officials to support supranationalism. Prior experience of effective governance at multiple levels makes them less inclined to view relations between constituent states and European institutions in zero-sum terms, and they are keener to support multi-level governance in the European Union. As the column with standardized coefficients in table 4.2 shows, federalism and country size are number one and two in terms of effect on top officials' preferences.

Party identification

The hypothesis that party identification may predict where top officials stand on supranationalism finds mixed support in the data. Europe's main party families have adopted distinctly different positions on European integration since the 1990s. So if partisan top officials internalize their party's views, one would expect to see this reflected in their preferences, especially among younger officials. However, my data do not bear this out. For most party families, relationships go in the hypothesized direction: conservatives are more intergovernmentalist than any other category, social democrats and Christian democrats are more supranationalist than liberals, young social democrats are more supranationalist than their older colleagues, while the opposite is true for young and old Christian democrats, and young liberals are less supranationalist than their older

Table 4.3 *Supranationalism by party identification*

Party identification	Number	Mean[a,b]	Median[a]
Older social democrats	12	2.7	2.5
Young social democrats	13	2.6	2.7
Older Christian democrats	5	3.3	3.0
Young Christian democrats	7	2.3	2.2
Conservatives	6	2.4	2.3
Older liberals/centrists	6	2.6	2.7
Young liberals/centrists	12	2.5	2.3
Older non-partisans	23	2.6	2.3
Young non-partisans	21	2.5	2.3
All	105	2.6	2.3

[a] Values on the supranationalism index range from 1.0 to 4.0:
neutral = 2.5.

[b] These means are not statistically different based on one-way
anova testing of difference of means.

party fellows (see table 4.3 for mean and median for each party family as well as non-partisans). Yet these associations are weaker than expected, and moreover they fade in a multivariate analysis. There is one significant exception: the prediction that young Christian democratic officials have more Euro-skeptical preferences – in contrast to their older Christian democratic colleagues – finds considerable support in the multivariate analysis. It is the fourth-largest effect in the model.

It is likely that this mixed result is partly a statistical artifact. The small number of cases in several categories raises the bar for obtaining statistically significant results. In addition, self-selection may explain why partisan top officials seem to diverge less strongly on supranationalism than national parties do. It may be, for example, that conservative party members who join the Commission come from the more pro-European wing of their parties.

Notwithstanding a relatively weak *general* effect of party identification, the strong statistical effect of the Young Christ Democrat dummy is consistent with my expectation that partisan top officials should reflect changing party positions on European integration.

Commission powerhouses

Let us now turn to the utility variables, beginning with positional power inside the Commission. The positional power hypothesis predicts that officials with greater policy autonomy will be supranationalist. Officials in competition policy, agriculture, external trade, or regional policy should be more supranationalist than those in education, culture, or tourism. Support for this thesis receives some statistical support in the bivariate analysis, and the parameter gains significance with controls.

Positional power becomes highly significant in the presence of controls because it interacts with national socialization, federalism, and national clubness. Officials with experience in national administrations are not influenced by whether they work in a Commission-led or Council-dominated policy area; there is no association between supranationalism and their DG's power ($R = .04$, $p = .71$). However, there is an association between supranationalism and Power-DG for individuals without national state experience ($R = .33$, $p = .02$). Federalism interacts with positional power in a similar way. Officials from unitary countries lean towards intergovernmentalism irrespective of what they do in the Commission ($R = .04$, $p = .78$). But officials from federal countries are responsive to the opportunities in their DG ($R = .48$, $p = .02$). Similarly, officials from strongly networked nationalities are quite immune to the influence of positional power ($R = .13$, $p = .33$), whereas their colleagues from weak networks are not ($R = .45$, $p = .03$). So Power-DG picks up residual variance once these variables have been taken out. This limited bite of Power-DG is reflected in table 4.2, where Power-DG has the smallest standardized coefficient among the statistically significant effects.

National interest and national networks – at the margin

I distinguish three ways in which country may influence top officials' preferences on supranationalism. One is to conceive of country as the political system in which top officials may be socialized into particular views on the territorial allocation of authority, and I have demonstrated above that it matters a great deal whether top officials come from federal rather than unitary, or from small rather than large political systems.

Another conceptualization, which I consider in this section, is country as a focus for economic interest. This is a utility variable. According to this logic, officials' preferences on supranational governance should reflect the economic interest of their country, and I find some support for this hypothesis. As one can see in table 4.2, the variable is significant at the .10 level in the multivariate model ($p = .05$). The association for perceived benefit is weaker than that for real economic benefit, so I report only the latter.

The third way to conceive of country is as a determinant of top officials' nationality or citizenship. Nationalities with extensive support networks are better armed to get information or support in a promotion system where nationality trumps merit. The hypothesis that these officials are more likely to lean to intergovernmentalism finds support in the data. It is the strongest bivariate association, but the variable weakens considerably when controlling for other factors.

National networks may help an official's career because they create bonds between potential applicants, supporters, gatekeepers, and recruiters of the same nationality. They also matter in subtle ways for people at the top, who use them to nurture relationships with influential compatriots in other parts of the Commission or in other EU institutions, to exchange information or canvass support for Commission initiatives, and to persuade compatriots of particular courses of action. In their anthropological study of the Commission, Abélès and his collaborators characterize the role of national networks as following:

Each nationality has its club, its network, its association of European officials, its "church," and they are especially frequented by those officials who are most destabilized by the multinational work environment. These happen to be more often Irish or Danish than German or Italian. Membership of the Irish club provides gossip, which makes it possible to keep up with local news. Equally, the Dutch, the Danes... try to find pubs in Brussels where they can bump into one another without having to make prior arrangements – a national habit. The Portuguese club groups ambassadorial diplomats and permanent representatives to NATO and the European Community. With its thematic dinners spiced up by reputable speakers, it performs a social and intellectual function. The French participate in political associations or, for the products of the ENA [Ecole Nationale d'Administration], in "old boys' networks." The Spanish form a cohesive colony, though the nocturnal social life has had to give way to the exigencies of the [Brussels] climate and the work rhythm in the Commission. The British, members of a club in London, do not see the need to belong to a club in Brussels. (Abélès, Bellier, and McDonald 1993: 25–6; my translation)

The two utility incarnations of country have respectively the fifth- and sixth-largest causal effect on top officials' preferences concerning supranationalism. Both are considerably weaker than the domestic socialization variables of federalism and country size.

Table 4.4 summarizes how these different conceptualizations capture preference variation among top officials from fifteen different countries. The correlation between average scores on supranationalism by nationality and a total score based on the four country variables is .78. Supranationalism is somewhat lower among Portuguese, Irish, and to some extent Danish officials than these variables predict, and Finnish and German

Table 4.4 *Four variables that capture variation among nationalities*

	Dependent variable	Independent variables[b]				
Nationality	Supranationalism[a]	Federalism[c]	Country size[d]	National economic interest[e]	National clubness[f]	Total score
Spanish	3.3	2	0	2	1	5
Finnish	3.3	0	2	1	1	4
Belgian	3.2	2	2	0	2	6
Greek	2.9	0	1	2	2	5
Italian	2.8	1	0	1	2	4
Austrian	2.8	2	2	0	0	4
German	2.7	2	0	0	0	2
Luxemburg	2.7	0	2	0	1	3
Portuguese	2.7	1	1	2	1	5
Dutch	2.6	1	1	0	1	3
Irish	2.6	0	2	2	0	4
Swedish	2.6	0	2	1	0	3
Danish	2.3	0	2	0	1	3
French	2.3	1	0	0	0	1
British	2.1	0	0	0	0	0

[a] The following averages are statistically different at the .10 level according to one-way anova testing for differences of means: Belgian, Greek, and Italian vs British. All other averages are not statistically different.

[b] I re-categorize nationalities: category 2 means that a nationality's value on this factor induces strongly to supranationalism, category 1 stands for values that induce moderately to supranationalism, and category 0 for values that do not induce to supranationalism. To make sure that these categories have the same meaning for every variable, I reverse values for country size and clubness. For example, a large population (high value on country size) becomes category 0, and a small population (low value on country size) category 2.

[c] 2 = federal systems; 1 = semi-federal or regionalized systems; 0 = unitary systems.

[d] 2 = small countries; 1 = medium-sized countries; 0 = large countries.

[e] 2 = high financial benefit; 1 = moderate financial benefit; 0 = low financial benefit.

[f] 2 = weak clubness; 1 = moderate clubness; 0 = strong clubness.

officials appear more enthusiastic than one would expect on the basis of country characteristics. On the whole, these four variables provide considerable leverage for explaining variation among nationalities.

As I explained in chapter 2, my strategy throughout this book is to substitute proper nouns where I can by conceptual categories. So rather than using country dummies, I am interested in discovering what particular characteristics of "country" may shape top officials' preferences, and how. Having grown up in a political system in which exclusive sovereignty is not highly valued, being a citizen of a net beneficiary of EU membership, and belonging to a nationality that is weakly networked in Brussels tend to make one more susceptible to supranationalism. These factors provide a theoretically more satisfactory explanation than country dummies.[8]

No Trojan horses

I find no support for the hypothesis that people parachuted into top positions from outside the Commission bureaucracy are more intergovernmentalist than are recruits from the Commission's middle management. The variable does not come close to significance. This goes against conventional wisdom, which depicts parachutists as Trojan horses for intergovernmentalism.

Parachutage is too blunt an instrument for national governments that desire to fill the Commission with loyal intergovernmentalist officials. National governments can usually block candidates with the "wrong" party membership or nationality, but they would be unwise blatantly to screen candidates for national loyalty. The multinational College of the Commission, which decides on senior appointments by simple majority, would not accept nominees who openly champion the interests of one country. What is more, restrictive tenure regulations protect top Commission officials against national control once appointed. Their government cannot fire them, and even the College of commissioners can take such a step only in exceptional circumstances. Parachuted officials can afford to distance themselves from the government that supported their candidature, because national government control ends with their appointment.

Conclusion

Top officials in the Commission bring with them rich experiences of previous occupations and of prior territorial settings, and these help predict their preferences on European integration.

Two experiences in particular predispose their views on supranationalism: service in a national administration, and growing up in a domestic political system characterized by multi-level governance. Individuals who served their country as national employees are likely to defend a European Union with member states as key pillars – an intergovernmental Europe.

---

[8] Of course, an OLS regression with country dummies instead of these four country-specific variables yields a larger R^2. It produces a model with an adjusted R^2 of .37, which is higher than the model in table 4.2. In addition to National Administration, Power-DG, and the dummy for Young-Christ Democrat, eleven of the fourteen country dummies are statistically significant (the reference category consists of the British officials). Yet dummies leave unspecified the particular country characteristics that are responsible for the systematic relationship with the dependent variable.

For them, national sovereignty stands for effective, efficient, and, above all, legitimate government.

Commission officials from political systems in which political authority is concentrated in national central institutions usually do not find much appeal in a supranational European Union. They believe that national institutions are capable of effective control over diverse policy areas. The political system that is most conducive to these preferences is that of a large, unitary state. Officials from political systems where authority is not concentrated, i.e. those from small countries or federal systems, have less to lose, and perhaps much to gain, by shifting some authority to the European level. Supranationalism gives those in small countries greater say in decisions that would otherwise be beyond their control. For those in federal countries, supranationalism extends multi-level governance to another level. There is, then, considerable support for the thesis that socialization shapes top officials' preferences on supranationalism.

However, top officials are also motivated by utility maximization, though the causal effect of these variables is decidedly weaker. One utility argument concerns how EU actors interact and organize themselves by nationality in Brussels. All other things equal, officials who are members of strong national networks – the Irish, Danish, and French, in particular – are likely to embrace intergovernmentalism. There is also some support for the hypothesis that officials' support for supranationalism indirectly reflects the national economic interest of their country of origin. Positional power in the Commission is the third utility variable. Officials in a Commission stronghold usually have more marked supranationalist preferences than managers of policy areas under Council control. Greater positional control makes top officials strive for even greater Commission discretion.

My data are not consistent with the popular belief that parachuted officials are more intergovernmentalist than their non-parachuted colleagues. Parachutage, the appointment of candidates from outside the services to top positions, does not appear to allow national governments to constrain supranational agents.

The predominance of domestic political socialization, national career socialization, and party socialization (for a small subgroup), as well as evidence of strategic positioning influenced by national networks and national economic interests, are living proof that the Commission is not insulated from the EU's system of multi-level governance. Top officials' preferences for a supranational or intergovernmental European Union are primarily shaped by outside influences – not inside the Commission. Only one Commission-specific influence – positional power–survives controls, and it is the weakest predictor.

The European Union emerged out of contending visions of supranational and intergovernmental cooperation in Europe and, since its birth, these have divided politicians and policy-makers inside and outside the Commission. The battles are ongoing, and sometimes exhausting. And so, when I ask the soft-spoken yet combative supranationalist official what he would like to do next in his professional life, he dreams of a less contentious existence, a simpler role on a smaller stage:

I would love to be mayor – the mayor of my village in France. It is the one thing I would like to do because that concerns a human dimension. To have opportunities to do things for people is a great gift; it is so real. When I studied Latin, I was always struck by the following little diversion. When Caesar crossed the Alps on his way to Gaul he stopped in a little village and dined with the chief of the village. Of course, they smoked a pipe near the fire and suddenly the chief told Caesar: "You have the world at your feet, you are a forceful figure." ... This was still the Roman Republic governed by three consuls – one of them being Caesar ... And Caesar responded: "No, I am only one of three consuls, while you are the only chief here. You are the first, and I am the second or the third." You see, this chief could get things done that Caesar could only dream of. (Official #70)

5   Capitalism against capitalism

In search of market liberals

For a long time, Europe's left was reluctant to support European integration. In its 1952 party program, the German social democratic party castigated supranational Europe as "a conservative and capitalist federation of the miniature Europe" (Haas 1958: 137). It is true that socialist parties in all six founding states helped to ratify the Treaty of Rome, but their support was often qualified – concerned as they were that European economic integration would make it more difficult to pursue socialist policies. Ambivalence or opposition also initially characterized left parties in Britain, Ireland, and Denmark in the 1970s, Greece in the early 1980s, and Sweden in the 1990s. The least one can say is that the left has not been in the vanguard of European integration. The uniting of Europe was crafted by parties of the center and the right (Featherstone 1988: 2).

The left's suspicion was understandable. Until the 1999 Treaty of Amsterdam, there was a powerful institutional bias in EU Treaties and legislation in favor of market-creating (i.e., negative) integration and against market-correcting (i.e., positive) regulation (Dehousse 1992; Majone 1992, 1994a, 1996; Pinder 1968; Scharpf 1996; Streeck 1991, 1996; Streeck and Schmitter 1991). A close examination of the Treaties leads Mark Pollack to conclude that, "from Rome to Maastricht, the fundamental thrust of the treaties has been neo-liberal, in the sense that each of the Community's constitutive treaties facilitated the creation of a unified European market, while setting considerable institutional barriers to the regulation of that same market" (Pollack 1999: 268). That changed with the Amsterdam Treaty of 1999, which addresses several concerns of regulated capitalism, including employment, social policy, women's rights, human rights, environment, and the powers of the European Parliament. Yet it remains the case that European integration is predominantly a market-liberal project.

A casual observer of the European Union may infer from this that the European Union's executive institution, the European Commission, should therefore prefer market liberalism. After all, is it not the Commission's primary responsibility "in order to ensure the proper functioning and development of the common market, ... [to] ensure that the provisions of this Treaty and the measures taken by the institutions pursuant thereto are applied" (Art. 211)? However, as chapter 3 shows, support for European regulated capitalism is far greater than support for market liberalism among the Commission's top officials.

Market liberals exist, of course, but they form a small minority. They believe that the European Union should be a lever for liberalizing domestic economies. A top official in a market-oriented DG argues for comprehensive deregulation to increase European competitiveness:

Official: To promote the competitiveness of industry in Europe, ... [it is not] efficient to have a sectoral policy or selective industrial policies. This has not worked. And to a certain extent this was the Commission's past policy, but it is absolutely clear that this is *not* what we are trying to pursue [now]. We want to have horizontal action; we want to promote *opportunities* for industry to be competitive. [We want to] create the right conditions. *This* is important – not to try to strengthen one sector by supporting or subsidizing a particular industry in need.

Interviewer: The Davignon approach is dead?

O: Well, that approach is very dangerous. For example, [the Dutch aerospace company] Fokker did not survive because neither the Dutch government nor the Commission was prepared to support the survival of a company in bad shape. This is an extremely important message. We are trying to achieve the following in our industrial policy: to create the conditions [for European competitiveness] and, beyond that, it is up to the industry to use these opportunities. Horizontal action is absolutely necessary and very important.

I: What are the main instruments for creating these conditions? It is not regulation; it is certainly not subsidies ...

O: No, it isn't. By promoting what could have an effect on competitiveness through *general* means: research and development, a good climate for innovation, a favorable tax situation. We want to deregulate so that companies are not bogged down by rules and regulations that do not serve a strong public interest. We want to open up and get rid of hurdles for industry to promote competition. This is very important in order to make companies stronger. We want to promote an open trading system, so that we do not put up a protectionist wall, because inside a protective area one will never become competitive.

I: So the policy of European champions is dead.

O: Yes, it is. [Another objective is to promote] the use of information technology. We want an information society. What also is extremely important – and here we have not yet been able to do very much, is to *deal* with – I was about to say "attack" – the main differences between Japan and the United States on one side and Europe on the other side. The public sector in Europe is too costly, and so are welfare policies, and taxation policies.

I: Does Europe have to converge to the American and Japanese models? Is that the message?

O: I do not know what you mean by that, but I think that we need more private initiative in the welfare system, for example with respect to insurance policies, or greater cost sharing in health care, or privatization of retirement schemes.... We need to explain that, by reducing public costs, we increase competitiveness, and we will be able to create new jobs, and this leads to a healthier, wealthier society. The purpose of all this is to create the best conditions and benefits for the citizens in Europe as a whole. It has no other purpose.

I: So it does not have to be an American or a Japanese model?

O: I do not think we can ever get so far, and I don't think we *should* try to get a Japanese or an American system in Europe. We have to find a *European* system, where one cares perhaps more for the individual citizen than other systems. We just have to find the right balance. And that is difficult – it is politically extremely difficult. (Official # 197)

Market liberals conceive of the combination of economic and monetary union and enlargement as a golden opportunity to scale down European policies that distort market forces and absorb European taxpayers' money. However, few support an Americanization of European society. In this sense, they are reluctant to embrace the social changes in the United Kingdom ushered in by Margaret Thatcher's neoliberal policies in the 1980s and 1990s. Instead, most favor a political economy that specializes in high-quality, high skilled niche production – the kind of co-ordinated market economy (Soskice 1999) characteristic of continental Europe:

Official: On the economic side, the European Union should *help* at least to turn the tide to decline, the relative loss of dynamism of Europe. North America is not a model for Europe. North America has many social problems. And it has that horrible tendency to neglect those who do not make it. Europe does not do that, and yet we have 11 percent unemployment, with unemployment rates like 25 percent in Spain – 50 percent among the youth in Spain or in the south of Italy. This is alarming. There is something definitely wrong.

Interviewer: What needs to be done?

O: The key problem is that we need to change the minds of the people. What is happening in two words is that those of us who have a job have given ourselves sufficient guarantees and entitlements to make sure that the mechanisms are unsustainable – so that our children will not have a job. So, that is the situation. There is much work to be done to change this. The problem is that the people with jobs and income form the core of national political systems, so they vote against changes.

I: So you have to *convince*...

O: One has to convince, and of course the rising costs of the status quo will [ultimately] convince these citizens. The problem is – how fast. That is the problem of decline.

I: Trying to turn the tide in terms of creating economic growth and employment
... One of the things Europe does not have is mobility of labor. And that is
probably not going to change very much even if one gets rid of regulations.
O: We need to empower people. The quality of the workforce is declining. The
school systems are declining. *This* is the key condition for mobility. The
other mobility – the mobility of the immigrants – I do not think we want
much of that, of a poor, destitute underclass. We need a mobility of skills ....
Managing change is difficult. We have to change the minds of people to make
them understand that an inflexible society has to be made more flexible.
(Official # 10).

The debate in the Commission on Europe's market economy takes
place within relatively narrow parameters. Most officials appear to be
either moderate market liberals or mild regulated capitalists. What
unites them is their rejection of an Anglo-Saxon liberal market economy. They diverge in the extent to which the European Union should be
proactive in retooling European societies. Allan Larsson, former minister
of finance in a Swedish social democratic government and, at the time of
the interview, director-general of social policy in the Commission, epito-
mizes a mild regulated capitalist. He believes that the European Union
should prevent regime competition through market regulation. Yet he is
also convinced that the EU should do more; it should help create jobs
and make employment policy a European priority:

Every labor market is a local market. That means that both national and local level
are important, but we can do much at the European level too. . . . In my opinion,
employment policy at the European level ought to go from a zero-sum game to
a positive-sum game. Zero-sum is the outcome when member states take action
in favor of employment in one country at the expense of jobs in other countries.
Take for example fiscal dumping, when one uses tax money to keep jobs in one
country at the expense of others. Or social dumping, when one undermines wages
and social conditions. Or monetary dumping. In short, it means giving priority
to your own district. The European Union is first and foremost about *avoiding*
this type of negative measures. But [the European Union] also has a positive side.
That is to give priority to employment, which is what the [proposed employment]
chapter in the intergovernmental conference [of Amsterdam] is all about. The
positive side means that Europe has a strategy to deal proactively with the nature
of changes in working life.

Surveys show that support for European regulated capitalism is relatively high throughout much of Europe among Europe's elites and public
opinion.[1] European regulated capitalism also finds strong backing in the

---

[1] Several sources on elite opinion are consistent with this. In an expert survey on positions concerning European integration for 142 national parties in 1999, party experts
were asked to assess support for certain EU policies on a scale from 1 (opposition) to 7
(support). On key policies of European regulated capitalism, mainstream party families

Commission, and that is borne out by a high mean value on the items that constitute the dependent variable in table 5.1. Yet there is a substantial dissenting minority. Let us examine why some officials are keener than others to advocate European regulated capitalism.

"Une bataille brute, une bataille des idées"[2]

Allan Larsson personifies a political entrepreneur in Europe long ignored by traditional studies of European integration. He began his career as a civil servant in the employment ministry in Sweden, then proceeded to become a social democratic member of parliament, minister of finance, a negotiator for Sweden during the country's EU accession talks, and chair of a working group on employment for the Party of European Socialists (PES) (hand-picked by PES president Felipe Gonzales). I met him in 1996 – "back in administration" as Commission director-general for social affairs. Larsson has moved back and forth between administration and politics, and between national and European arenas. A varied career indeed. Yet one quality has never changed – his commitment to one substantive objective: that an open, internationally competitive economy

proved on the whole fairly supportive: on EU cohesion policy, ranging from 5.3 for liberals to 5.8 for social democrats; on EU environmental policy, from 5.0 for conservatives to 6.2 for social democrats; on EU employment policy, from 4.4 for conservatives to 6.0 for social democrats. Only radical right parties appear strongly to oppose these policies (Hooghe, Marks, and Wilson 2000). One can draw similar results from an elite survey conducted by Eurobarometer in the spring of 1996, which polled elected politicians, high-level civil servants, business and labor leaders, and media and cultural leaders in all EU member states. They were asked to evaluate whether policy areas should be decided at national/regional or European level, with a value of 1 referring to exclusively national/regional competence and a value of 10 to exclusively European competence. The survey reports mean scores ranging between 4.3 and 7.6. Leaders want primary EU competence for environmental policy (7.6), scientific and technological research (6.7), employment policy (6.0), and social policy (5.4). They support secondary EU competence for regional development (4.6), health insurance (4.5), and education policy (4.3). This question constitutes a hard test of support for European regulated capitalism. It assesses the extent to which national elites are willing to tolerate exclusive supranational competence; European regulated capitalism, however, does not require *exclusive* supranational decision-making but promotes partnership – shared decision-making – between European, national, and regional governments in the above policies. (European Commission 1996). I do not know of directly comparable data for the general public. Eurobarometer regularly presents respondents with a list of policy areas, and it asks them whether they want these policies to be decided at national or at European level. This is a very crude measure for assessing support for European regulated capitalism. Nevertheless, a 1996 survey shows that for an absolute majority of respondents the following areas central to European regulated capitalism should be decided at European level: science and technology research (70%), protection of environment (65%), regional support (63%), and fight against unemployment (53%). There is minority support for European-level policy making for health and social welfare (34%), education (37%), and workers' rights vis-à-vis employers (53%) (European Commission 1997).

Table 5.1 *Top officials on European regulated capitalism*

Item	Yes	Yes, but	Neutral	No, but	No	Mean[a]
1. Europe has developed a unique model of society, and the Commission should help to preserve it: extensive social services, civilized industrial relations, negotiated transfers among groups to sustain solidarity, and steer economic activity for the general welfare.	42.5%	38.7%	4.7%	9.4%	4.7%	3.21
2. No united Europe without a mature European cohesion policy.	46.7%	31.4%	1.9%	18.1%	1.9%	3.24

[a] Values range from 1.0 (No) to 4.0 (Yes); neutral = 2.5. A high value is consistent with European regulated capitalism, and a low value with market liberalism.

such as Sweden's should be made compatible with social democratic principles – growth should go hand in hand with high-quality jobs, fair wages, and comprehensive welfare. Director-general Larsson's views on regulating market forces in the European Union are an outflow of his long-standing social democratic values.

Allan Larsson is not the only politico among the Commission's top officials. As I noted in chapter 2, most have been active in politics in some fashion, though few have put their professional lives so unambiguously at the service of their ideological convictions as Larsson. It seems reasonable to expect top officials' preferences on regulating market forces to reflect, at least in part, their ideological orientations. Yet ideology is just one of several plausible influences on top officials' preferences. What can be learned from existing studies for understanding preference formation on regulating market forces in the European Union?

[2] I borrow this expression from a Commission official, who exclaimed at the end of an interview about the structural funds reform in the late 1980s: "C'était une bataille brute, mais c'était aussi une bataille des idées!" (Brussels, October 1993). With the "bataille brute" he was referring to the tug of war over resources and competencies that involved four or five Commission directorates-general, and that also pitted the Commission against national administrations. But in the same breath, he emphasized that underlying such fierce power politics was a deeply rooted ideological conflict. This chapter illustrates that there is often tremendous tension between power or interests on the one hand and ideas or ingrained practices on the other hand.

Early theorizing on European integration – neofunctionalism and liberal intergovernmentalism – did not pay much attention to where political actors stand on market and state relations in Europe. European decisions were analyzed as a function of whether they strengthen or weaken the national state, not whether they alter the role of government in the economy. From that perspective, it seems plausible to assume that actors' positions on supranationalism or intergovernmentalism predispose their position on regulating European capitalism. As one top official put it, "[ideology] is the wrong axis. We are most divided on another axis: pro-integration or anti-integration" (official #58). The tug of war – *bataille brute* – that counts is the one that pits national against supranational interests.[3]

The implications of international governance for national sovereignty have rarely been high on the agenda of comparativists.[4] As far as European integration is concerned, the working assumption was for a long time that domestic politics was only marginally affected anyway. Few comparativists paid attention to political economy issues *beyond* national boundaries. Only in the 1990s did a growing number begin to emphasize the pivotal role of European integration in reconfiguring relations between state and market in Europe (Hix 1994). EU decisions affect national industrial regimes, welfare states, and party systems. They bear on equality and the role of government – issues that were traditionally associated with the left/right cleavage in the domestic arena (Hix 1998; Hooghe and Marks 1999). This perspective makes concerns about national sovereignty subservient to substantive policy goals. So comparativists are inclined to argue that political actors use European decisions to achieve substantive goals they were formerly seeking exclusively within states.

Comparative political economists (CPE) led the pack of comparativists in examining consequences of the blurring of domestic and European politics (Crouch and Streeck 1997; Gorges 1996; Leibfried and Pierson 1995; Rhodes 1995, 1996; Rhodes and van Apeldoorn 1997; Scharpf 1996; Streeck 1991, 1996; Teague and Grahl 1992; Turner 1996; Wilks 1996). CPE scholars study the effects of European market integration on domestic institutional arrangements, or they assess the odds for a European industrial relations system, a European welfare state, or a

---

[3] A corollary of this argument is that there should be a strong association between top officials' positions on supranationalism and those on regulated capitalism. Yet, the correlation between these two factors is close to zero (see footnote 5 in chapter 3). Dispositions to supranationalism in the European Union do not shape preferences on regulating Europe's economy.

[4] Except for students of state building. See for example Thomas Ertman (1997), Hendrik Spruyt (1994), and Charles Tilly (1975, 1990).

European social and redistributive policy.[5] Pioneering this line of work was Wolfgang Streeck and Philippe Schmitter's 1991 article on the dim chances for a European industrial relations system. In the second half of the 1990s, a theoretical shift in the field of international political economy (IPE) swelled the number of people studying the domestic sources of international cooperation, of which European integration is the most extreme example (Fioretos 1998; Mattli 1999; Milner 1997; Moravcsik 1998). IPE scholars argue that governments engage in international cooperation to pursue domestic economic interests. They conceive of domestic economic groups' preferences as the primary factor shaping international institutions.

This political economy work focuses on the objectives and strategies of factors (trade unions, capital, farmers), sectors (e.g. private versus public sectors, or exposed versus sheltered sectors), or national governments – not Commission officials – but its insights are illuminating nevertheless for understanding Commission preferences. The key assumption is that actor preferences on regulating capitalism at EU level are colored by experiences in domestic social and economic institutions. So officials from divergent industrial regimes – the Swedish coordinated market economy versus the British liberal market regime, for example – should have different preferences on regulating European capitalism. The fact that the Swede Larsson comes from an industrial regime with strong affinities to European regulated capitalism may help explain why he is an ardent regulated capitalist.

Political economists identify domestic economic institutions as potential constraints on actor preferences. Students of party and electoral politics, on the other hand, point to the role of ideology and partisanship in shaping preferences on new European issues (Anderson 1998; van der Eijk and Franklin 1995; Gabel 1998b, 1998c; Gabel and Hix 2000; Hix 1999; Marks and Wilson 2000). They argue that – as in domestic politics – one's position on the left/right ideological dimension reflects one's stance on regulating capitalism. In the European Union, these left/right views may cut across national interests. Sure enough, scholars who emphasize ideology in shaping EU politics are most interested in understanding the preferences of political parties, party leaders, or voters – not top Commission officials. However, if one accepts the comparativist assumption

---

[5] Critical political economists in the classical Marxian or Gramscian tradition have consistently denounced European integration as a capitalist enterprise undermining socialism in Europe. However, most of these studies are abstract macro-structural analyses, which do not lend themselves easily to micro-level hypothesizing concerning actor positions. It is difficult to extract from them systematic expectations concerning variations in actor response. For an overview of this literature see Lankowski (1997) and Cocks (1980).

that domestic and European politics have become blurred, there is little reason to exclude *a priori* Commission officials from being influenced by competing ideologies and partisanship. Director-general Larsson is not the only top official with a party-political history.

A third group of comparativists starts from the assumption that the bureaucratic or policy environment shapes civil servants' preferences. One approach sees bureaucrats as maximizers of resources, competencies, or status. This conception of bureaucratic interaction as ongoing *batailles brutes* underlies the bureaucratic politics model and the principal – agent model, which have both been applied to the European Commission.[6] Another strand of theorizing conceives bureaucratic interaction primarily as *une bataille des idées*. Policy paradigm approaches accentuate how ideas and policy legacies – rather than material interests – may motivate policy makers (Coleman 1998; Hall 1993; Majone 1989, 1991; Rose 1991; Skogstad 1998). Ministerial departments, and by extension Commission directorates-general, often espouse distinct worldviews that may influence people working in this environment. The principal – agent and bureaucratic politics models on the one hand and the policy paradigm studies on the other hand are all consistent with a view of the Commission as a multi-organization, where variations in decision rules, resources, and styles among policy sectors create distinctive environments for Commission officials (Cram 1994, 1997). Yet they disagree on how these environments shape preferences, whether by structuring incentives for maximizing professional success, or by molding values.

As in the previous chapter, the causal analysis in this chapter needs to disentangle the influence of interests and internalized values, and of contexts outside and inside the Commission. A top official who worked in at least five different DGs during his long Commission career, before landing in a social-oriented DG, illustrates how the line between *bataille brute* and *bataille des idées* may be a fine one:

If the director-general of DG *Y* or *Z* does not have a philosophy that coincides more or less with the thinking in that DG, he or she is a bit out of place. In other words, if I take on this job in social affairs, I have to be interested in the broader social scene. I have to be interested in other things than the market economy. I have to be interested in other issues than supply and demand, or pricing. If I am not interested in people, the development of people, the kinds of policies that run in that direction, I have no business in this post. Now imagine that I am faced with the director-general for economic affairs, whose concerns are quite clearly

---

[6] For the bureaucratic politics model: Allison (1969), Bendor and Hammond (1992), Rosati (1981); applications to the European Commission: Peters (1992). Leading works on the principal – agent model: Downs (1967); McCubbins, Noll, and Weingast (1987); Moe (1997); Wintrobe (1997); for a critical view: Worsham, Eisner, and Rinquist (1997); on the Commission: Franchino (1999, 2000); Pollack (1997).

economic convergence, which I share, the development of economic monetary union, which I share, budget rigor and the reduction of public deficits – I share that view as well. I would inevitably say to him: "Wait a minute! It is not just a matter of economic convergence. It is not just a matter of economic and monetary union. We have to recognize that there is more to the development of the Community, the competitiveness of the Community, than just these policies. We have to make space for other policies." So I would get into a conflict in two minutes with my good friend Giovanni Ravasio, director-general of economic and financial affairs. (Official #30)

Why top officials may diverge

Why are some officials more in favor of European regulated capitalism (ERC) than others? As in the previous chapter, I draw from socialization and utility logic to proffer possible answers to this question. Top officials may have internalized preferences on regulating capitalism through their work in the Commission, through previous work experiences in national administrations, through participation in their particular domestic industrial regime, or through party-political linkages. Then I turn to three situations in which top officials' preferences may be motivated by their concern for professional success. This may be in response to incentives in their DG, to the influence of national governments, or to Commission presidents. Figure 5.1 plugs these hypotheses into the broader model of preference formation.

Logic of influence (causal mechanism)	Source of influence (type of institutional context)	
	Type I Inside the Commission	Type II Outside the Commission
Socialization	Length of service in Commission Length of service in ERC-DG	Experience in national administration Experience in national system (corporatism) Political party identification
Hybrid category	Delors factor ↓	
Utility maximization	Position in ERC-DG	National economic interest

Figure 5.1 Hypotheses on top officials' preferences for European regulated capitalism.

Commission socialization

Neofunctionalism and liberal intergovernmentalism imply that political actors' preferences on a supranational or intergovernmental Union predispose their stance on regulating European capitalism. Constitutional issues take precedence over substantive or ideological concerns. This view leads one to expect that the European Commission supports European regulated capitalism because these policies require greater supranationality. Socialization theory then predicts that Commission employees internalize these preferences.

H_1: *The longer an official has worked in the Commission, the more he or she prefers European regulated capitalism.*

I use the same indicator for *Commission Socialization* as in chapter 4, which is the number of years served in the Commission prior to the interview.

Experience in national administration

For the same reasons that Commission officials are expected to endorse European regulated capitalism, former national civil servants are likely to be skeptical. Whereas the former are presumed to like it because it promises to strengthen supranationalism, employees from national state institutions are anticipated to fear it because it threatens state autonomy. Many former civil servants were successful regulators in their home administration, and they may well believe that national institutions are intrinsically valuable settings for political regulation. Also, they may consider national regulation intrinsically more legitimate.

H_2: *The longer an official worked for a national administration, the less he or she prefers European regulated capitalism.*

As in the previous chapter, I use as indicator for *National Administration* the number of years served as a national civil servant prior to joining the Commission.

National system: corporatism

Comparativists argue that European politics is an extension of domestic politics. An implication is that what shapes views on regulating capitalism in one's own country can be expected to influence preferences on regulating capitalism in the European Union. This reasoning turns the prior argument on its head: substantive objectives shape preferences concerning institutional design.

One such factor is the character of the domestic capitalist system. David Soskice (1999) distinguishes between coordinated and liberal market economies in Europe. In coordinated economies, non-market actors, such as the state authority or peak organizations for employers and labor, play a large role in regulating economic relations; these regimes are usually corporatist. In liberal market economies, economic actors use market mechanisms to bring structure to their relationships. Organizations of labor or employers usually play only a minor role – these tend to be non-corporatist societies.[7]

Each regime has distinct institutional arrangements, and these mold the preferences and behavior of firms, labor, and state elites – and perhaps also of Commission officials. Yet this categorization does not predict the direction of the association; here one needs recourse to socialization theory.

One hypothesis builds on the concept of belief consistency (Sears 1993). Individuals want to extrapolate their experiences to the European arena; they are inclined to bring European institutional arrangements in line with national ones. European regulated capitalism is closer to the corporatist, coordinated economies of Germany/Benelux and Scandinavia than to the state interventionist/family-coordinated model in Southern Europe, and it is furthest removed from Anglo-Saxon capitalism. So one may hypothesize the following:

H_{3a}: *The more the economic regime of an official's country of birth resembles a coordinated market economy, the more he or she supports European regulated capitalism.*

A different argument starts from the notion that individuals draw lessons from past experiences. This view emphasizes that socialization is not an automatic process. European regulated capitalism, even in Jacques Delors' ambitious formulation, is unlikely to replicate the postwar social contract of Europe's most advanced societies (Hooghe and Marks 1999; Rhodes and van Apeldoorn 1997; Schmitter 1996; Streeck 1996; Streeck and Schmitter 1991). Individuals from corporatist economies may therefore conclude that European regulated capitalism would undermine national practices (Streeck 1996). In contrast, weakly corporatist societies could employ European regulation to upgrade lower standards and

---

[7] There are many labels to describe the same basic distinction. Michel Albert (1993) contrasts the Rhine model with Atlantic or Anglo-Saxon capitalism. Colin Crouch and Wolfgang Streeck (1997) pit institutional capitalism against neoliberal capitalism. Stephen Wilks (1996) analyzes continental/social democratic and neo-American models. Martin Rhodes and Bastiaan van Apeldoorn (1997) compare the Anglo-Saxon market-oriented model with two network-oriented versions, the German social market model and the Latin state interventionist model. Esping-Andersen (1999) labels the latter family-coordinated capitalism, because of the crucial role of the family as a non-market coordinating agent in the economy.

entrench corporatist practices at home. This leads to the following counter-hypothesis:

H_{3b}: *The more the economic regime of an official's country of birth resembles a coordinated market economy, the less he or she supports European regulated capitalism.*

In measuring the type of capitalism in Europe, political economists usually employ rough categorizations, and these often do not include all EU member states. I use as proxy an index of *Corporatism* developed by Markus Crepaz for the early 1990s, which relies on twelve judgments made by experts attempting to quantify corporatism (Crepaz 1992). Crepaz does not include Portugal, Spain, and Greece, so I estimate scores for these countries separately. I also simplify Crepaz' standardized scores into rankings, where the most corporatist EU member state has a value of 15 and the least corporatist a value of 1.

Party identification

Regulating capitalism in Europe involves regulation of market forces, the provision of collective goods and social services, and income redistribution. These issues have long defined party politics in national states. One may expect that Commission officials who identify with a party reflect their party's preferences.

Recent party research demonstrates that left-wing parties have become more pro-European as the European Union has become a more propitious arena for social democratic goals. With the goal of an internal market achieved, parties on the economic right have become reluctant for fear that further integration would strengthen EU capacity to re-regulate market forces. Christian democratic parties used to be strong supporters, but they have become less enthusiastic as economic and social conservativism has grown in their ranks. On the basis of this, one may hypothesize that older socialists will show qualified support, and their younger colleagues stronger support, for European regulated capitalism; older Christian democrats strong support, and younger party sympathizers weak support; older and younger liberals reluctant support; conservatives deepening skepticism.

H_4: *For officials with a party identification, those who place themselves on the ideological left are more in favor of European regulated capitalism than are those on the right. This contrast sharpens among the younger generation.*

I use the same dummy indicators for *Party Identification* as in the previous chapter. So my baseline for the party dummies consists of non-partisans, that is, officials who did not disclose their party allegiance.

Utility vs. socialization in ERC-DGs

So far I have conceived of Commission officials as members of wider European or national arenas. However; they spend most of their time inside the Commission. The new governance model draws attention to institutional variation in bureaucrats' immediate policy world. Commission policy areas may influence officials' preferences in two ways.

A socialization argument links length of service in particular policy tasks to support for European regulated capitalism. Commission officials are most likely to internalize pro-ERC values as they spend more time in directorates-general that espouse such values or worldviews.

H_{5a}: *The longer top Commission officials have worked in units dealing with social and redistributional issues, the more they support European regulated capitalism.*

In contrast, a utility maximization argument assumes that officials want to maximize professional success, and they adjust their preferences accordingly. If that is the case, then it is more important to know the kind of job an official does today than how long he has been working for DG X or DG Y. Position holders in ERC services may support European regulated capitalism because that way they can expect more jobs, a greater share of the EU budget, or a higher status for their DG. The adage of bureaucratic politics that "you stand where you sit" suggests the following counter-hypothesis:

H_{5b}: *Top Commission officials in units dealing with social and redistributional issues are more likely to support European regulated capitalism.*

For the variable *ERC-Soc* I calculate years spent in DGs dealing with European regulated capitalism, that is, DGs involved in provision and redistribution, social regulation, and supply-side policies. Nearly 48 percent of Commission officials have worked in a regulated capitalism-friendly DG. I test the counter-hypothesis with a variable *ERC-DG*, which is a dummy that allocates a value of 1 to current employees in ERC-friendly services. Just over 35 percent work in such a DG.

National economic interest

Whether the European Union promotes European regulated capitalism or liberalization influences costs and benefits for individual member states.

A group utility argument therefore links national economic utility to the political-economic preferences of Commission officials.

H_6: *Officials from countries with net gains from European regulated capitalism will favor European regulated capitalism, whereas officials from net contributors are reluctant supporters.*

My indicator *National Economic Benefit* is the same as in chapter 4.

Delors factor

Formal recruitment rules ensure that the political Commission is well placed to select officials on the basis of their preferences *if it so wishes*. During his ten years in office (1985–94), former Commission president Jacques Delors was the driving force behind an action plan for European regulated capitalism. According to George Ross' authoritative study, "Delors, with Pascal's [Lamy, Delors' chef de cabinet] advice, had very carefully replaced a considerable number of high Commission officials, directors-general and division heads, in critical areas" (Ross 1995b: 67). Delors appeared to have a strong interest in influencing the ideological make-up of his top bureaucracy. This suggests the following utility hypothesis:

H_7: *Top officials appointed under Delors are more supportive of European regulated capitalism.*

The variable *Delors* is a dummy, which takes on a value of 1 for officials appointed under the Delors presidencies. Of the 105 Commission officials, 54 fall into that category.

As in the previous chapter, I examine the relative power of these hypotheses with the help of multivariate linear regression. My measure of *European regulated capitalism* is an index of two items. The first item in table 5.1 summarizes the most comprehensive formulation of European regulated capitalism to date, Jacques Delors' concept of "organized space." His conception draws heavily from the coordinated market economies of Germany and the Benelux, and it is in contradistinction to the Anglo-Saxon liberal market economy. It probes whether European institutions should help bring about a social market economy. The second item taps into Commission officials' support for the flagship policy of European regulated capitalism, EU cohesion policy. Values range from 1 (unconditional opposition) to 4 (unconditional support), with a mean of 3.2 and a median of 3.5.[8]

---

[8] The standard deviation is 0.68. The distribution is heavily skewed to European regulated capitalism: 4 percent of officials are radical market liberals and another 4 percent moderate market liberals, as against 51 percent radical and 24 percent moderate regulated capitalists; the remaining 17 percent balance these principles quite evenly.

Explaining European regulated capitalism

The analysis in table 5.2 demonstrates that top officials' preferences are to a considerable degree explained by party-ideological factors. Party identification overshadows all others in the multivariate analysis. Partisanship is alive and well in the top layers of the Commission bureaucracy. I discuss the influence of party identification first, and then move on to the remaining hypotheses.

Party identification trumps all

Party identification is the single most powerful predictor of where officials stand on European regulated capitalism. In the bivariate regression, the coefficient of determination (R^2) equals .23, and this rises to .31 for the 61 partisans (not shown in table 5.2).

The results for Christian democrats are consistent with the hypothesis that top officials reflect the shift in the Christian democratic party family from a position strongly in favor of European regulated capitalism to a more market-liberal stance. The Christian democratic dummy is positive, whereas the young Christian democratic dummy is negative. In the immediate postwar period, support for regulating capitalism was a logical choice for Christian democrats who had embraced the philosophy of Mounier and Maritain. Social personalism became the political and social-theoretical basis for European Christian democracy in the 1950s and 1960s (Hanley 1994; van Kersbergen 1997, 1999). Jacques Delors, a socialist but also a practicing Catholic of the older generation, relied explicitly on social personalism to explicate his vision of a European organized space (Delors 1992; Ross 1995b). It is then not a surprise that older Christian democratic top officials, like Delors, are hardcore supporters of European regulated capitalism. However, with religion rapidly losing salience in Europe, Christian democratic parties are increasingly emphasizing social and economic conservatism. This sits uncomfortably with European regulated capitalism. In the Commission, younger Christian democratic officials reflect this repositioning of recent years.

The data are less clear-cut on the hypothesis that socialists have shifted from lukewarm to very strong support. Nevertheless, table 5.3, which displays average support for old and young for each party family, demonstrates that, of all top officials, young socialists are very strong supporters of European regulated capitalism. They are second only to older Christian democrats. However, they do not differ significantly from older socialists, which is why the dummy does not survive controls.

The findings for conservatives and liberals are in line with expectations. Conservative officials are least likely to support European regulated

Table 5.2 *Explaining European regulated capitalism: multivariate OLS regression*

Variable	Correlation coefficient	Regression coefficients		
		Model 1[a]	Model 2[a]	Model 2 (standardized)
Commission Socialization	.21**	.002	–	–
		(.008)		
National Administration	−.35***	−.024**	−.026***	−.271***
		(.010)	(.008)	
National System Corporatism	−.20**	−.024	−.028*	−.164*
		(.014)	(.014)	
Party Identification Socialist	.14*	−.116	–	–
		(.186)		
Christian Democrat	.05	.533*	.589**	.278**
		(.273)	(.253)	
Conservative	−.39***	−1.152***	−1.137***	−.391***
		(.246)	(.231)	
Liberal	−.08	−.062	–	–
		(.248)		
Young Socialist	.18**	.194	–	–
		(.244)		
Young Christ Democrat	−.11	−.891**	−.913***	−.338***
		(.343)	(.327)	
Young Liberal	−.07	−.072	–	–
		(.279)		
ERC-DG	.19**	.286**	.309***	.219***
		(.119)	(.112)	
National Economic Benefit	.19**	.143**	.140**	.213**
		(.060)	(.055)	
Delors	.16*	.017	–	–
		(.117)		
R^2		.42	.41	.41
Adj. R^2		.34	.37	.37
Durbin–Watson		2.25	2.23	2.23

Note: $N = 105$.
[a] Unstandardized regression coefficients, with standard errors in parentheses.
Significance levels (one-tailed): ***$p < .01$ **$p < .05$ *$p < .10$.

capitalism. The dummy is strongly negative. A combination of nationalism and economic conservatism predisposes conservative parties to be reluctant supporters of greater European regulation and redistribution, and conservative officials espouse this stance. The liberal party family is diverse, and so liberal and centrist officials do not receive consistent cues

Table 5.3 *European regulated capitalism by party identification*

Party identification	Number	Mean[a][b]	Median[a]
Older social democrats	12	3.2	3.1
Young social democrats	13	3.6	3.5
Older Christian democrats	5	3.8	4.0
Young Christian democrats	7	3.0	3.0
Conservatives	6	2.2	2.3
Older liberals/centrists	6	3.1	2.9
Young liberals/centrists	12	3.1	3.0
Older non-partisans	23	3.4	3.5
Young non-partisans	21	3.2	3.5
All	105	3.2	3.5

[a] Values on the regulated capitalism index range from 1.0 to 4.0; neutral = 2.5.

[b] The conservatives are statistically different from socialists (both old and young), old Christian democrats, and non-partisans (old and young). The other means are not statistically different from one another based on one-way anova testing of difference of means.

from their party allegiance. This is reflected in the insignificance of the liberal dummies.

The strong showing of party identification challenges theories of European integration that have downplayed the impact of encompassing ideological frameworks and party-programmatic appeals. For officials with close party allegiance, partisanship is the primary prism through which they evaluate EU issues.

More national administration than Commission socialization

Partisanship does not exhaust variation among top officials. Socialization through service in a national administration is the second-strongest predictor of their stance on European capitalism, albeit at a respectable distance from party identification. Former national officials are far less outspoken in their support for European regulated capitalism than are former professors, business people, or professionals. Just as former national civil servants are less likely to be supranationalist, they are also less likely to endorse regulating capitalism at the European level. National administrations seem effective in socializing individuals into Euro-cautious preferences.

Commission socialization, on the other hand, is significant in the simple regression, but it fizzles out when controlling for other factors. The main reason is that it is only strongly positively associated with European regulated capitalism for non-partisans. The forty-four non-partisan officials are almost equally strongly influenced by Commission ($R = .40$, $p = .007$) and national socialization ($R = -.41$, $p = .006$) in the simple regression, though Commission socialization (but not national administration) weakens considerably when adding controls. For the sixty-one partisans, in contrast, it matters a great deal whether an official has had a prior career in the national state sector ($R = -.35$, $p=.006$), but length of tenure in the Commission is unrelated ($R=.10$, $p=.495$). For the majority of European Commission officials then, current association with the European Commission leaves a far weaker imprint than a prior stint in a national administration.

Corporatism

Top officials' preferences on supranationalism were strongly influenced by values internalized in their respective national political systems. Officials from countries with experience in multi-level governance are keener on sharing national authority with a supranational EU. Can the same be concluded for preferences on regulating capitalism? Do top officials extrapolate experiences in their country's capitalist system to the European Union?

The association with corporatism – my proxy for measuring divergent capitalist institutional arrangements – is negative and significant ($R = -.20$), and this relationship holds in the multivariate analysis. Yet the relationship is not particularly strong; it has the lowest standardized coefficient reported in the last column of table 5.2. The reason is that corporatism captures only part of variation in capitalist experience. When one crosstabulates degree of corporatism with type of capitalist system, weak corporatist countries fall into two quite different categories: liberal market economies and family-coordinated economies. Officials from liberal market economies do not desire increased European regulation, but those from family-coordinated systems want it very much (table 5.4). Weak corporatism is desirable in liberal market economies because market mechanisms efficiently coordinate economic activity; a proactive state or enforceable labor–business agreements could disrupt market coordination. However, in a capitalist system with inadequate market mechanisms, weak corporatism is a sign of weakness. There has to be some non-market mechanism for coordinating economic relations and, if organized labor and business are unable to do this, other non-market actors must step in. In the Southern European economies, families try to fill the void, but they do so haphazardly (Esping-Andersen 1999). Non-market coordination at the EU level seems attractive because it could help ratchet up domestic coordination.

Table 5.4 *European regulated capitalism by type of capitalism
and corporatism*

| | Corporatism[b] | | | | |
Type of Capitalism[a]	Low	Medium	High	All	Number
Liberal market economies[c]	2.9	3.0	–	3.0	22
Family-coordinated market economies[d]	3.5	3.6	–	3.5	45
Sectoral coordinated market economies[e]	–	3.8	2.9	3.2	27
National coordinated market economies[f]	–	3.3	2.6	2.7	11
All	3.3	3.3	2.6	3.2	
Number	59	17	29		105

[a] Capitalism classification after Kitschelt et al. (1999) and Esping-Andersen (1999).
[b] Degree of corporatism from Crepaz (1992).
[c] UK and Ireland.
[d] France, Greece, Italy, Portugal, Spain.
[e] Austria, Benelux, Germany.
[f] Denmark, Finland, Sweden.

ERC-DGs: more a matter of utility

The utility maximization hypothesis that position holders in ERC-DGs, such as regional or social policy, tend to favor more European-wide regulatory competencies finds support in the multivariate analysis.

To test the relative causal power of utility maximization versus socialization, I also examine whether length of service in an ERC-friendly DG is positively associated with support for European regulated capitalism. I find that, though the simple correlation for ERC socialization is higher than for ERC utility ($R = .24$ instead of $R = .19$), this effect weakens considerably in a model with controls. The socialization hypothesis finds support among non-partisans, but much less so among partisans. When I substitute utility maximization for socialization in the general model, the basic explanatory structure of the model remains unchanged, but the overall fit is considerably lower than in a model with ERC utility.[9]

Regression analysis does not answer conclusively whether it is concern for professional success or socialization-on-the-job that motivates some officials to endorse European regulated capitalism and others not. Both of these are probably at work – the Commission is a diverse environment in which ambitious officials fight power battles *and* champion

---

[9] The statistics for the full model with ERC socialization are: $R^2 = .37$ and adjusted $R^2 = .33$. The correlation between the socialization and utility variables is a high .58, and multicollinearity makes it not advisable to test them simultaneously in the same model.

distinct worldviews. Yet on the basis of my data I am drawn to conclude that utility maximization offers a more robust explanation than socialization.

National interest – at the margin

Officials from countries reaping net financial benefits from EU structural policy are more inclined to favor further EU regulation and redistribution. Though the association with this variable is modest in the bivariate analysis, it gains strength in the multivariate analysis. The reason is that it picks up consistently higher support among officials from the cohesion countries, that is, the greatest beneficiaries of EU structural policy (Greece, Ireland, Spain, and Portugal). Whereas average support outside these countries is 3.2 out of 4.0, it is 3.6 for officials from those four countries.[10]

National interest matters, but its impact is mediated by partisanship. Party identification is especially powerful among northern officials. Northern socialists (3.3) are more in favor than northern Christian democrats (3.3), who are in turn considerably more supportive than liberals (3.0) and conservatives (2.2). Non-partisans are in the middle of the pack (3.3). Similarly, southern socialists (3.9) are more enthusiastic than Christian democrats (3.5), who are more in favor than conservatives (2.00), though not more than liberals (4.00); again, non-partisans sport median values (3.5).[11] So European regulated capitalism can count on bonus support in cohesion countries, but national economic interest does not change the nature of the relationship between party identification and support for regulated capitalism.

Weak Delors factor

An assertive Commission could shape the outlook of top officials through targeted ideological recruitment. The three consecutive Delors Commissions between 1985 and 1995 were assertive, and so one might expect Jacques Delors – the champion of European regulated capitalism – to have used his powers of appointment to promote people with similar

---

[10] These figures should be interpreted with caution. With only fifteen officials from the cohesion countries in the sample, much depends on whether these fifteen individuals are representative of their subgroup. I have no evidence that suggests the contrary but, as I explained in chapter 2, the response rate for interviews and questionnaires was lowest among officials from cohesion countries.

[11] The small numbers stretch the reliability of these averages to the limit. There are only four socialists, three Christian democrats, one conservative, two liberals, and five non-partisans.

views to his to top positions. However, the Delors effect is quite weak, and it peters out in the multivariate model.

These results for all officials mask major differences between partisans and non-partisans. The association is positive and powerful for partisans ($R = .31$, $p = .01$), but it is non-significant and negative among non-partisans ($R = -.15$, $p = .32$). Moreover, the Delors effect works only for some categories of partisans. Whether by design or by luck, Delors improved on partisanship for those partisans who otherwise were likely to be less supportive of European regulated capitalism. Hence, Delors selected the most pro-European regulated capitalist old socialists (3.6 against 3.1 for non-Delors recruits), the most favorable young Christian democrats (3.5 against 2.6), and the most ERC-friendly liberals (4.0 against 2.7 for old liberals; 3.4 against 2.9 for young liberals). Only for conservative partisans is there no Delors effect (2.0 for Delors recruits against 2.3 for non-Delors recruits.) This suggests that Jacques Delors and his team were reasonably effective in screening most partisan appointments, but far less effective – or interested – in selecting sympathetic non-partisans.

Conclusion

Institutional constraints outside the Commission – party and country – profoundly affect the way top officials think about regulating capitalism in Europe. They easily trump influences from inside the Commission.

Political parties constitute by far the most formative setting for top officials. Officials reflect their party's positions on European regulated capitalism, with left parties generally more in favor than parties on the right. More precisely, they reflect their party's preferences on European regulated capitalism at the time of their socialization. So older Christian democrats show strong support, and younger party fellows weak support; older socialists show more qualified support than do their younger colleagues; and conservatives demonstrate deepening skepticism. The strong impact of party identification is consistent with a growing EU literature rooted in comparative politics that emphasizes the role of non-territorial factors, particularly ideology and party identification, in shaping EU contestation. It challenges theoretical models that conceive of EU politics as a function of international bargaining among national governments in pursuit of national economic benefit.

This does not mean that territory does not matter. It is important in the guise of national administration, national economic interest, and national corporatism, though all take second stage to partisanship. Former national civil servants are more reluctant to support European regulated capitalism. National interest plays for officials from cohesion countries, who are the strongest supporters of European regulated capitalism.

Past experience with regulating capitalism tends to shape current preferences for European regulated capitalism. Officials from family-coordinated economies are most likely to support European regulated capitalism. This is consistent with the fact that these economies have reason to believe that European regulated capitalism could provide non-market coordination where national capacity for coordination is weak. The situation is different in systems where non-market coordination through state authority (Scandinavia) or through generalized exchange between organized business and labor (Benelux, Germany, and Austria) is entrenched. A decentralized, more voluntarist European version might disrupt rather than buttress national corporatism. And for the liberal market economies of the United Kingdom and Ireland, EU-induced non-market coordination threatens existing practices.

There is some evidence that the immediate policy world of the Commission is capable of altering preferences formed outside the Commission. Position holders in ERC-friendly services are strongly in favor of European regulated capitalism, and they appear to be so because it advances their professional success.

Overall, in shaping its top employees' preferences on regulating capitalism in Europe, the Commission is no match for external bodies – parties, national administrations, national governments, or domestic economic institutions. It is not an effective socializing agent nor does it offer a particularly compelling structure of material incentives. Fifty years after its creation, the Commission is a porously bounded institution. The upshot of this is that top Commission officials are in the thick of political contestation in the European Union. Like other actors in the European arena, they voice ideological preferences on what constitutes "good common life" in the European Union. And, when given the opportunity, they may let these preferences guide their actions:

Interviewer: Can the Commission steer away from taking politically sensitive stances, and can it stick more to technical management? Should the Commission do that? Or does one have to accept that there are certain political choices that the Commission as a whole, as an organization – including, probably, the senior officials – has to take?

Official: The job is not a purely technocratic job. By the way, the profound changes through monetary union pose an interesting problem, because we are pushing Europe into a [neo]liberal direction. I am referring particularly to the independence of the European Central Bank: it is an autonomous institution above the others, a *cinquième pouvoir*. That is in principle a [neo]liberal mechanism, which very much goes against socialist ideas. It is, of course, to some extent also brought about by the globalization of the world economy. But it stands over and above politics – it is pre-configuring our policy lines by promoting competition. That is a [neo]liberal policy line, and it is related to the internal market. And that means, of course, the confinement of traditional socialist ideas.

I: And in a way, these decisions have been taken on seemingly technical grounds while they actually have enormous political implications.

O: Indeed.

I: Do you think it is part of the Commission's role to make the implications clearer: "Look, there are political choices involved in this?"

O: Well, I personally make that always very clear in my speeches on monetary union. But I think Mr. Delors, for example, was fishing in dark waters.

I: It is ironic because Delors, a social democrat, was the man who realized the internal market. And he also started economic and monetary union.

O: Yes, but you see, I always say that what the Germans consider to be the neoliberal imperative, the Freiburger imperative, that is for the French *la gloire de la France*. The fact that the French are so interested in bringing about monetary union is not so much a neoliberal trait, but it is deeply rooted in the fact that they cannot stand the idea of being dependent on the Bundesbank. But you can, of course, say: "Never mind, whatever. Whether this is *pour la gloire de la France* or not, the result will be the same." And the result is that we are moving into a neoliberal system. (Official # 200)

6   Principal or agent

Crisis in spring: Commission resigns en masse

"Et l'intendance suivra," Napoleon said when going to war, meaning, roughly: "And the supply train will follow." The masters of the European Union, in their common institutions and in national governments, have favoured a similarly lofty view of priorities in constructing their political and bureaucratic empire. When great campaigns for a single market or a single currency are going forward, they have tended to presume that matters of basic housekeeping can be left for later.

These words prefaced *The Economist's* biographical sketch of Mr. Erkki Liikanen, at the time the commissioner for budget, administration and personnel matters (*The Economist*, December 19, 1998, p. 66). Mr. Liikanen received praise in this article for his efforts to improve sound and efficient financial management. Yet, on March 15, 1999, he resigned with the entire Santer Commission after the publication of an independent expert report exposing six cases of fraud or mismanagement and several instances of nepotism in the Commission.

The unprecedented en masse resignation of the Commission was the climax of a six-month tug of war between Europe's executive and the European Parliament. It began, in the fall of 1998, with parliamentary inquiries into the Commission's financial management. Leaks from a disgruntled Commission official to the Green party fraction had triggered these. A parliamentary resolution of January 14, 1999, called for an official investigation by independent experts into alleged cases of fraud and mismanagement of Commission funds. The committee, created on February 2, made its results public six weeks later.[1]

Few insiders were surprised by the crisis. For years, the Court of Auditors' annual reports had warned about gaps in control, mismanagement, and fraud. During my interviews, which took place *in tempore non-suspecto*

---

[1] For extensive coverage, consult the *Financial Times*, March 16 through March 25, 1999. The report from the committee of independent experts was released on the European Parliament's website.

between July 1995 and February 1997, these issues were on top officials' minds.

In March 1995, the Commission endorsed a reform program entitled "Sound and Efficient Financial Management – SEM 2000."[2] The program envisaged reform in three stages. First, the Commission intended to rationalize its management procedures and train more managers. A second stage would start changing the culture by inducing officials to be receptive to management and by altering the regulatory framework. In a third stage, the Commission would involve national civil servants more closely in managing EU policies. Through this stepwise approach, reformers sought to build a pro-management constituency in-house that would be networked with like-minded allies in national administrations (Cini 1996; Laffan 1996; Metcalfe 1992, 1996a, 2000; Peterson 1997b). In 1998, the Commission started another initiative, entitled "Designing Tomorrow's Commission." Every Commission service, including all Commission offices in EU member states and more than 120 delegations around the world, underwent a screening of its organizational and managerial practices (Peterson 1999). These efforts were inspired by public sector reforms in national bureaucracies importing NPM (New Public Management) and DPM practices (Deregulation, Privatization and Marketization) (Campbell 1995; Lane 1997a; Peters and Savoie 1995, 1998; Pollitt 1993).

Poor financial management was not the only criticism leveled at the Commission. It was reportedly not open enough and not democratically accountable. Many were convinced that it had tried to cover up mismanagement during the parliamentary investigations (Metcalfe 2000).[3] Commission president Jacques Santer came under severe criticism for "his extraordinary insensitivity and poor judgment, [as he] adopted a tone of indignation and self-righteousness" (Dinan 1999: 57). Santer insisted on keeping investigations under control, and he appeared to resent demands for transparency (*Financial Times*, January 7, 1999).

And yet, over the past years, the Commission had taken many steps to improve accountability. In February 1994, it unveiled a package of ten measures. The "transparency package" contained, among other things, procedures to broaden and regulate consultations with interest groups, to increase public hearings and information seminars, and clear and more liberal rules on access to information (Peterson 1995b). The Commission stepped up these measures over the following years. It was also anxious to appear more receptive to political supervision by the European

---

[2] The two Nordic Commissioners, the Finnish Erkki Liikanen and the Swedish Anita Gradin, were the political authors of the reform program.

[3] The independent expert report alluded in its conclusions to an attempted cover-up.

Parliament (Nicoll 1996). On transparency and accountability, the Commission has made more progress than the still-secretive Council of Ministers (Hayes-Renshaw and Wallace 1997; Lodge 1994; Schmitter 2000). But it was all too little, too late.

Two basic questions underlie and predate the recent tumult in the Commission. First of all, should the European Union be democratic, like its constituent member states, or should it be technocratic, like other international organizations for economic cooperation?[4] A second basic question sits squarely on the first one. What should be the role of the Commission? Should it be the autonomous executive of the European Union, or should it become a conventional civil service? Should it be a principal or an agent? Let us examine these questions – first in general terms, and then for top Commission officials – in light of a broader debate on international governance. I shall then seek to explain variation in top officials' preferences on whether the Commission should defend its role as an initiating principal or emphasize its administrative and managerial responsibilities as an agent.

Governance beyond national borders

How should international governance be organized? For over two centuries, policy makers have sought forms of international cooperation that are consistent with maintaining national states as basic units of political organization. Of course, nineteenth- and early twentieth-century imperialism squared the circle for only a small group of nations, which increased their economic markets while preserving political sovereignty by subjugating other populations. Since World War II, policy makers have tried to combine integration with national democracy by creating international regimes (Keohane 1984; Keohane and Nye 2000a, 2000b; Murphy 1994). Because they are elitist, technocratic, and closed, such regimes have been termed "clubs." In that light, the European Union appears simply as "the most significant and intrusive international organization" (Keohane and Nye 2000b: 2). Yet, as the ties woven by these international regimes have grown denser and stronger, governance through international regimes has become contested. I distinguish two dimensions to this debate, and I discuss each with particular reference to the European Union.

---

[4] There is an extensive literature on democracy in the European Union. See essays by Edgar Grande, Michael Greven, Claus Offe, and Michael Zürn in Greven and Pauly (2000). Also see Biersteker (1999), Héritier (1999a), Höreth (1999), Majone (1996, 2000), Merkel (1999), Risse (1997), Scharpf (1997a, 1998, 1999), Schmitter (2000).

Dimensions of international governance

Technocratic or democratic decision-making. The first dimension defines basic principles of authoritative decision-making: whether governance beyond national states should be democratic or technocratic.

Democracy can take many forms, but in essence it is "a regime or system of governance in which rulers are held accountable for their actions in the public realm by citizens, acting indirectly through the competition and cooperation of their representatives" (Schmitter 2000: 3; Schmitter and Karl 1991). It requires that all citizens have a minimum of political rights and duties, and it calls for a political class that *competes* to be allowed to represent citizens and that, on behalf of citizens, holds rulers accountable. At the other end of the continuum are technocratic forms of collaboration. Paraphrasing Schmitter and Karl's definition of democracy, one can define a technocratic regime as a system of governance in which rulers are held accountable for their actions by technical experts, acting directly in epistemic communities – networks of actors with authoritative claim to knowledge (Haas 1992) – or indirectly through appointed representatives, based on objectives and means defined by scientific analysis of cause-and-effect relationships.

The difference between democracy and technocracy is not that one is accountable and the other not. It is that accountability is of a different sort. In a democracy, rulers are accountable if their decisions are contingent upon the consent of a representative part of the population. Technocratic rulers are accountable if their decisions are contingent upon their acting according to prevailing scientific knowledge.

In the European Union, these two principles have divided those who seek collaboration through democratic institutions and those who want functional, expert-based cooperation (Haas 1958, 1964; Lindberg and Scheingold 1970; Radaelli 1999). The European Coal and Steel Community gave experts a pivotal role in making supranational policy. Through a system of *engrenage*, these experts were expected gradually to involve interest groups, organized labor, and business (Mazey 1992). European decisions would be taken by technocratic consensus. The High Assembly, the predecessor of the European Parliament, was added to the initial design at the eleventh hour. Democrats found much wanting in this technocratic design, but this was the path European integration was set on – different in degree, but not in kind, from most other international regimes created at that time. Yet, over time, the European Union has adopted many conventional democratic practices, and the European Parliament has been the main beneficiary.

Monnet – a technocrat – feared the impact of an elected assembly on the autonomy of the Commission, but democrats saw it differently:

[Monnet's] gamble was very simple: the more you limit competence to areas which might be economically and politically important but less sensitive for the public at large and for political parties, the more you were likely to get real powers for a body of more or less independent decision-makers. Hence Monnet's initial reluctance to create an Assembly and to give it the right to sack the Commission. [Yet] in the long run, the existence of the parliamentary assembly has become a crucial source of political legitimacy for the Commission as it has helped to enhance its political role and establish it as the executive of the European Union independent from the member states. (Neunreither 1995: 6)

The Commission resignation crisis was a rare occasion when democrats and technocrats joined forces – but for different reasons. For democrats, the European Parliament's decisive role in prompting the resignation of the Commission was proof that political supervision can and should work in the European Union. In a lead article, the *Financial Times* called the outcome "a victory for EU democracy" and "a dramatic shift in power from bureaucrats to parliamentarians" (*Financial Times*, March 18, 1999). For technocrats, the downfall of the Commission was the inevitable outcome for a technocratic body trying to play politics. The European Parliament was instrumental in exposing this Commission weakness, but strengthening the European Parliament is not the solution. Technocrats wish to restore technocratic governance, for example by channeling technical decision-making into European regulatory agencies.[5]

Principal or agent. The second dimension draws a distinction between making and implementing decisions at transnational level – the international body as principal or agent.

The role of an international body in facilitating international collaboration has been subject to scholarly controversy for a while (Cox 1996; Cox and Jacobsen 1973). When an autonomous international government makes decisions, it acts as principal. But it is also possible that the constituent units make decisions, and that they employ an international secretariat as an agent to take care of implementation and monitoring.

In the European Union, the Commission's role has been contested throughout much of its history. Initial incomplete contracting – a largely

---

[5] The division of labor between elected politicians and non-elected specialists has been subject to controversy in many democracies. A long-standing issue is the role of courts in adjudicating conflict. Two more recent examples concern the shift of monetary policy from politicians to independent central banks, and the delegation of certain forms of regulation to semi-autonomous agencies. On agencies, see a special issue of the *Journal of European Public Policy* (1997), with contributions by Kreher, Dehousse, Majone, and Shapiro. For a comparison of the European central bank's democratic accountability with that of other central banks, consult Jakob de Haan and Sylvester Eijffinger (2000). In the United States, courts and regulatory agencies have historically played a greater role than in Europe (Majone 1991).

deliberate strategy by the founders – left participants guessing whether the Commission was principal or agent (Duchêne 1994; Tsebelis and Kreppel 1998). In the 1960s, French president Charles de Gaulle forced the issue into the open when he declared that it was the *Commission's* objective to install itself as an independent government and *his* goal to thwart such plans. Commenting on the 1965 empty chair crisis in his memoirs, he explains:

> For these champions of integration, the European executive was already alive and kicking: it was the Commission of the Economic Community, made up, admittedly of representatives nominated by the six states but, thereafter, in no way dependent on them. Judging by the chorus of those who wanted Europe to be a federation, albeit without a federator, all the authority, initiative and control of the exchequer, which are the prerogatives of government in the economic sphere, must in future belong to this brigade of experts. . . . The fundamental divergence between the way the Brussels Commission conceived of its role and *my own government's insistence, while looking to the Commission for expert advice, that important measures should be subordinated to the decisions of the individual states,* nurtured an atmosphere of latent discord. (de Gaulle 1971; reprinted in Nelsen and Stubb 1998: 37–38, my emphasis)

Here are two opposing views of the role of the Commission. Proponents of the Commission as principal – as government – want it to become an institutional partner equal to the European Parliament, the Council, and the Court of Justice. According to the other view, the Commission should become a conventional civil service, and thus the agent to European or national principals.

The Commission resignation crisis rekindled conflict. Proponents of the agent/civil service option usually want the Commission to give priority to efficient management and to curb policy initiation. Supporters of the principal/government option resist such a shift.

Dimensions and top officials. Where do top officials stand on technocratic and democratic principles? And how do they square their preferences on this issue with the Commission's role?

Table 6.1 shows that top Commission officials conceive of these as separate dimensions. The two technocratic items and the democratic item are not significantly associated. The items on the internal market and on administering things efficiently express an agent role for the Commission. Officials with high scores on these items favor an administrative and managerial Commission, whereas those with low scores favor a principal role for the Commission as initiator of new policies. The item on the European Parliament taps the democracy/technocracy dimension.

Table 6.1. *Correlations: dimensions of international governance*

Item	Concentrate on internal market	Administering efficiently
1. The Commission should concentrate on maintaining the internal market	1.000	
2. The Commission should concentrate on administering efficiently	.321***	1.000
3. The Commission should support full legislative powers for the European Parliament, even if the price would be to lose its monopoly of initiative	−.127	−.134

Significance levels: ***$p < .01$ **$p < .05$ *$p < .10$.

Types of international governance

Figure 6.1 presents these two dimensions in an effort to capture possible outcomes of European integration. My conjecture is that the European Union will end up within this space.

The four polar types in figure 6.1 have general labels: diplomatic, consociational, (neo)functional, and quasi-federal. The abstract labels reflect my belief that the choices facing the European Union apply in principle to any attempt to organize governance beyond national boundaries. Unpacking these ideal-types enables one to make plain the parameters within which the European polity is likely to evolve. These choices have tangible implications for citizenship. I draw primarily on Karl-Heinz Neunreither's work to characterize the distinct social contracts with citizens that each governance type implies (Neunreither 1995).

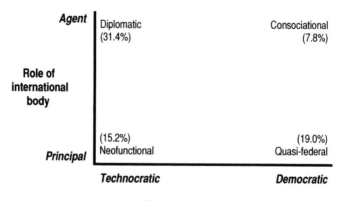

Figure 6.1 Top officials and types of international governance.

Figure 6.1 also shows where top officials stand. I use the European Parliament item of table 6.1 as the indicator for the democracy/technocracy dimension, and an index of the two other items for the principal/agent dimension.

Diplomatic governance. The predominant type of international governance in the postwar period is diplomatic governance – in the upper-left corner of figure 6.1. Decision-making is primarily technocratic, that is, clubs of technical negotiators bargain on specific issue areas. Diplomatic regimes generally stay out of the public eye, and public input is weak. Authority remains firmly in the hands of national institutions; the international body is an agent. The pivotal actors here are usually national diplomats, who shuttle back and forth from the national to the international to convey government orders. Diplomatic regimes were designed as creatures of national governments, and for the most part they remain so (Keohane and Nye 2000b).[6]

In the history of European integration, this type is often associated with Charles de Gaulle. De Gaulle intended to plant the European Community firmly in the upper-left corner of figure 6.1, where national governments instead of supranational organizations determine the pace.

The citizens of diplomatic governance are primarily market-citizens or *consumer-citizens*. They appeal through their national government for international governance on issues pertaining to market failure. Citizens consume decisions taken by national elites on their behalf. Citizenship in this type of governance is apolitical, and substantively narrow. It is much weaker than what citizens are accustomed to in national democracies.

Diplomatic governance finds considerable support among top officials. It is the largest group – more than 31 percent. These officials combine reluctance for EU democracy with support for an administrative and managerial Commission.

Neofunctional governance. The European Union is different from other international regimes created after World War II. From the start, diplomatic governance had to share the limelight with neofunctionalist governance, the type in the lower-left corner of figure 6.1. Neofunctionalist and diplomatic governance are similar in that, in both, decisions are primarily taken according to technocratic principles. The underlying assumption is that democracy beyond national borders is neither

---

[6] The presumption is that national governments engage in diplomatic governance to create collective goods that enhance national welfare. This presumed primacy of national economic benefit explains why international relations scholars, particularly of the liberal institutionalist school, argue that, to understand why and when states cooperate, one needs to examine domestic economic interests (Milner 1997; Moravcsik 1998).

necessary nor possible (Dahl 1999; Greven 2000; Offe 2000). The types differ sharply on the second dimension. In neofunctionalist governance, an international body has authority to make autonomous decisions – not merely delegated authority to implement others' decisions.

Jean Monnet was the archetypal proponent of neofunctionalist governance. He sought real independent powers in a few policy areas for the High Authority – note the term – in the expectation that these limited responsibilities would spill over into other areas. Transnational experts would identify common needs and initiate practical solutions. Addressing the problems of, say, worker-citizens would draw attention to citizen needs in parenting, health care, or education.

What kind of citizenship is implied in neofunctionalist governance? Citizenship appears as more multifaceted than in a diplomatic regime, but it is fragmented because citizens interact with the supranational principal along multiple functional lines – and not generalized political lines. They interact as economic producers, parents, patients, students, or consumers; their relationship with the supranational principal is apolitical. Karl-Heinz Neunreither termed this "segmented citizenship" (Neunreither 1995). In paternalistic fashion, international governance seeks to "improve" individuals' conditions in segments of their life.

Just over 15 percent of top officials support Jean Monnet's neofunctionalist conception of an activist Commission in a largely expert-driven decision-making regime.

As Neunreither remarks, consumer and segmented citizenship "leave out the basic quality of citizens – that they are political beings. Citizens in the European Union's approach are the object of care-taking policymaking, not its subject" (Neunreither 1995: 10). Democratic decisionmaking, on the other hand, presumes a notion of citizenship that appeals to individuals as political beings.

There is a growing literature on how one may design democratic institutions beyond the national state, beginning with pioneer David Held (1991, 1995). Yet much work on democracy and international governance concerns the European Union, including Edgard Grande (2000), Michael Zürn (2000), and recent work by Philippe Schmitter (2000). This turns the spotlight onto the right-hand side of figure 6.1. In naming these types I have chosen labels reminiscent of types of national political organization.

Consociational governance. According to this type, the international body is a neutral site for bargaining among relatively self-contained national democracies. It is an agent of national principals. The international body in consociational governance remains ultimately deferent to the constituent national states. Its composition and working usually reflect national diversity. Yet, in contrast to diplomatic governance, democratic principles tend to govern decision-making, that is, there is a political class that *competes* to represent citizens and, on behalf of citizens, holds rulers accountable. Whether the rulers are international or national politicians is not so important. The crux is that those who hold rulers accountable represent their respective national states. Moreover, national elites act on behalf of the various national peoples, who do not themselves get involved. In a consociational regime, democracy is the game, but control is filtered through national elites and institutions.

Several scholars have examined consociational features of the European Union (Chryssochoou 1998; Gabel 1998a; Schmidt 1998; Taylor 1991, 1996). Yet they sometimes find it difficult to distinguish consociational from diplomatic/intergovernmental governance. The basic difference lies not with the role of the international body, but with the character of decision-making. Whereas in diplomatic governance decisions are taken through epistemic communities, and are knowledge based and consensual, decision-making in consociational governance is political, that is, value laden and contested.

Citizenship in a consociational regime is encompassing, and indirect. As Neunreither emphasizes, *indirect or derived citizenship* means "that political European citizens are not given their own rights as the new Sovereign of the European Union by a sort of constituent act. Rather, this new quality is introduced in a somewhat timid way, via his or her former, still existing, quality of being a citizen of one of the member states. Consequently, ... if we can speak of a new 'political citizen', even in an embryonic state, this citizen must be qualified as an indirect citizen or as a derived one" (Neunreither 1995: 10). A European Union passport can be acquired only through national citizenship. All European citizens are hyphenated citizens.

Consociational governance is not popular among top officials. In the upper-right corner of figure 6.1, less than 8 percent feel comfortable with a combination of democracy and Commission as agent.[7]

---

[7] This low result may be an artifact of the indicator. The European Parliament item is not a very good indicator for measuring support for democratic control consistent with consociational governance – *in*direct political control through national actors, which could be elected national leaders, national parties, or national parliaments. The European Parliament is primarily a non-territorial chamber, though national parties could use it as a venue for national democratic control. National leaders are more likely to use the Council structure, the EU's closest equivalent to a territorial chamber. And national parliaments would require a new institution, such as the much talked-about interparliamentary conference. The crudeness of the indicator therefore makes it difficult to separate diplomatic governance proponents from consociational governance supporters. It

Quasi-federal governance. The lower-right corner of figure 6.1 captures quasi-federal governance. This combines democracy with an international principal. Decisions are negotiated in autonomous supranational institutions that are subject to direct political supervision. I choose to call this type "quasi-federal" rather than federal to emphasize that this conceptualization is broader than federalism in the classical sense.[8] Classical federalism implies a constitutionalized division of powers between territorial levels of government, whereby the constituent units co-decide on constitutional change. Quasi-federal governance in the European Union may be more fluid in structure. It may not be rigidly (or explicitly) codified, and it may involve power sharing between functional as well as territorial constituent units.[9]

Citizenship in the quasi-federal type is direct. Full direct or interactive citizenship enables citizens to control rulers through competition and cooperation between their representatives. This requires, among other things, intermediary organizations that channel citizens' demands to the international level – without national gatekeepers. Directly elected legislative bodies that represent territorial, ideological, or functional diversity are the more conventional institutional expression of this. In the European Union, the institution that comes closest to embodying this citizenship concept is the European Parliament. Proponents of direct European citizenship also want to build a political identity for the EU, through the creation of symbols of identity (a flag, an anthem), the adoption of general rights (incorporation of the Human Rights convention), or intermediate channels of political representation (European political parties or interest groups).

In the lower-right corner of figure 6.1, 19 percent of top officials favor democracy in combination with a principal Commission.

is quite possible that some top officials who reject the European Parliament item would be happy to support consociational forms of democracy, such as a stronger Council of Ministers, or a new representative institution for national parliaments, or a reorganization of the European Parliament along territorial lines. I suspect that consociationalists are undercounted, and diplomats overcounted.

[8] Federalism is a familiar, but contested, concept in the context of European integration. A speech by German foreign minister Joschka Fischer in May 2000 sparked animated debate on whether it still makes sense to strive for a federal European Union. Fischer entitled his speech "From Confederacy to Federation." A group of scholars connected to the European University Institute responded to this speech with an edited volume that debates alternative options arrayed along the continuum from quasi-federal to consociational governance (Joerges, Mény, and Weiler 2000).

[9] Philippe Schmitter's two-by-two typology of future EU polities opens up a wide space for institutional variation. Depending on whether aggregation of interests is fixed or variable, and territorial or functional, he distinguishes between stato, confederatio, consortio or condominio (Schmitter 1996). In subsequent work, he reflects upon strategies for democratizing the most novel and fluid form of these, the condominio (Schmitter 2000).

These four types and their corresponding conceptions of citizenship delineate the array of choices for the European polity. Proponents of more democracy may or may not favor a principal Commission. Similarly, supporters of technocracy may prefer to bestow authority on the Commission – the Monnet design – or vest authority with member states while the Commission acts as agent – the de Gaulle design.

Why do some top officials favor technocratic over democratic decision-making? Why are some keen on seeing an administrative and managerial Commission, whereas others are reluctant to weaken its executive initiative? In the remainder of the chapter I take up the second of these questions.

Principal or agent?

Throughout the European Union's history, Commission observers have always been aware of a tension between the Commission's political and administrative roles. Yet the terms of the debate have shifted over time, and explanations for why some officials may choose to focus on implementation and others on political initiative have changed as well.

Jean Monnet, the founder of the European Commission's predecessor, the High Authority, wanted the organization to steer clear of routine administration and provide political leadership. According to Monnet, one could not do both simultaneously. He downplayed the Commission's administrative and managerial tasks – a choice not always appreciated by his colleagues. In his biography of Monnet, François Duchêne recounts:

A charge often made against [Jean Monnet], especially by opponents like the head of the French Steel Association, Pierre Ricard, was that he was far too involved in the politics of Europe – code at the time for the European Defense Community – and far too little involved in coal and steel. There was truth in this. Monnet told David E. Lilienthal [a long-time American friend of Monnet] in April 1952 that coal and steel were "the least important part" of the new Community. What mattered was that "the people of Europe" were ready "for a deep change." Monnet and a good proportion of the staff of the High Authority had certainly not gone to Luxembourg out of fascination with the scrap market. Ricard's criticism was echoed by those members of the board of the High Authority who felt that their first priority must be coal and steel. (Duchêne 1994: 239–40)

Monnet believed that, given the right institutional design and targeted recruitment, the High Authority would gain the political initiative. The institutional format he had in mind was one of deliberate under-organization by structuring tasks around small, flexible teams. Officials would be independent. The ideal "political leader" would be financially autonomous – a high salary earner; professionally independent – on secondment rather than tenured; and a high-flying technocrat – equipped with particular expertise rather than a generalist (Duchêne 1994; Neunreither 1995; Radaelli 1999). There was no place for Max Weber's ideal-typical bureaucrat in Monnet's High Authority.

David Coombes' study of the Commission reinforced this dichotomy between politics and bureaucracy, but his conclusions are quite opposite from Monnet's (Coombes 1970). As its administrative tasks grew, the Commission became swamped by administration. It adopted the "conservative, mechanistic and impartial" character of traditional bureaucracies, and could no longer "be called on to take initiatives or to hold convictions" (Coombes 1970: 298). The Monnet design was dying; Weber began to move in.

Coombes attributed the decline of political initiative largely to the ascendancy of a new generation. Many came from national administrations, often seconded, and appeared keen to apply their bureaucratic expertise to the Commission. A second, professionally more diverse, type was attracted by the policy opportunities at EU level. These people were usually young, professional, bright sparks, but they demonstrated little or no interest in the larger political agenda of European integration. According to Coombes, former national officials and young, apolitical policy entrepreneurs were instrumental in the bureaucratization, professionalization, and compartmentalization of the Commission. Only among the founding officials did the original Monnet spirit appear to be alive and well. So, by 1970, Coombes' conclusions were disconfirming Monnet's premonitions. He found that the will to give priority to political initiative was most strongly entrenched among those who had made a career out of the Commission. He identified generational change and prior career experience as influences on how Commission officials define their role.

Since Monnet and Coombes, this dichotomy between politics and administration has dominated thinking about the Commission. Much work has assumed that political initiative goes hand in hand with weak bureaucracy, limited professionalism, and a cavalier attitude to rules. Yet, under the influence of comparative public administration, Commission observers have begun to develop more nuanced views. One product is the introduction of a new concept – policy or bureaucratic entrepreneurship – to characterize instances in which the Commission exploits rules to extract decisions that would otherwise not have occurred (Cram 1997; Majone 1989, 1993; Moravcsik 1999; Nugent 1995).

How does this entrepreneurial notion of initiative relate to the traditional concept of political initiative defined by Monnet and Coombes? In his analysis of the Commission, Edward Page distinguishes between two types of political role for Commission officials (1997: 145–58). One is the Monnet role: Commission officials mobilize support and persuade other institutions and groups to deepen European integration. These officials thrive in a non-hierarchical, somewhat chaotic political environment. But there is another, less spectacular type that initiates policies within its field of expertise. To deliver such bureaucratic or policy entrepreneurship, top officials need professional staff, organizational resources, and technical expertise. In other words, they need bureaucratization. Neither Monnet nor Coombes took notice of this second type of activism.

These political roles contrast with two managerial roles. One concerns routine administration, which refers to the conventional caretaker role of Weberian bureaucrats. As Page describes, routine administration involves "obeying orders, following instructions, enforcing regulations; reacting to events and changes in the world outside on the basis of written rules" (Page 1997: 148). Like bureaucratic entrepreneurs, routine administrators need bureaucratic resources. But the former use these resources proactively, and the latter reactively. The second administrative-managerial role type is political adjudication: the Commission engages in political negotiation to ensure the implementation of policy, such as in competition policy or in trade disputes. Not all non-bureaucratic activities require initiative.

Monnet and Coombes contrasted initiative and bureaucracy. Page contrasts initiative and administrative management. The Commission's initiative emphasizes its capacity to be a principal in the European Union; its administrative and managerial role stresses its function as an agent. Disputes surrounding the Sound and Efficient Management program (SEM), the 1999 resignation crisis, and subsequent tensions in the Commission concerning the Neil Kinnock reforms can be conceived as episodes in an ongoing battle between proponents of a principal Commission and supporters of an administrative and managerial Commission. So when may officials prefer administrative management to initiative – or the reverse?

Why top officials may diverge

Officials may have been socialized in a number of contexts to internalize preferences for administrative management: while working for the Commission, through prior work experiences, or through party membership. Alternatively, utility maximization expects rational actors to bring their preferences in line with the institutional opportunities available to obtain professional success. Officials may respond to incentives in their directorate-general, or to the influence of national governments, or to

Logic of influence (causal mechanism)	Source of influence (type of institutional context)	
	Type I Inside the Commission	Type II Outside the Commission
Socialization	Length of service in Commission	Experience in national administration Private sector experience Party identification
Hybrid category	Delors factor ↓	
Utility maximization	Years to retirement Position in admin/management DG	National economic interest

Figure 6.2 Hypotheses on top officials' preferences for administrative management.

Commission presidents. Figure 6.2 displays how these hypotheses fit in the theoretical framework.

Commission socialization

A first hypothesis links length of Commission service to opposition to an administrative and managerial Commission. Monnet set the High Authority on course to be a principal. Decades of Commission activity, institutional self-interest, and formal rules have reinforced the strong bias in Commission culture to be a creator more than implementer of European policies. As Coombes observed in 1970, this leads to the following hypothesis:

H_1: *The longer officials have worked for the Commission, the less they support an administrative-managerial Commission.*

The indicator for *Commission Socialization* is number of years served in the Commission prior to the interview.

Experience in national administration

National bureaucracies strive to embody Weberian principles of impartial administration, implementation according to rational and legal criteria,

and subservience to political guidance. The extent to which national bureaucracies are Weberian in practice varies (Ertman 1997; Page 1985,
1995; Page and Wright 1999a). Yet, even in the least Weberian administrations, top officials' prior experiences should contrast quite sharply
with a Commission culture that values independent entrepreneurship.

How do these prior experiences influence former national bureaucrats'
views on the Commission? One view in socialization theory is that individuals generally want consistent beliefs, and therefore they can be expected to extrapolate internalized values to new settings. So officials from
strongly Weberian bureaucracies may want to extend Weberian values and
norms to the Commission, which would induce them to support a conventional administrative role. An alternative interpretation starts from the
assumption that individuals use internalized values as a basis to evaluate
a new context. Individuals draw lessons, and this may lead them to take
different positions. So former officials from weakly Weberian administrations may be keenest on a Weberian Commission, perhaps because they
see it as a counterweight to inefficient, politicized, or clientelist practices
at home. Former officials from Weberian administrations, on the other
hand, may realize that a Weberian administration has characteristics –
limited personal creativity, rigid routines, and limited attention to special
group needs – that would make it unworkable in the complex Commission environment. This leads to the following two competing hypotheses:

H_{2a}: *Former state officials from strongly Weberian administrations give strongest support to an administrative-managerial Commission, whereas their colleagues from least
Weberian administrations provide weakest support.*

H_{2b}: *Former state officials from strongly Weberian administrations give weakest support to an administrative-managerial Commission, whereas their colleagues from least
Weberian administrations give stronger support.*

I use multiple indicators to divide bureaucracies into least, medium,
and strong Weberian administrations (see Appendix II), which I use to
produce three dummy variables – *Strong Weberian, Medium Weberian,* and
Weak Weberian. For example, *Weak Weberian* has a value of 1 if the Commission official is a former national civil servant from a weakly Weberian
administration. The reference category consists of top officials without
prior service in national administration.

Private sector experience

Top officials with a private sector background can be expected to sym-
pathize with plans for an administrative and managerial Commission,
because they would introduce some private management techniques into

the public sector (Lane 1997b; Peters 1996; Pollitt 1993). In chapter 2, I described how several countries have catapulted managers with industrial or banking experiences into leadership positions to accelerate public sector reforms (Hood 1998b; Lane 1997a; Marsh and Rhodes 1992; Page and Wright 1999a; Rockman and Peters 1996; Wright 1994b).

More than 12 percent of top Commission officials entered the Commission straight from a job in private industry or banking (national bank not included), and another 11 percent had worked there at some point in their professional life.

H_3: *Officials with prior private sector experience will support an administrative-managerial Commission.*

To examine this hypothesis, I construct *Private Sector*, a dummy taking on a value of 1 for top officials with prior experience in industry or banking.

Party identification

Calls for public sector reform and the introduction of private management techniques have usually come from the economic right. One may expect officials on the economic left to be wary of attempts to concentrate the Commission's efforts on the internal market and efficient administration, because these seem proxies for scaling back on social-democratic policies. Commission entrepreneurship was critical in securing progress in EU social policy (Cram 1997; Falkner 1998; Leibfried and Pierson 1996), environmental policy (Bomberg 1998; Liefferink 1997; Sbragia 1996), and cohesion policy (Ansell, Parsons, and Darden 1997; Bache 1998; Hooghe 1996, 1998).[10] Economic liberals should support administrative management for the reasons that social democrats oppose it. This leads to the following hypothesis:

H_4: *Right-of-center officials support an administrative-managerial Commission, whereas left-of-center officials oppose it.*

For *Party Identification* I use dummies for social democrats and liberals.

Maximizing utility and years to retirement

Career incentives in the Commission privilege initiative. Younger officials' chances for promotion depend on whether commissioners notice them. The surest way to draw attention is by furnishing creative solutions to

---

[10] Some scholars have contested the extent to which Commission entrepreneurship has been decisive in these cases (Golub 1996; Moravcsik 1999).

political puzzles. So younger officials have persuasive career incentives to take risks, exploit opportunities for initiative, bypass hierarchies, and avoid the unglamorous work of administering existing programs. Older officials are probably by inclination more cautious and conservative. What is more, being *fin de carrière* they do not need to pay much attention to career incentives. One may expect them to focus more on administration and management.

H$_5$: The younger officials are, the less they support an administrative-managerial Commission.

I test this life-cycle hypothesis with a variable *Age*, which is the age for each official in 1996, the mid-point of the interview period.

Maximizing utility in administrative/management DGs

Starting from the assumption that bureaucrats are rational beings who want to expand their power, the bureaucratic politics model proposes that bureaucrats tend to "stand where they sit." Administrators and managers in the Commission have long been considered second-rung, and so these officials have much to gain from a shift in the Commission's role from political initiative to administrative management.

H$_6$: Officials from DGs with a primarily managerial role support an administrative-managerial Commission.

I construct a variable *Admin/Management DG*, which has a value of 1 for officials in DGs with tasks that are primarily administration, implementation, or adjudication.

National economic interest

A clampdown on Commission initiative is likely to impose costs on member states that benefit from positive integration. Fewer Commission initiatives in regional and urban policy, research and development, education, tourism development, rural development, transport and environmental infrastructure, or social policy, and greater concentration on monitoring the internal market and implementation of core economic regulation, would reduce immediate benefits for poorer countries. A group utility argument links national economic utility to top officials' preferences on the Commission's role.

H$_7$: Officials from countries with expected net gains from Commission initiative are reluctant to support an administrative-managerial Commission.

As an indicator for net country benefit I use *National Economic Benefit*, a measure for EU structural funds intervention by member states.

Delors factor

At first blush, it seems odd to hypothesize support for administrative management among Delors recruits because Delors' impatience for the minutiae of implementation and management is well documented (Cini 1996; Grant 1994; Peterson 1999; Ross 1995a,b). In that respect – as in others – Jacques Delors took a leaf out of Jean Monnet's book. Yet there are several reasons Delors recruits may want administrative management.

The implementation of the internal market program was the jewel in the crown of Delors' ten-year period in office. Self-selection and targeted recruitment by Delors make it likely that many Delors appointees are strong supporters of the internal market. And Delors made them – in the words of a Delors recruit – his lieutenants for bringing about the internal market. This is likely to instill in Delors appointees a particularly strong sense of responsibility for consolidating the internal market. Career incentives reinforce these dispositions. Delors conceived of the internal market as the technical steppingstone to a grander federal design. Yet he also knew that a failing internal market could jeopardize all – including his name in history. Similarly, top officials who achieved positions of Commission leadership on the back of the internal market program are likely to think that their ongoing professional success depends on the consolidation of the internal market.

H_8: *Delors recruits are supporters of an administrative-managerial Commission.*

Delors is a dummy with a value of 1 for officials recruited under the Delors presidency.

I examine these hypotheses in a multivariate regression (OLS). I measure preferences for administrative management with an index for *Management* composed of the items in table 6.2. The first item states that "the Commission should concentrate on administering things efficiently." Improving personnel and resource management has been the objective of the SEM program under the Santer Commission, and the Kinnock reforms under the Prodi Commission. The second item taps the administrative challenges of the internal market. Values for *Management* range between 1.0 (unconditional opposition) and 4.0 (unconditional support for administrative management), with a mean and median of 2.5 (standard deviation = 0.72). The Commission is almost perfectly divided between administrators and political initiators.

Table 6.2. *Top officials on administrative management*

Item	Yes	Yes, but	Neutral	No, but	No	Mean[a]
1. The Commission should concentrate on administering things efficiently	17.1%	38.1%	1.9%	32.4%	10.5%	2.6
2. The Commission should concentrate on maintaining the internal market	11.4%	36.2%	1.9%	35.2%	15.2%	2.4

[a] Values range from 1.0 (no) to 4.0 (yes); neutral = 2.5. A high value is consistent with favoring administrative management.

Explaining administrative management

Why do a fair number of top officials support administrative management for the Commission? Why are they willing to let go of the Commission's unique executive power that emanates from its sole right of initiative? This result seems at odds with the dominant paradigm in public administration, which expects that bureaucrats want to expand power or status. The results in table 6.3 shed some light on this puzzle. A mixture of six utility and socialization factors in parsimonious model 2 explains 29 percent of the variance (adjusted $R^2 = .24$).

Commission – socialization plus utility

I hypothesized that the Commission as institution may influence top officials' preferences in two ways. Socialization theory suggests that longer service in the Commission leads top officials to internalize the Commission's culture of being a principal. This hypothesis finds considerable support in the simple regression, and the effect is the second-most powerful in the multivariate analysis (last column). Asked to describe what he would miss most if he left the Commission, a long-serving top official responds:

The Commission is the *first* truly creative [international] enterprise. I would never have gone to another administration, be it at national or international level. The single-most important thing is the creativity one can employ here. This is a new organization, and this brings with it that one has an enormous margin to do something new. There are always new topics popping up. (Official #7, his emphasis)

Creativity, action, and – ultimately – power are difficult to give up, as a former national civil servant attests:

Interviewer: What is the one thing you would miss most if you left the Commission?

Table 6.3. *Explaining administrative management: multivariate OLS regression*

Variable	Correlation coefficient	Regression coefficients		
		Model 1[a]	Model 2[a]	Model 2 (standardized)
Commission Socialization	−.20**	−.023**	−.017**	−.248**
		(.009)	(.007)	
National Administration				
Weak Weberian	.25***	.321	.474**	.211**
		(.238)	(.199)	
Medium Weberian	−.05	−.263	–	–
		(.215)		
Strong Weberian	.04	−.112	–	–
		(.186)		
Private Sector	.08	−.029	–	–
		(.152)		
Party Identification				
Socialist	−.21**	−.276*	−.256*	−.152*
		(.155)	(.150)	
Liberal	.20**	.267	.293*	.154*
		(.179)	(.174)	
Age	.07	.036**	.032**	.237**
		(.015)	(.013)	
Admin/Management DG	.18**	.091	–	–
		(.136)		
National Economic Benefit	−.16**	−.160**	−.179***	−.246***
		(.068)	(.065)	
Delors	.22**	.442***	.460***	.320***
		(.135)	(.130)	
R^2		.31	.29	.29
Adj. R^2		.23	.24	.24
Durbin–Watson		2.14	2.19	2.19

Note: n = 105.
[a]Unstandardized regression coefficients, with standard errors in parentheses. Significance levels (one-tailed): ***$p < .01$ **$p < .05$ *$p < .10$.

Official: I think it is the action. I go sometimes back to my former national ministry, and I walk around there, and I think it is very quiet. I would not be able to work there anymore. It is also the international dimension. Even though one can find national jobs with a strong international affairs component, it is never as intensive as here.

I: Are you referring to the multinational environment here in-house?

O: Also, yes, but I am mainly thinking of the *scope* of the work, which is not just limited to one member state. It is simply much bigger, and so it makes it

. . . [Pause.] In the end, we are probably interested in having power. And I suppose, if one is really honest, one has to admit that. (Official #41, his emphasis)

A second hypothesis predicts that career incentives in the Commission lead younger officials to avoid administrative management. As table 6.3 shows, age becomes highly significant once one controls for Commission socialization and Delors recruitment. It appears indeed that, *ceteris paribus*, younger officials are in the frontline of those opposing administrative management. It seems plausible to link that to a utility argument. Younger officials have more professional time ahead of them, and so they are likely to be more susceptible to career incentives. So far, these have been overwhelmingly favorable to policy entrepreneurs. The authors of the SEM program tried to tackle this bias. They suggested that the Commission weigh management experience more heavily in appointment and promotion decisions (Laffan 1996). Neil Kinnock's reforms are putting these recommendations into practice. These changes may affect career incentives in the future.

Former career experience – mixed impact

The hypothesis that prior state experience may influence officials finds support among former civil servants from weakly Weberian administrations, who are considerably more likely to prefer a conventional bureaucratic role for the Commission (*Weak Weberian* in model 2). The direction of the effect suggests learning and lesson drawing. Former officials from, say, Belgian, Italian, or Greek administrations – no paragons of Weberian purity – appear most intent on making the Commission a showcase for efficient management. An administrative and managerial Commission would perhaps counter pathologies at home and set an example for national reform.

In contrast, the association between private sector and administrative management is surprisingly weak. The variable does not pick up strength when controlling for other factors either. This finding flies in the face of the new management literature: former private sector managers are *not* natural allies of public managers.

Party identification matters

I hypothesize that social democrats are inclined to reject administrative management, whereas those on the economic right – market liberals – support it. The results in table 6.3 for the dummies *Socialist* and *Liberal* are consistent with this.

No utility effect for leaders of administrative/management DGs

I hypothesize that top officials in charge of administration, implementation, or oversight activities want administrative management because it is likely to enhance the status of their job. As table 6.3 shows, the correlation is significant and in the predicted direction. Yet the effect washes out when controlling for Delors recruitment. Among Delors recruits, the effect of this variable is zero.

National interest counts

Officials from cohesion countries – the greatest net financial beneficiaries of European integration – strongly oppose more administrative management in the Commission. The association with *National Economic Benefit* is negative and significant, and it gains strength to the .01 level when controlling for other variables. This group utility variable is the third-strongest effect in the parsimonious model.

The Delors factor

By far the strongest predictor of top officials' preferences is whether officials are Delors recruits. This hybrid between socialization and utility is highly significant in the bivariate regression, and gains strength in the multivariate analysis. Delors recruits, then, are particularly concerned about the Commission's capacity to manage efficiently. As table 6.4 demonstrates, this result is robust across ideology, country of origin, and type of directorate-general in the Commission. A Delors recruit who joined the Commission to negotiate the liberalization of financial services expresses this view:

Table 6.4. *Delors recruits on administrative management across subgroups*

Subgroup	Recruited by Delors		Not recruited by Delors		All	
	Score	No.	Score	No.	Score	No.
Weak Weberians	3.2	6	2.8	7	3.0	13
Liberals	3.4	7	2.5	11	2.9	18
Administrators & managers	2.7	27	2.7	16	2.7	43
Social democrats	2.5	13	2.1	12	2.3	25
Nationals from cohesion countries	2.4	12	1.3	3	2.2	15
All officials	2.7	53	2.4	52	2.5	105

Economic and monetary union is important, but I tend to think that consolidating the internal market is even more important. *That* is the basis of what we do in the Community. Economic and monetary union will follow by itself. Consolidating the internal market, that is, making sure that member states apply the rules that they signed up to, will secure equal treatment throughout the Community of countries, nationalities, and economic actors. ... If the population cannot trust the Community because there is still discrimination between nationalities, there is no Community. It is as simple as that. And they will not be prepared to accept a common foreign policy, or economic and monetary union. *That* is the mechanism. If you ask me what the Commission should do, *that* is what it should speak for. (Official #41)

The men (and women) of the 1992 campaign want to safeguard what they accomplished. This requires, they believe, monitoring compliance day after day, and administering patiently, routinely, and efficiently. A decade of Delors activism has left an unexpected legacy. It has created a cohort of committed administrators and managers.

Should the Commission be primarily a principal – initiating and governing – or an agent – managing and administering? A loose, yet fairly consistent, coalition supports each view. Those who give priority to administrative management are likely to be Delors recruits; they are often economic liberals; they tend to be relative newcomers; and yet they are older than the average official. The most ardent promoters of an administrative and managerial Commission are thirteen former national civil servants from Weak Weberian administrations (mean = 3.0, against 2.5 for all). The greatest surprise is that former bankers or business people are *not* more likely to promote management.

Supporters of the other view tend to come from cohesion countries; they are long-serving Commission officials, yet younger than their colleagues; and they are often left of center. The strongest opponents of a more administrative and managerial Commission are the fifteen officials from cohesion countries (mean = 2.2). In previous chapters we found that the Commission is unable to instill supranationalism or regulated capitalism into its employees. Here it is different. The institution uses socialization and career incentives, quite effectively, to induce officials to defend Jean Monnet's legacy of principal power. Officials whose professional future is linked to the Commission's have sustained – not lost – their desire for political initiative. Jean Monnet feared it would be different.

Conclusion

Over the past decade, the Commission has shouldered the brunt of criticism against the European Union. What role could the Commission play in a contentious European polity? Should it make more of administrative management and less of political initiative? Should the Commission be primarily agent or principal? In the wake of the 1999 resignation crisis, top officials concur that the Commission's future role hinges on its capacity to reinvent itself as a useful and legitimate institution. They are less in agreement on what this new role might be.

I have anchored this question in a broader discussion on international governance. Two basic issues are at stake. One dimension defines principles of decision-making: whether international governance should be democratic or technocratic. The second dimension draws a distinction between making and implementing decisions beyond states: the international body as principal or agent. There is no simple relation between these two dimensions in international governance, nor is there one in the European Union. Democrats do not necessarily support a governmental Commission, and technocrats do not necessarily want an administrative and managerial Commission. Decoupling the Commission's role from that of democracy in the European Union frees one to explore each question imaginatively. For example, Philippe Schmitter formulates a long list of "modest" to "not quite so modest" democratic proposals – all the while remaining non-committal about how the Commission would fit in (Schmitter 2000).

Although top Commission officials have views on the democratic or technocratic character of the European Union, it is the future of the Commission that preoccupies them most. A fairly strong, and growing, constituency – about half of all officials – supports a humbler organization with fewer tasks, more administration and management, and under tighter political supervision.

At first blush, it seems surprising that many top officials want to trade initiative for more administrative management. It appears to contradict the notion that bureaucrats are loath to weaken their organization's power. Yet top officials may have personal reasons to do so. First, ideological or policy concerns may override one's desire for power. Supporters of administrative management tend to be on the economic right, or concerned about creating an efficient counterweight to ineffective, politicized national civil services. Second, top officials may support management for self-interested reasons. Emphasizing the Commission's legislative instead of its bureaucratic role may not help to maximize their personal power. George Tsebelis and Geoffrey Garrett (2000) argue that the codecision procedure has shrunk the Commission's legislative influence, and yet at the same time, the Commission's bureaucratic and adjudicative discretion is likely to increase. The reason is that, under the new codecision procedure, supermajorities in Council and Parliament are required to enact legislation, and this makes it harder to overrule the Commission's administrative, implementing, and adjudicating decisions. If this reasoning is correct, rational Commission officials may want to strengthen the Commission's capacity for administration and management to maximize *their* power under changing legislative rules.

Professional self-interest goes a long way in explaining why many top officials appear happy to give up Commission governmental power. Yet why does a sizable group of top officials persist – against the tide – in supporting a governmental Commission? They do so because a clampdown on Commission initiative would hurt positive integration and redistributive policies, which these officials value. A shift to administrative management announces harder times for social democrats and for countries that are net beneficiaries of EU political regulation.

7 Accommodating national diversity

In search of eurofonctionnaires

A Commission without ready access (at least until 4 or 5 pm) to cappuccino, espresso, or lemon tea – and fresh croissants or Danish pastries – would be difficult to imagine. The cafeteria, often tucked away in a corner of the building, serves as an escape valve in an intense work environment, where officials unwind with political commentaries, playful flirtation, and culturally tinged pleasantries. French is still the dominant social language, though this is changing rapidly with English on the upswing. Yet old-timers claim that social gatherings have become increasingly mononational: Spanish meet Spanish, Irish socialize with Irish, and so forth. The cafeteria is also a desirable location for informal work meetings. At any point during the day, one may observe a group of four to six officials sharing jokes or opinions with their *chef d'unité* (head of unit). Sometimes it is easier to vent frustration or air new ideas in the friendly and neutral setting of the cafeteria.

The occasional visitor may not pick up subtle differences between these two types of gatherings. A closer look reveals telling contrasts. Whereas social gatherings are usually genuinely egalitarian, work meetings are shaped by a fair dose of hierarchy. This is, after all, a public administration – and, in theory, one built on Weberian principles of organization. More remarkable still are the differences in the composition of these groups. The former gatherings are often nationally monocultural, but the latter always consist of different nationalities. Geographical diversity down to the unit level is firmly entrenched in this administration.

No Commission official is born a European. Though one may change one's nationality – albeit with great difficulty – it is impossible to give up nationality altogether. With national citizenship come a mother tongue, cultural affinity with other (usually neighboring) nationalities, and particular national stereotypes. In their anthropological study of the Commission, Abélès and his collaborators recount how a German Commission official tried to re-invent herself as Spanish. She was desperate to escape the perceived stigma of being German: overbearing, hierarchical, humorless, and dull (Abélès, Bellier, and McDonald 1993). Few people go to such lengths to elude stereotypes, but top officials are often acutely aware that one's nationality may work for or against oneself. A Greek official argues how national prejudices may hurt the career chances of his compatriots:

Although I try to be detached, I cannot ignore that people from different nationalities, all of which merit a promotion, do not always receive their promotion equally easily ... I once said that for a Greek to prove that he is not stupid, he has to work very hard; but for another nationality to prove that he is not stupid, he has to work very little. Certainly, and this is something I must say even though I hate it, nationality in the sense of saying "the Greeks do this," "the Italians do this," "the Germans do that" is very much ingrained in the Commission. One should judge a person on merit irrespective of sex or nationality. I am not an idealist, but the further we go in that direction, the better. (Official #63)

Common nationality lowers the threshold for instrumental as well as social connections. When I was setting up interviews, I exploited the fact that a disproportionate number of secretaries are Belgian, and more particularly that we share Flemish/Dutch as our mother tongue. Though it is impossible to know to what extent my play on common nationality actually boosted my response rate, national linguistic bonds elicited goodwill among gatekeepers to my interviewees.

Nationality also matters in that it is usually accompanied by a mother tongue. In a multi-linguistic environment, to be French or British/Irish is an obvious advantage because French and English are the Commission's working languages.[1] An official who speaks a minority language points the finger on this:

Official: It is not the same thing, when, in a meeting of directors or heads of cabinet, you negotiate in French and English with people for whom this is their first language, their mother tongue.

Interviewer: Apparently, simultaneous translation is now used in the meetings of *chefs de cabinet*, for the first time. It was changed when the new members [Austria, Finland, and Sweden] came in.

O: That is astonishing. That is very bad. No, I think the best solution is what David Williamson [then secretary-general of the Commission, and British] does. David Williamson ... never speaks English to a non-English. For example, he knows that I speak better English than French but, when I see him on a bilateral basis, he speaks French to me. He does that because he wants to have the same handicap. And I find it a very nice thing to do. So if we could

---

[1] After the unification of Germany, and again after the accession of Austria, some German-speakers in the European institutions wanted to upgrade German to the third working language, but this pressure has since subsided.

envisage English-speaking people speaking French, and French people speaking English, then I would not mind having these two [working] languages.

I: Several years ago, the College of Commissioners tried to limit the usage of language to two languages, French and English. But then, someone said, that is fine – provided that the French use English and the English use French. It did not go through.

O: Of course it was not accepted. You know, it is a serious handicap, which should not be underestimated. If, say, a Frenchman throws a joke in French, he can grab the attention, and at the same time, by altering a nuance, he can then give the sentence a totally different meaning. A non-French-speaking person simply cannot achieve this in the way a native speaker can. (Official #61)

Most top Commission officials have what it takes to thrive in a multi-national environment. Many are fluent in several languages.[2] Nearly half of all top officials studied or worked abroad before, which means that multinationality is not new to them, nor is working in a language different from their mother tongue. Several grew up in multinational families, or live in one. A large number find that their multicultural work environment makes their time in the Commission much more fascinating. Nearly 50 percent of Commission officials indicate this as the one thing that they would miss most if they were to leave the Commission.[3] Most Commission officials see national difference primarily as a plus-point of their work environment.

Yet, at the same time, their job is made more complex by the fact that they work for, and with, multiple deeply rooted nationalities. Joint EU policies create friction among nationalities as often as they rally common interests, and top officials are supposed to put these policies into practice irrespective of how they are received by the various nationalities. How, then, should a supranational organization reconcile national difference?

[2] Yet one should not exaggerate polyglot talents in the Commission. All top officials, for example, are not equally well versed in the two working languages, let alone in third languages. It became apparent during the interviews that some top officials who work primarily in French may have difficulty following discussions in English, or, at any rate, writing reports in English. They came usually from Southern European countries (of course, except for the French, French is already their second language), and most of them were close to retirement. I rarely observed the reverse with officials whose preferred language (either native tongue or first foreign language) was English. Several enlargement recruits from the UK, Ireland, and Denmark told me that their knowledge of French was one reason they were selected for the job. I do not know for sure whether this criterion has held for subsequent recruitment, though it seems difficult to imagine how a senior official could do an effective job without a working knowledge of French. Even top officials from the three most recent member states appeared to have been screened for their ability to function in a French-speaking environment.

[3] This was an open question during the interview. The second-most often mentioned feature is "power, the capacity to influence events, to make a difference."

The relationship between civil servants and those who claim a stake in policies is a defining feature of every civil service (Page 1997). Like national civil servants in national arenas, European officials need to define their relationship with stakeholders in EU public policies. Yet as employees of an organization at the nexus of the national/international boundary, they have a harder time justifying what their "added value" is.

National civil servants can credibly claim to speak for the public interest, that intangible though influential notion of the public good. Modern civil services, especially in continental Europe, were shaped to be part of a legal order that stands above the mix of civil society – the *Rechtsstaat*. In Weberian ideal-typical fashion, bureaucrats are expected to embody and guard the principles of the *Rechtsstaat*. Many features of the typical Weberian bureaucrat reflect this: a preponderance of legal professionals, tenure, and seniority as an important principle for promotion. All these insulate bureaucrats from the hurly-burly world outside the civil service. Bureaucratic reality may never have quite lived up to the ideal-type, and, over the past two decades, the conception itself has been challenged. Yet the Weberian conception is still the prevailing ideal-type for most national administrations (Page and Wright 1999c).

International civil servants, on the other hand, are likely to be asked *which* public and *which* interest they defend. Officials in international organizations face powerful alternative loci of authority in the form of national governments – not simply the mix of civil society. National communities may ultimately be imagined (Anderson 1983). Yet a diversity of experiences reinforce these imagined boundaries – national anthems, flags, welfare services, legal systems, constitutions, local government, membership of the United Nations, or votes in the EU Council of Ministers. The notion of *national* public interest has a hard, tangible core. *International* public interest has a much shallower base in reality. True, the European Union has acquired some trappings of nationhood – an anthem, a flag, a public holiday, membership of some international organizations, a driver's licence, a passport... Moreover, Commission officials are endowed with the explicit authority to formulate recommendations or opinions if they consider these necessary for the proper functioning and development of the common market (Treaty of the European Communities, Art. 211). Yet this is a far cry from being the guardian of a European common good. These are some reasons why Commission officials are likely to be torn between the concrete world of national communities and the more abstract realm of the European community (Abélès and Bellier 1996; Page 1997). A seasoned top official contrasts collective will in the Commission and national administrations:

There is a clear difference between national administrations and the Commission. National administrations have a broad consensus on objectives. All civil servants are interested in pulling the same cart, and they know in which direction and when to pull the cart. They may disagree about marginal adjustments or speed, but they basically all agree on where they want to go and what the national interest is. To use the word "national interest" gives immediately away why this cannot be the case inside the Commission. Even though we are supposed to work for the common interest of the Community, nobody forgets his background, his nationality. Much of the conflict between national interests has been transferred to the Commission. Some [officials] are almost unashamed of it; they go straight for it and make it no secret. Others – and I think this is also a question of how long you have been in the Commission – work much more for the common benefit. They tend to take a rational, reasoned balanced Community approach, whereas others choose a national-interest approach. So, national tensions are transferred to the Commission, and that makes it impossible to have everybody agree *ex ante* on common objectives. There *are* no common objectives.... This is still a relatively young, expanding and maturing institution, which has not yet found its own identity. (Official #78)

It is difficult to be a Eurofonctionnaire if one is defending a rather weakly developed sense of European civil service. Top Commission officials live a precarious existence in the twilight zone between international and national governance.

The Commission's challenge to reconcile national diversity with its role as a supranational civil service goes to the heart of governance in the European Union. It raises the broader question of how a polity fragmented into highly differentiated socio-political systems – national states – is able to make decisions that are accepted as legitimate by its components. Let us first examine theoretical views on how a plural polity such as the European Union may reconcile diversity with unity, and then see how this tension is reflected in the Commission.

Governing a multinational polity

EU politics is to a significant degree shaped by institutionalized conflict among fifteen or so nationalities. The European Union is a plural polity. Students of the European Union have been slow in comparing the European Union with other plural polities. Similarly, students of divided or plural societies have rarely ventured outside the traditional boundaries of national politics to study rule in transnational settings.

Majoritarian and non-majoritarian rule

The plural democracy literature examines the conditions under which a culturally divided society may achieve prosperity, democratic stability, and democratic quality. This literature emerged out of a direct challenge to the prevailing pluralist paradigm of politics, which argued that democratic stability is facilitated by a homogeneous political culture (Almond 1956). The United Kingdom and the United States were considered prime examples of cultural homogeneity, and hence the best candidates for democratic stability.

Spearheaded by Arend Lijphart, some scholars began to question this view in the 1960s. They looked at four smaller countries – Austria, Belgium, the Netherlands, and Switzerland – and found that, though all these countries were culturally heterogeneous, they enjoyed a high level of democratic stability. This paradox produced the consociational theory (Lijphart 1969, 1984, 1999; McRae 1974). The key argument is that distinctive political institutions induce elites in these plural societies to adopt a consociational style of decision-making, and steer them away from the "first-past-the-post" competitive decision-making common to Anglo-American democracies (for recent essays on consociationalism, see Steiner and Ertman forthcoming). This enables these societies to maintain stability despite the centrifugal forces of cultural heterogeneity. The precise institutions that are required to produce this result vary somewhat from one student of consociationalism to another, but one can usually distinguish three characteristics: (a) it requires that elections are held on the basis of proportional representation, not first-past-the-post; proportionality also applies to bureaucratic positions, the police, the military, and the allocation of government funding or public procurement (in contrast to recruitment and promotion purely on merit); (b) it requires governments to be grand coalitions of all major groups – not minimum-winning cabinets; (c) it entails that groups have veto power on issues of vital interest – in contrast with majority decisions. The common thread here is that consociationalism aims permanently to include all relevant groups in decision-making.

Consociationalism is just one means for constraining majority rule. Kent Weaver distinguishes three more types of non-majoritarian rule: delegatory mechanisms, arbitral rules, and limited government (Weaver 1992; Lijphart, Rogowski, and Weaver 1993). Delegatory mechanisms allow each group to govern its own affairs. Federalism fits here as a means to avoid domination by one territorial group over others. Arbitral rules restrict majority rule by placing authority in the hands of unelected officials who are selected on the basis of merit. Examples include judicial review and regulatory bodies, where executive officials are appointed for life or with extended tenure. Finally, limited government strategies contain majority rule by making some or all government decisions difficult: by forbidding them outright (e.g. constitutional provisions against entrenchment of a specific church), by requiring supermajorities, or by putting in place multiple veto points.

These four non-majoritarian types have in common that they loosen the link between "one man, one vote" and decision-making; instead, they establish an association between "one group, one voice" and decision-making. Non-majoritarian rule replaces majoritarian rule. These two paradigms of political organization have defined the literature on democracy over the past three decades. They have also influenced constitutional practice. Non-majoritarian practices have become more widely used in western democracies, and majoritarian rule has declined (Anderson 1999).[4]

Non-majoritarian models have always seemed more appropriate for the European Union. Some EU students apply the theory of consociationalism (Chryssochoou 1998; Gabel 1998a; Schmidt 1998; Taylor 1991, 1996). Many EU features resemble those found in national consociational democracies. The EU has highly institutionalized national groups (national states). It facilitates elite accommodation through vetoes and grand coalitions. EU institutions use national quotas: vote distribution in the Council of Ministers is loosely proportionate to population, and there are national quotas for positions in the Commission and the European Court of Justice. Finally, although most EU legislation now falls under majority voting, the informal rule, certainly in the Council, is to avoid majority voting as much as possible.

Most EU scholars employ a somewhat broader notion of non-majoritarianism in the Madisonian sense – which is that power should be shared, dispersed, limited, and delegated rather than concentrated in the hands of the (elected) majority. Applying insights from federalism, Alberta Sbragia draws attention to quasi-federal practices in the European Union, which ensure participation and autonomy to national states (Sbragia 1993). Philippe Schmitter proposes to recalibrate citizenship and decision-making with a mix of majoritarian and non-majoritarian amendments. His proposals range from the conventional – enacting an explicit bill of rights – to the radical – concurrent majorities in Council (e.g. measures needing majorities among small states, medium-sized states, and large states) – to the revolutionary – citizen vouchers to finance public interest activities by EU-level associations acting as a counterweight to business interests and/or national government lobbying (Schmitter 2000). To lighten the decisional burden in the multinational European Union, Giandomenico Majone makes the case for devolving certain decisions

---

[4] Jeffrey Anderson shows that virtually all EU member countries have become more non-majoritarian over recent decades.

to politically independent institutions such as courts, a central bank, or regulatory agencies (Majone 1996, 1998, 2000).

At the same time, some recent democratic reforms seek to move the European Union away from excessive non-majoritarianism in an effort to make decision-making more efficient. The bulk of legislation, including all internal market legislation and much of environmental and regional policy, is co-decided with a qualified majority in the Council of Ministers and a simple majority in the European Parliament. A number of proposals under debate have a majoritarian tinge, most prominently that small countries give up their automatic right to a commissioner and the Council presidency (Dehousse 1995; Majone 1998). As the European polity deepens and pressures for democratization grow, conflict about the desirable balance between majoritarian and non-majoritarian rule is likely to intensify.

Inside the Commission

The tension between majoritarian and non-majoritarian rule is reflected inside the Commission where it fuels conflict between opposing conceptions of political-bureaucratic organization. One conception starts from the viewpoint that civil servants should defend the general public interest rather than sectional interests. This is the Weberian ideal-type, which has strong roots in the great national bureaucracies of continental Europe. According to this view, merit should shape personnel selection and task organization, and legal-rational criteria should guide policy-making. The "power of senior officials is likely to be exceptionally strong, therefore, because they are the apex of a hierarchically structured organization, with a clear line of command transmitting instructions through a chain of subordinates to its very base" (Page and Wright 1999c: 2).

This stands in contrast with a bureaucratic organization based on the principle that it should include, reflect, and represent the mix of interests in the polity. A non-majoritarian logic drives this type, with features that closely resemble consociationalism. Jobs and tasks are distributed according to the principle of proportionality among constituent segments, and a concern for consensus and recognition of each group's vital interests shape policy-making. This consociational type has characterized the bureaucracies of plural democracies such as Austria, Belgium, and Switzerland (Page 1985). Civil servants act as umpires for group elites or, more often, they are sounding boards – perhaps even ambassadors – for "their" group. There is no clear hierarchy among civil servants because relationships are characterized by ongoing deliberation. Top officials' power is constrained; they are merely the most senior deliberators, with limited command over their troops.

Weberian and consociational principles have always been at odds in the Commission. The High Authority was originally conceived as a Weberian organization (Coombes 1970; Duchêne 1994). Its first president, Jean Monnet, wanted his team of officials to embody a higher European inter-est, to formulate common problems and propose solutions to the College of Commissioners, and on their behalf persuade national representatives to adopt supranational arrangements (Monnet 1962).[5] However, as EU competencies grew, national governments became increasingly reluctant to let go of control over Europe's bureaucracy. This is reflected in the growth of the Council machinery to counterbalance the Commission's organizational resources, and in the expansion of comitology to curb the Commission's executive autonomy. It underlies more recent attempts to control the Commission from within through national quotas for recruit-ment, by influencing the appointment of top officials (most particularly through parachutage), by questioning tenure for Commission officials, and by encouraging their substitution with seconded national officials. Against the backdrop of this ongoing tug of war between institutions, how consociational has the Commission become, and how much of its initial Weberian character has survived?

A consociational or a Weberian bureaucracy?

When commissioner Neil Kinnock unveiled a spate of personnel mea-sures at his press conference on September 29, 1999, he began to swing the pendulum back from a consociational to a Weberian administration. Since then, a flurry of press releases, documents, and speeches have cul-minated in a *White Paper on Reforming the Commission* (March 28, 2000), which is due to be fully implemented by the end of 2002. Interested EU observers can follow progress on the web.[6]

---

[5] For Jean Monnet, a supranational authority transcending sectional diversity was critical to the new method of common action which he described as the core of the European Community. In an article published in 1962 (after the High Authority had been replaced by the European Commission) he characterized this new method of common action as "common rules which each member is committed to respect, and common institutions (i.e. first of all the European Commission, and secondly the European Parliament and the European Court of Justice) to watch over the application of these rules. Nations have applied this method within their frontiers for centuries, but it has never yet been applied between them. After a period of trial and error, this method has become a permanent dialogue between a single European body, *responsible for expressing the view of the gen-eral interest of the Community*, and the national governments *expressing the national views*" (Monnet 1962, my emphasis).

[6] The website is *http://europa.eu.int/comm/reform/index_en.htm* (last accessed on Febru-ary 14, 2001).

If it works, it will constitute a departure from Commission history. Over the past two decades, the organization of the Commission has reflected primarily consociational principles. Proportionality and extensive consultation of national representatives prevail in recruitment and promotion at top levels. Senior posts are divided among nationalities according to quotas that roughly reflect the distribution of votes in the Council of Ministers. A subset of these top positions is de facto reserved for particular nationalities. In Commission-speak, these positions have a "flag." Furthermore, external candidates may take up top bureaucratic positions if no suitable internal candidate can be found – this is parachutage. Although parachutage has declined over the past decade and a half, nearly half of my interviewees were recruited that way; the other half are career Commission officials.

Commission cabinets broker senior appointments. Each political commissioner – two each for the five largest member states and one for small member states – has a group of five–ten political aides, who are almost to the person of the same nationality as their commissioner. Negotiations for top appointments usually take place between the cabinet of the commissioner with functional responsibility for the vacant post, the cabinet of the commissioner for personnel (or, for the most important positions, the Commission president's cabinet), and the cabinet of the commissioner of the nationality of the applicants. The role of cabinets in the recruitment and promotion of senior officials has increased over the past two decades (McDonald 1997; Nugent 1995; Peterson 1999; Ross 1995a,b). But their influence also reaches deep into the policy-making process. Because of their unique consociational characteristics, commissioners and their cabinets have been described as "national enclaves" (Michelmann 1978a,b; see also Edwards and Spence 1994; Egeberg 1995; McDonald 1997; MacMullen 1997; Nugent 1995; Peterson 1997b, 1999; Ross 1995a,b). So even though, in principle, top officials are appointed on the basis of merit, in practice they need the right nationality, support of their national commissioner, and (preferably) the blessing of their national government.[7]

Consociational principles such as proportionality and mutual veto are also present in the administrative organization of the Commission. As a matter of principle, the most senior civil servant of each directorate-general must have a different nationality from the responsible

---

[7] The Kinnock reforms emphasize that merit should guide recruitment and promotion. Article 33 in the white paper is entitled "promotion based on merit." The fine print specifies that merit should determine promotion from grade to grade (e.g. from A7 to A6), whereas seniority should guide promotion within a particular grade (e.g. from A7/step 4 to A7/step 3) (*White Paper on Reforming the Commission*, March 28, 2000).

commissioner.[8] Officials in adjacent positions in the chain of command are generally not of the same nationality. And all directorates-general, directorates (large subdivisions), units (next subdivision), and task forces (temporary units) have a policy of maximizing "geographical diversity" among their personnel, which means that they aim to have a variety of nationalities and, in addition, a balance between north and south.[9]

Explicit recognition of national diversity in the administrative organization of the Commission does not prevent officials from promoting the interests of their nationality, but it makes such national-interest behavior less effective. Multinational balance in units and across hierarchical levels makes it difficult for individual officials to bestow favors on their nationality. It also discourages colonization of particular units by a nationality or group of nationalities. These claims find support in systematic empirical research on nationality in the Commission. Edward Page has compared the actual distribution of nationalities in DGs with what one would expect in non-colonized DGs, and he has detected no evidence of colonization, at least not at the level of directorates-general (Page 1997). Morten Egeberg has focused on national favoritism by individual officials, and he has found very little: there are some traces in less than one-quarter of Commission units (Egeberg 1995; MacMullen 1997).

How does one interpret these findings? Egeberg concludes that the Commission has significant Weberian qualities: "What has emerged seems to be more than just a secretariat to the Council, or a neutral broker . . . . Intentionally or unintentionally shaped, the services seem to have achieved some autonomy for promoting common European interests" (Egeberg 1995: 28). However, these findings are precisely what one would expect in an operative consociational system, where segmental elites successfully guard the neutral status of the central state apparatus by mixing national representatives strategically (Taylor 1996). Not only

---

[8] Exceptions are rare. The two instances during my field research concerned two Spaniards on Latin America and the Mediterranean (DG Ib) and two Britons on transport (DG VII). Several interviewees expressed concern about the former, although the situation was remedied when the Spanish director-general retired in 1997. They perceived the latter instance as accidental and unproblematic.

[9] The Kinnock reforms do not want to abolish geographical balance, but aim to cut down on excesses: "Ensuring a reasonable geographical balance among staff is one of the aims of the Commission's recruitment policy in accordance with Article 27 of the Staff regulations. This will be addressed in the first place by ensuring a wide publication of the notices announcing competitions and by ensuring that the tests used take account of the multicultural dimension of the European Union. In this way, equal treatment of candidates from all member states will be ensured. Neither competitions organized by nationality, national quotas nor a general move to competitions by language, would be appropriate. The Commission will reflect on further means of ensuring reasonable geographical balance" (Article 26 in *White Paper on Reforming the Commission*, March 28, 2000).

Table 7.1 *Top officials on nationality in the Commission*

Item	Yes	Yes, but	Neutral	No, but	No	Mean[a]
1. It hurts the Commission's legitimacy that certain DGs tend to be dominated by particular nationalities, such as agriculture by the French, competition by the Germans, regional policy by the Spanish, environment by the north ...	11.4%	27.6%	1.9%	32.4%	26.7%	2.3
2. Too many Commission civil servants let their nationality interfere in their personal judgments.	9.5%	20.0%	2.9%	45.7%	21.9%	2.2

[a] Values range from 1.0 (no) to 4.0 (yes); neutral = 2.5. Values below 2.5 indicate a preference for a Weberian approach to nationality in the Commission; values above 2.5 indicate a preference for a consociational approach.

do effective consociational mechanisms curtail national favoritism and national colonization, they also discourage Commission officials from advocating the general European interest.

How do these consociational principles of organization affect Commission officials' perceptions on nationality? Table 7.1 gives some indication. The first question taps into the national colonization issue; 39 percent of Commission officials think that national colonization is a problem. Individual national favoritism – the second item – is perceived as somewhat less problematic: close to 30 percent believe that too many Commission officials let their nationality interfere with policy decisions. A substantial minority is not happy with current practices, and 12 percent protest unequivocally (combined index, not shown). These officials seek to strengthen rational-legal principles of organization in the Commission. Yet the majority are satisfied with the current consociational setup, and 27 percent of these candidly reject concerns about national capture (not shown). As a group, top Commission officials seem to lean to the consociational status quo end of the scale.

Why top officials may diverge

Imagining a European public interest requires a leap beyond the real world of diverse nationalities. Conversely, accommodating national diversity in consociational fashion presupposes a relaxation of modern

Logic of influence (causal mechanism)	Source of influence (type of institutional context)	
	Type I Inside the Commission	Type II Outside the Commission
Socialization	Length of service in Commission Cabinet experience	Experience in national administration
Hybrid category		Parachutage↓
Utility maximization	Position in soft-policy DG	Character of national network National quota

Figure 7.1 Hypotheses on top officials' preferences for consociational accommodation.

Weberian conceptions of bureaucracy. Why do officials display one or the other disposition?

Socialization theory predicts that individuals who spent time in institutional environments supporting Weberian or consociational principles may have internalized these norms. I hypothesize that officials may have taken up Weberian principles through their service in the Commission and in state administrations, and they may have picked up consociational values while working for a cabinet. A utility maximization line of theorizing starts with the proposition that consociational and Weberian rules of organization have calculable professional consequences for top officials. Weberian criteria insulate them from political and national manipulation; consociational criteria increase the likelihood that nationality trumps merit in career and policy decisions. I discuss how rules related to particular policy tasks, rules for recruitment, and characteristics of the nationality to which officials belong may affect professional incentives. Figure 7.1 provides a visual presentation of where these hypotheses fit in the broader theoretical framework. As in the other chapters, I work my way from the upper-left corner to the lower-right corner – that is, from socialization inside the Commission to utility maximization outside the Commission.

Commission socialization

Jean Monnet's vision of the High Authority was Weberian in spirit. He wanted his officials to advocate a higher European interest, albeit in an organization free from hierarchy, routine, and permanency. The last thing he wished his High Authority to become was a consociational organization that entitled member states to their quota of positions.

To the extent that these Monnet values are embedded in the Commission as an institution, one may hypothesize that the longer officials work in the Commission, the more they internalize these norms. One finds echoes of this expectation in anthropological studies of the Commission (Duchêne 1994, on Jean Monnet; Abélès, Bellier, and McDonald 1993; Bellier 1995; McDonald 1997).

H_1: *The longer officials have worked in the Commission, the less likely they are to support a consociational Commission.*

The indicator for *Commission Socialization* is the number of years served in the Commission prior to the interview.

Cabinet experience

Monnet modeled the High Authority on his own French Commissariat de plan. Others imported into the new supranational organization another distinctly French institution: the *cabinet*. The purpose of the cabinet system was exactly opposite to what Monnet had in mind. It was supposed to instill in this supranational organization apposite respect for national sensitivities.

In his study of the Delors period, George Ross describes the role of cabinets in balancing national interests, party-political priorities, and European political goals with technocratic policy-making (Ross 1995b; see also Grant 1994). Being able to sound out nationalities and taking seriously national sensitivities or interests are at the center of a cabinet member's job. One may hypothesize that officials with cabinet experience are more consociational.

H_2: *Prior cabinet members are more likely to support a consociational Commission.*

Cabinet is a dummy with a value of 1 for officials who served in a Commission cabinet.

Experience in national administration

Some national bureaucracies rest on Weberian principles, others are consociational. Socialization theory predicts that former civil servants extrapolate their respective national experiences to the Commission.

Civil servants in consociational and partisan-politicized environments are often critical of their own administration and their role in it (Aberbach, Rockman, and Putnam 1981; Dierickx 1998; Dierickx and Beyers 1999;

Dierickx and Majersdorf 1993). Their experiences tend to be negative, and so it is quite likely that they are keen to avoid similar circumstances in the Commission. This leads to the following hypothesis:

H_3: *Former state officials from weak Weberian administrations oppose a consociational Commission, whereas their colleagues from Weberian administrations are less likely to oppose a consociational Commission.*

I use the same set of multiple indicators as in chapter 6. So I produce three dummy variables: *Strong Weberian*, *Medium Weberian*, and *Weak Weberian*, where, for example, *Weak Weberian* has a value of 1 if the Commission official is a former national civil servant from a weakly Weberian administration. The reference category consists of top officials without prior service in a national administration.

Maximizing utility in soft-policy areas

Commission officials handle competition cases behind closed doors to prevent undesirable meddling by interested parties. Keeping one's distance from stakeholders actually helps competition officials to enhance their status as impartial, effective, and powerful arbiters. But not all policy issues are like that. Many EU policy areas require extensive consultation and cooperation with member states. Utility maximization logic predicts here that officials in charge of such policies can benefit from a Commission that is tailored to reflect national sensitivities – a consociational Commission.

Top officials who are most likely to benefit from consociationalism are those in charge of issues of divided EU/national competence. Yet, divided competencies by themselves may not be sufficient. It is only when competencies are parceled out in ways that require all sides to coordinate policy-making on an ongoing basis – that is, nothing gets done unless all are on board – that a consociational style becomes attractive. In addition, extensive national variation in preferences and institutional arrangements encourages consociational decision-making. When preferences and resources diverge considerably, member states are more likely to subvert or ignore a Commission edict that they dislike. So a hard-nosed unilateral or top–down legislative approach would not get the Commission very far. Officials get better results when they use "soft" policy instruments, such as benchmarking, peer group pressure, making technical arguments for a joint effort, or promoting networking.[10] Policies where these instruments are used frequently are often labeled "soft policy areas" (for a general discussion on soft law and persuasion, see Cram 1997;

[10] Helen Wallace dubs this the "OECD technique" (Wallace 2000: 32).

on specific areas, see Craig and De Burca 1999; Falkner 1998). Most of these are in the general socio-cultural area. This leads to the following hypothesis:

H_4: *Commission officials in charge of soft policy areas, where ongoing policy coordination with national governments prevails, are more in favor of a consociational Commission.*

My measure *Soft-DG* is a dummy with a value of 1 for officials in charge of such issues.

Utility and nationality

Nationality organizes the Commission. Although some positions are quasi-permanently reserved for a particular nationality ("national flags"), the bulk regularly changes "ownership." From time to time, then, nationalities engage in intense competition with the aim of earmarking a vacant job as "Italian," "Spanish," or "German." Certain nationalities are more effective in obtaining prized jobs and weighing in on policy. Officials of "less effective" nationalities are unlikely to enjoy the status quo; they have a professional interest in insulating Commission organization from national influences. Nationalities that do not benefit from current consociational rules are therefore expected to prefer a Weberian Commission.

I hypothesize that the utility of nationality for professional success is influenced by two factors. First, a quota-based promotion system creates the perception of considerable career constraints, and these are especially apparent to officials from small countries. Small nationalities, such as Danes or Belgians, can claim between seven and ten top positions, whereas the four largest nationalities claim between twenty-seven and thirty-two. In normal years, the annual turnover rate at the top is usually below ten positions, and it can be fewer still in years of enlargement. So it may take several years before a position opens up for small nationalities. Under a merit system, Danish or Belgian officials could compete annually; under a nationality-based system, they wait for a vacancy for which Danes or Belgians are encouraged to compete. This leads to the following hypothesis:

H_{5a}: *Officials from nationalities with a small personnel quota are less likely to support a consociational Commission.*

A second factor relates to the effectiveness of national networks of support that reach throughout Brussels institutions. Officials from strongly networked nationalities have liberal access to national support and, in a consociational system, such support is essential to compete effectively for the best positions:

H_{5b}: *Officials from strongly networked nationalities are likely to support a consociational Commission.*

For *National Quota* I allocate to officials the number of votes in the Council of Ministers (according to the Amsterdam Treaty) for their country of origin; they range between 2 and 10.

National Clubness is the same index of chapter 4. It combines four indicators of networking: cultural cohesion, financial and organizational resources, intentional government policy, and cabinet resources earmarked for personnel policy. Values are 0 (weak clubness), 1 (medium clubness), and 2 (strong clubness).

Parachutage

A final utility maximization hypothesis links national government influence over recruitment to officials' preferences. The leverage of national governments is presumed to be strongest for appointments through parachutage, the recruitment of external candidates for A1 or A2 positions. Many external candidates have ties with the national government that proposes them, and more than half are former national civil servants or diplomats.[11] One may expect officials who owe their appointment to their national government to be responsive to national concerns.

H_6: *Parachuted officials are more likely to support a consociational Commission than are non-parachuted officials.*

Parachutage is a dummy variable that takes the value of 1 for parachuted officials.

As in the previous chapters, I use multivariate linear regression (OLS) to examine how these hypotheses stack up against the data. I measure top officials' preferences for a consociational Commission through an index for *Consociationalism* composed of the two items in table 7.1 (reversed coding).[12] Values range between 1.0 (Weberian) and 4.0 (consociational). The mean is 2.8 out of 4.0, and the median is 3.0.

Explaining consociational accommodation

Why do many top officials want the Commission's people, organization, and practices to reflect national diversity, and why do others reject

---

[11] Before entering the Commission, 55 percent of parachutists were in paid national service as a civil servant or diplomat, against 27 percent for non-parachutists.

[12] A scale reliability test produces a Cronbach's alpha equaling .63 (standardized: .63).

Table 7.2 *Explaining consociational accommodation: multivariate OLS regression*

Variable	Correlation coefficient	Regression coefficients		
		Model 1[a]	Model 2[a]	Model 2 (standardized)
Commission Socialization	.15*	−.004 (.011)	–	–
Cabinet Experience	.18**	.273* (.141)	.260* (.133)	.157*
National Administration				
Weak Weberian	−.22**	−.325 (.240)	−.357 (.216)	−.148
Medium Weberian	−.23**	−.370* (.208)	−.390** (.169)	−.210**
Strong Weberian	.21**	−.014 (.193)	–	–
Soft-DG	.22**	.642*** (.160)	.639*** (.156)	.339***
Nationality				
National Quota	.29***	.046 (.028)	.047* (.026)	.168*
National Clubness	.43***	.357*** (.093)	.351*** (.082)	.362***
Parachutage	−.16**	−.183 (.194)	–	–
R^2		.40	.39	.39
Adj. R^2		.34	.35	.35
Durbin–Watson		2.11	2.09	2.09

Note: $N = 105$.
[a] Unstandardized regression coefficients, with standard errors in parentheses.
Significance levels (one-tailed): ***$p < .01$ **$p < .05$ *$p < .10$.

this? In other words, why do some prefer a consociational to a Weberian Commission?

As table 7.2 shows, four variables account for 39 percent of the variance in the parsimonious model 2. The most striking finding is that nationality is strongly associated with consociational or Weberian views. When one knows where a top official comes from, one stands a reasonable chance of predicting whether she prefers a consociational or a Weberian Commission. Let us now examine the six hypotheses one by one. As in the previous chapters, I report both unstandardized and standardized coefficients. The latter enable us to compare the relative explanatory power of various factors; coefficients vary between 0.0 and 1.0, and the closer a coefficient to 1.0, the more significant the influence is.

Cabinet experience vs. Commission socialization

To many Commission observers, Jean Monnet's notion of an independent body transcending national particularities captures the true nature of Commission culture. In contrast, the cabinets are the undesirable "foreign" intruders set loose to corrupt the Commission's real culture. How does this stand up to reality?

If Monnet's cultural legacy ever infused the Commission, there is little trace among the Commission's current generation. Top officials with long tenure in the Commission are not more likely to be Weberian. On the contrary, the bivariate association in table 7.2 is positive rather than negative, though the effect drops out in multivariate analysis. We know from earlier chapters that the Commission is not a greenhouse for supranationalism or regulated capitalism; it also does not nurture a European public interest over and above national sensitivities.

In contrast, the hypothesis that officials with cabinet experience are more in favor of a consociational Commission finds support in the multivariate analysis. The "foreign" cabinet culture has stronger roots among top officials than the mythical Commission culture. The effect is only moderately powerful for the whole population (standardized coefficients). That is because the effect is strong only for internal recruits, officials who were promoted to top rank from inside the Commission. It is negligible for parachutists. As table 7.3 shows, ex-cabinet members are significantly more consociationalist than are internal recruits without cabinet experience. Parachutists, on the other hand, are uniformly less in favor of consociationalism, whether they served in a cabinet or not.

Internal recruits and parachutists join cabinets for different reasons. Internal recruits who clock cabinet service – and 40 percent do – enter a cabinet *before* they achieve top rank, and they do so because it is one

Table 7.3 *Consociational accommodation for internal recruits and parachutists by cabinet experience*

	No cabinet experience	Cabinet experience	All officials Score	No.
Internal recruits	2.7	3.2	2.9	61
Parachutists	2.6	2.7	2.6	44
All officials	2.7	3.0	2.8	105

Note: The cells are averages on a scale from 1.0 (Weberian) to 4.0 (consociational).

of three major routes to a high-flying career.[13] Commissioners tend to select cabinet members who understand the interests of the commissioner's country and are willing to lend an ear to national sensitivities. Cabinet politics makes officials attuned to diverse national interests. Self-selection, handpicking by commissioners, and learning all point in the same direction: ex-cabinet members should be open to consociational principles. Parachuted officials are different. When they enter a cabinet – and 30 percent do – they do this *after* they have climbed to the top. A cabinet posting is usually not a stepping-stone to a senior position but a political interlude in an already successful Commission career. Parachutists join because they believe in a cause or a person, or want a change of scene.

National administration – moderate effect

Prior state experience influences top officials' views on consociationalism. Ex-civil servants from weak or medium-weak Weberian administrations – the more non-cohesive, permeable, and politicized administrations in Europe – are more likely to oppose the Commission's consociational tendencies. In the final model, *Medium Weberian* is significant at the .05 level and *Weak Weberian* falls just shy of significance at the .10 level ($p = .10$).

As in chapter 6, I find that former national servants do not mechanistically extrapolate internalized bureaucratic norms to a new setting, but rather conclude that norms learned in a national setting may be undesirable in the Commission. Chapter 6 argues that officials from bureaucracies with an inferior track record in administrative management are more likely to support an administrative and managerial Commission. Here I find that officials from weakly or moderately Weberian administrations are more likely to want a Weberian Commission.

This makes sense when one considers that officials from consociational bureaucracies know very well the costs of consociationalism. Civil servants face more veto points inside the administration, which raises the hurdles for policy-making. Their status is lower, and so is their policy autonomy. And they often feel alienated because temporary political aides or tenured civil servants with the right party-political affiliation monopolize

---

[13] As several top officials told me, there are three major routes to higher administrative echelons. One, reportedly the most effective route, runs through cabinet service. Another is by lobbying support from one's national home base – national government, party connections, or national administration. And the third is to build up a reputation for one's policy expertise or managerial excellence; a prized venue for displaying one's meritocratic qualities is by serving as assistant to a director-general. One objective of the Kinnock reforms is to upgrade this third channel to top promotion.

policy-making. Officials with these experiences do not want to repeat them in the Commission.

Prior experiences count, but not in a reflexive fashion. Reasonable, well-informed individuals rarely give themselves over to passive socialization; they reflect critically, and draw lessons.

Soft-policy areas – soft on consociationalism

Socialization goes some way towards explaining why some Commission officials want a consociational Commission and others do not. How can utility maximization improve upon this?

Let us begin by examining whether the idiom "one stands where one sits" works in this case. I hypothesize that officials are more likely to support consociationalism when they deal with soft policy. I mean by this policy issues where the Commission lacks the power of the purse or the legislative pen, and depends largely on ongoing policy coordination and soft mechanisms such as persuasion, peer group pressure, and recommendation. Social policy, culture, education, research, environmental policy, etc. fall under this rubric. As table 7.2 shows, *Soft-DG* has the second-largest effect in the parsimonious model.

It is of course possible that this utility argument masks socialization, but evidence for this counter-hypothesis is weak. To test for socialization, I construct a variable *Soft-DG Soc*, which for each official counts the number of years spent in soft policy areas. The correlation with the dependent variable is modest ($R = .16$, $p = .11$). A model with the socialization factor is significantly weaker ($R^2 = .31$, adjusted $R^2 = .28$) than the model with the utility factor in table 7.2 (model 2, $R^2 = .39$). When I include both, the socialization variable does not attain significance. Though statistical associations do not prove that utility trumps socialization, these results give further credence to my conclusion in earlier chapters: one is more likely to predict preferences when one knows where someone works in the Commission, rather than for how long he has worked there.

The pull of nationality

The hypothesis that officials' preferences on consociational principles in the Commission are influenced by how useful national citizenship is for furthering their career finds overwhelming support. The two variables are highly significant in the bivariate and multivariate models (combined $R^2 = .23$). Aspiring top officials from small countries regard national quotas more often as negative constraints on professional progress than do colleagues from larger member states.

The most powerful association in the model is with *National Club-ness*. Strong national networks are priceless resources for top officials – as venues where officials muster support for their next career move, mobilize scarce information in a difficult dossier, or find a sounding board for sensitive proposals. Top officials steeped in national networks not only incur debts with compatriots; they also build up credit when mediating between Commission and national sensitivities. They walk a two-way street paved by national connections. Reflecting on the role of commissioners and senior bureaucrats, a seasoned official puts it like this:

The Commission's best advisers on the impact of policies in a particular country are its commissioners from that country. They spend a long time saying to each other, "the specific situation in country X is the following . . ." It is their job to explain to the Commission the politics involved. So, there is nothing wrong with explaining the context of the impact of a Community policy on a particular country. But if you intervene on purely nationalist grounds to argue, "we are against this proposal because, say, we have 30,000 tons of rice exports," or alternatively, "this does not please our shippers," people will not deal with you. Your credibility is definitely reduced because, after all, everyone is conscious that we have to explain Community policies to national audiences. That is our role, and we fail at it mostly. Most of the hostility is not so much *in* the Commission between commissioners, but vis-à-vis the outside audience. And no doubt Spanish commissioners spend more time explaining at home why the Commission has to be tough on state aids than they do telling us that the Spanish are worried about the impact of the Iberia decision on Spain. Being the mediator, *the two-way go-between*, is extremely important, and, on balance, we would all find that we are most beleaguered by our own nationality, and not by each other. (Official #39, my emphasis)

In a polity where successful policy-making often depends on access to scarce information, officials with weak national networks are at a disadvantage.

No Trojan horses

Common wisdom has it that parachutists are likely to support consociationalism. Yet, as table 7.3 very clearly shows, the opposite is true. Parachutage is negatively associated with support for consociational principles.

Parachutage gives national governments the illusion of control, and this has led many EU observers to take parachutists for "Trojan horses" undermining the Commission's Weberian status. But this is difficult to believe – for the same reason that the expectation that parachutists are intergovernmentalists does not find support in the data (chapter 4). National governments do not have the final say over appointments – not even over national flags. Commissioners do. And, once appointed, tenure protects top officials against undue national pressure. A parachuted top official, questioned about parachutage, minimizes its effect:

> It is quite true that you have a certain number of de facto national flags. But you have to look and see what is actually happening. For example, would DG IV's policy [competition, reputedly dominated by Germans] be very different had, say, a Frenchman and not [a German been director-general]? I don't think that the nationality difference is very strong at all in terms of how people act. . . . [National governments] exaggerate the real effect of the decision, but let us recall that it can be very popular *chez-eux*. In their home base it is important that they can point at Mr. X as "one of ours." But in the reality of the day-to-day work, does it make a lot of difference? Quite frankly, it does not. (Official #1)

National governments' insistence on filling senior posts appears more driven by habit and status than by a rational concern to maximize national interests, as another official suggests:

> *Official:* These [national-specific appointments are the product of] *traditions* rather than anything else.
> *Interviewer:* So there is a French tradition in agriculture. . .
> *O:* For example, and a German tradition in competition, and so on. Strangely enough these traditions are always out-of-date. They probably reflect to a certain extent interests of the past. For example, there is a strong French tradition in DG VIII [development], which is understandable because at one point there was a *grande politique africaine de la France*. But these times are long gone and I am not sure that preserving this tradition is good for French national interests.
> *I:* Do you think that it may actually work against French national interests?
> *O:* Probably. Or it is indifferent to French interests. . . . I am simply suggesting that these traditions perpetuate regardless of real interests. And if one were to think in self-interested rational terms, one would probably conclude that the French should not stake so much on development policy but would be advised to concentrate their efforts elsewhere. (Official #217, his emphasis)

National pressure may be more real for internal recruits. A long-serving top official warns of the pernicious effect of national influence on *internal* top appointments:

> There is a general danger in the fact that from A3 level up [head of unit and higher] member states are perceived to have the last say in who [among internal candidates] they want to apply for a post. Of course, that creates a clear link and gratitude towards those who nominated you, and they might expect you at a given point, as a counter-service, to pursue the national interest. . . . It is dangerous when a member state picks candidates. This creates a dilemma for young people. As long as they are in a career up to A4, [what counts] is that they are doing their work efficiently and that they are not listening to "their master's words" in their member state. Autonomy from their member state is normally an

asset. But they change when they are very ambitious and want to move on. At some point, it will be payback time, because member states will say: "Well, you did not serve our interest." (Official #43)

Conclusion

How do top officials conceive of nationality in the Commission? In a Weberian ideal-typical administration, nationality does not count much. Merit infuses the organization, and officials are expected to reflect the general European interest. In a consociational model, nationality is central. The Commission reflects national diversity, and officials are counted on to represent their nationalities. This chapter shows that top officials lean to consociational accommodation. Yet they differ in how far they want to go in accommodating nationality.

Nationality is the single most powerful predictor of support for consociational accommodation. Officials from large and strongly networked nationalities are best placed to exploit a consociational career policy, and they want to sustain a consociational Commission for self-interested reasons.[14]

The work that officials do also provides incentives for supporting consociational principles. Officials in charge of soft policy issues support a consociational approach because they need cooperative relations with national actors, and they may not get these easily in a distancing, Weberian Commission. Furthermore, to some extent, officials' preferences are shaped by experiences inculcated over time. Prior national civil servants are less likely, and former cabinet members more likely, to support a consociational Commission.

Utility maximization trumps socialization. Self-interested career calculations best explain top officials' stances on national diversity in the Commission. Why is that so?

There is a qualitative difference between this issue and the issues examined in previous chapters. Whether the European Union becomes more or less supranational, promotes more or less regulated capitalism, or allocates more or less administrative and managerial responsibility to the Commission has little impact on a top official's immediate professional life. The effects lie in the distant future. Yet whether the Commission bureaucracy becomes more or less consociational could boost or shrink

---

[14] This manifestation of self-interest should not surprise us. Plural societies that in the past turned to consociationalism for mending deep divisions often find it difficult to shed consociational practices, even after the society has ceased to be deeply divided. Those who gain under consociational rules often want to preserve consociationalism (Lustick 1997; Nordlinger 1972; Tsebelis 1990).

a top official's professional fortune. It affects who is hired, promoted, or fired. That is why commissioner Kinnock's reforms, which tilt the balance to Weberian principles, have caused great unease in the Commission's ranks.

Many studies of European integration have assumed that the Commission is intent on substituting diverse national concerns with a uniform European interest. This chapter questions this assumption for the Commission's elite officials. These people generally want to recognize Europe's diversity in the Commission. I have focused here primarily on how this influences top officials' views on Commission personnel and task organization, and I have stressed that – in the prevailing circumstances – they have compelling utilitarian reasons to think in consociational rather than Weberian terms. Yet their inclination to acknowledge diversity is not merely driven by immediate professional concerns; for many, it is embedded in a conviction of how Europe could or should come together. In the words of an official:

I like my service to be a microcosm of the Community. I like my colleagues to reflect the diversity within the Community. There is a certain mystery as to how people with such different backgrounds can work together. (Official #30)

8   Conclusion

The conventional notion that the Commission is a unitary actor is misleading. In reality, the Commission is culturally diverse and politically divided. Visitors are struck by the linguistic and cultural variety within and among directorates-general (DGs). As one moves down the corridor of a typical DG, or takes the stairs to the next floor, one is beamed from a French-speaking into a predominantly English- or Spanish-speaking environment – dotted with one-to-one conversations in Danish, Greek, or Dutch. Administrative and social styles vary markedly. Some units swear by an egalitarian consultative style; others are run in a hierarchical and directive fashion. Here are a few cues for distinguishing one from the other: whether doors are open or closed; whether several small informal meetings of co-workers are going on, or one director-led assembly; whether secretaries are facilitators or gatekeepers; whether it takes a simple phone call (or email), fax or letter, or a formal application to the hierarchy to meet an official; whether *circulaires* (the famous trail of bureaucratic paperwork) are treated on a first-in first-out basis, or reach to the ceiling in the director's office.

Political preferences differ from office to office. Euro-federalists work with defenders of state power and politically agnostic policy wonks. Market liberals negotiate with social democrats and with independents. Officials concerned about the Commission's managerial deficit argue with colleagues opposed to trading the Commission's executive power for administration and management. Some regret that top positions in the Commission bureaucracy are subject to national quotas – in consociational fashion; others sigh that a standard Weberian bureaucratic format would not work; yet others rejoice in creating professional opportunities out of consociational necessity.

One needs to simplify to understand. Yet there is a trade-off between the simplicity of one's explanation and its precision. Many scholars of European integration have employed the unitary actor assumption, which assumes that the Commission and its employees are united in favor of deeper European integration. Commission officials are presumed to be supranationalist, to support EU policy competencies beyond market regulation, to defend the Commission's executive powers, and to prefer an organization insulated from national interference. This is in line with the prevailing paradigm of utility maximization in the study of bureaucracies. According to this literature, bureaus seek to maximize budgets, bureaucratic discretion, or status and work conditions (Blais and Dion 1991; Downs 1967; Dunleavy 1991; Migué and Bélanger 1974; Moe 1991, 1997; Niskanen 1971, 1994; Simon 1947; Tullock 1965). A similar reasoning underpins principal–agent theory, a widely used paradigm in public administration, which examines when agents (usually bureaucracies) are able to expand their own power and shirk the wishes of their principals (usually elected representatives, or, sometimes, the electorate) (for EU applications, see Franchino 1999, 2000; Pollack 1997). To what extent, though, does the goal of maximizing agency power actually motivate those who work in, or lead, bureaucracies?

This question raises two separate issues. In the first place, the prevailing model assumes that bureaucratic interest and individual motivation coincide. To what degree is this true in practice? Might individuals not be motivated to weaken as well as strengthen the autonomy of the bureaucracy in which they work? This book shows that top Commission officials typically do *not* hold preferences that merely reflect the Commission's presumed self-interest in greater institutional autonomy, and the next section develops a general argument for why that is the case. Second, the principal –agent model assumes that agents – and their employees – maximize their material utility. To what degree is this empirically valid? My study suggests that top officials' preferences on EU governance *cannot* be reduced to utility maximization, but instead are strongly motivated by the desire to hold consistent beliefs. I explain in the following section why that is so.

The Commission as non-unitary actor

With few exceptions, theoretical approaches to European Union politics have conceived of European Commission officials as instruments of deeper integration. The assumption is that institutional self-interest induces Commission officials to promote further integration. But is it appropriate to conflate the interest of a bureaucracy with that of its employees?

Bureaucracies vs. bureaucrats

Principal–agent models have been criticized for their lack of attention to collective action problems in organizations. One of these critics is Terry Moe, who focuses on the problems that principals (e.g. Congress) face in making unitary decisions. The same reasoning can be applied to agents as well as principals (Moe 1990, 1997).[1]

Whether one can conflate the interest of a bureaucracy with that of its officials is best examined empirically. To what extent, then, do top officials' preferences actually coincide with the Commission's institutional interest? Let us adopt for a moment the mantle of principal–agent theory, and operationalize the notion of maximizing bureaucratic power. If the Commission were intent on maximizing its power, it would take strong positions on each of the dimensions of EU governance dealt with in this book. It would be supranationalist to enhance its autonomy. It would promote European regulated capitalism to expand its policy responsibilities. It would champion an executive role for the Commission to maximize its agenda-setting powers. And, finally, it would campaign for a merit-based, Weberian internal organization to limit national interference. Accordingly, top officials would score high on each of these dimensions. My individual-level survey data make it possible to calculate where each individual stands in relation to the Commission's projected self-interest.[2]

We know from previous chapters that top officials do *not* have similarly high scores on these dimensions.[3] Figure 8.1 provides a visual representation of this. In a principal–agent world of self-interested bureaucracies,

[1] Terry Moe indirectly makes this argument for the US bureaucracy. He argues that whether bureaucracies are "effective," that is, capable of intentional unitary action, depends on how they are constituted. Bureaucracies reflect the politics of the political system they are part of. A political system in which power is fragmented and decisions are difficult to make or overturn prompts actors (politicians, interest groups, and bureaucrats) to rely on formal rules to protect their interests or solve their commitment problems. "The result is a bureaucracy that is vastly overformalized and disabled by its own organization" (Moe 1997: 472). The EU system of multi-level governance is strewn with as many veto points as the US system, and following Moe, one would expect this to affect the EU bureaucracy. Terry Moe would probably not be surprised to hear that the European Commission is relatively ineffective as a unitary actor.

[2] For each individual, I take the values on each of the four dependent variables, I reverse the values for Administrative Management and Consociationalism (1 becomes 4, . . . , 4 becomes 1), and I sum values on all four dependent variables and divide by 4. For example, a top official has the following values: 1.50 for Supranationalism, 3.50 for European Regulated Capitalism, 2.75 for Management (recoded: 2.25), and 4.00 for Consociationalism (recoded: 1.00). The total is 8.25 and so, divided by 4, her general score is 2.06. Compare that with the value of 4.00, which an impeccable defender of the Commission's self-interest is expected to have.

[3] Have I inadvertently loaded the dice by using extreme statements for tapping support of Commission institutional interest in combination with moderate statements for tapping disagreement? The former would raise the bar for top officials to agree; the latter would lower the bar for them to disagree. However, I do not think I have done so. Let us take for example the three items constituting the supranationalism scale (chapter 4, table 4.1). The two supranationalist statements are not extreme, though one could argue that item 2 is perhaps a little less moderate than item 3. Yet, despite their broadly moderate language, there is considerable spread in support and opposition on each item, and moreover average support is below the neutral point for both of these. This means that more officials oppose than support these moderate supranationalist items.

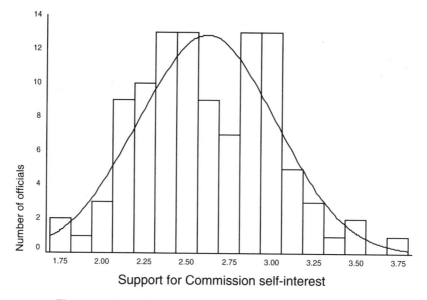

Figure 8.1 Top officials and the Commission's institutional interest.

top officials would have scores on the right side of this figure. They don't. They are spread across the entire spectrum from 1.7 to 3.8, with an average score for all top officials of 2.6 (median = 2.6).[4] Only a minority take positions that coincide with Commission self-interest.[5]

The intergovernmentalist item gives a yet clearer indication that I have not exaggerated differences between top officials' preferences and the Commission's institutional interest. Item 1 – "member states . . . ought to remain the central pillars of the European Union" – directly and bluntly echoes Charles de Gaulle's plea for a *Europe des parties*. It seems inconceivable that anyone who reflects the Commission's interest in supranationalism would support this statement, and yet more than 30 percent of top officials do.

[4] The results are the same, only starker, when I use a cruder measure. In this, I simply flag, for each basic question, whether an official's preference reflects the Commission's institutional interest. Less than 5 percent share the Commission's preferences on all issues ($n = 5$); 25 percent on three out of four issues ($n = 26$); 23 percent on two issues ($n = 24$); and 37 percent on one issue ($n = 39$); more than 10 percent do not support a single one of the four Commission preferences ($n = 11$). The distance between the preferences of top officials and those of the Commission as an institution is great.

[5] A possible counter-argument is that I have misspecified the relevant level of aggregation for Commission officials. A focus on the whole Commission may obscure the fact that individual officials' preferences coincide with functional subdivisions of the Commission. So I also examine functionally similar groupings of services: DGs with important authoritative competencies and/or financial resources, DGs concerned with policies central to European regulated capitalism, DGs concerned with soft policy issues, and DGs that primarily engage in routine administration, implementation, or adjudication. The first two groupings should benefit from deeper supranational integration; the latter two

This raises as many questions as it answers. Why do top officials' preferences not coincide with Commission self-interest? To answer this one must examine collective action problems in the Commission.

Why is the Commission not a unitary actor?

Attributing to individuals the preferences of the collectivities to which they belong is sometimes a reasonable simplification. Expressions such as "the trade union will not accept this," "the party wants that proposal," or "the government is considering several options," though imprecise, can be useful and elegant shorthand for the views of a controlling majority of union functionaries, party leaders, or cabinet ministers.

If it makes sense to conceive of parties, trade unions, or governments as unitary actors, why not do the same in the case of the Commission? However, the Commission is less coherent and less capable of intentional action than collectivities such as political parties, trade unions, or governments. Why is that so?

In his book *Games Real Actors Play*, Fritz Scharpf (1997b) thinks through the circumstances in which it is appropriate to conceive of aggregates of individuals – collectivities – as unitary actors. He begins by distinguishing between individual actors and composite actors. The notion of composite actor implies a will for intentional action by participating individuals at a level above the individuals involved. Composite actors may vary considerably in their actual capacity for intentional action, but the notion presupposes at a minimum that participating individuals intend to create a joint product or achieve a common purpose (Scharpf 1997b: 52–4). So mere exchange relationships do not qualify as composite action, but joint ventures do.[6] Aggregates of individuals that do not meet this criterion are not composite actors, but need to be disaggregated into their "components" – individual, intentional actors.

For a composite actor to be an intentional, unitary actor, yet more is required. Composite actors constitute potential; unitary actors are actuality.

---

should flourish under the status quo (or more intergovernmentalism). However, this does not appear to be the case. The bottom line is that the gap between top Commission officials and the Commission is wide no matter how one defines the Commission. No matter how one cuts it, one cannot easily identify Commission officials with the institutional interests of the Commission.

[6] Scharpf develops a sophisticated apparatus for distinguishing composite from noncomposite actors. Among composite actors he makes a further distinction between collective actors, which depend on the shared preferences of their members, and corporate actors, whose activities are carried out by staff members whose private preferences are expected to be neutralized by employment contracts. Each type specializes in one of the two critical resources for aggregates of individuals to become composite, and unitary, actors.

In order to be a unitary actor, individual participants must have non-conflicting preferences or, failing that, the composite actor must have the institutional capacity to resolve conflicts among employees/core members who disagree (Scharpf 1997b). According to Scharpf, what matters is the *extent* of *a priori* preference convergence and the *degree* of institutional capacity for conflict resolution. One or both, need to be high. The Commission is weak on both counts for reasons that I now turn to.

Divergent preferences. Preferences are rooted in experience. The more individuals have similar experiences, the more they are likely to hold the same preferences. Conversely, the larger the number of institutional settings that matter to individuals, the greater the likelihood of their experiences, and their preferences, diverging. That is why one expects greater divergence of preferences in a system of multi-level governance, in which individuals' diverse institutional experiences interact.[7] Multi-level governance connects individuals representing institutional actors with divergent norms or incentives; for example, EU decision-making requires civil servants from clientelist political systems in Southern Europe to engage in joint enterprises with Commission officials from clientelist-free Scandinavia. Moreover, multi-level governance softens the shell of institutions, and this facilitates connections between otherwise insulated institutional settings. It makes one's own institutional environment – for top officials, the Commission – more porous, and it makes other institutions appear larger and more relevant. So the sources of political preferences are more diverse in systems of multi-level governance than in political systems where authority is concentrated in a single, hierarchical institutional actor.[8]

---

[7] On multi-level governance, see Börzel and Risse (2000); Marks, Hooghe, and Blank (1996); Hooghe and Marks (2001); Scharpf (1988, 1994). There is a growing literature on how a system in which authority is diffused across territorial levels – a multi-level polity – influences the preferences and behavior of political parties (Bomberg 1998; Hix 1999; Marks and Wilson 2000; Marks, Wilson, and Ray forthcoming), trade unions (Ebbinghaus 1999; Ebbinghaus and Visser 1997; Turner 1996), social movements (Imig and Tarrow 1997, 2001; Marks and McAdam 1995; Tarrow 1995, 1999), firms and business representation (Coen 1997; Greenwood 1997), national and regional governments (Hooghe 1996; Marks 1996a; Marks et al. 1996), structures of interest intermediation (Falkner 1996, 1999), or policy networks (Kohler-Koch and Eising 1999).

[8] One exception to this expectation may be dual federalism or, more broadly, compartmentalized forms of governance in which authority is fragmented – but not shared – among different territorial levels of governance. In these circumstances, it is quite possible that preferences are formed almost exclusively by experiences in individuals' separate worlds, and that they do not have much interaction with individuals in other contexts. A stark example of this is the way francophones and anglophones in Quebec used to live next to, but not with, one another, until the barriers between the two communities came down during the silent revolution of the 1960s. The Canadian writer Hugh McLennan wrote a gripping novel about these separate worlds; he called it "two solitudes."

As figure 8.1 illustrates, there is little convergence of preferences on EU governance among top Commission officials. One could imagine a different outcome. Self-selection may spawn homogeneous preferences, as it tends to do in political parties, where people with similar political views are attracted to join. By the same logic, one might expect that only individuals with pro-European or pro-Commission views would opt for a Commission career. However, self-selection for a Commission job – to the extent that it occurs – is motivated by preferences along several dimensions. For example, under Jacques Delors, some new officials joined the Commission to be able to push forward internal market reforms. But that does not make them more likely to support maximal Commission power. In chapter 6, I find that these Delors recruits are *less* likely to support the Commission's longstanding executive powers; instead, they are happy to trade the Commission's initiative for better administrative management.

Top officials are extraordinarily diverse (chapter 2). Their educational, professional, and cultural background is far more heterogeneous than that of top officials in any national bureaucracy. Commission candidates do not get groomed in a Euro-bureaucracy school or recruited from a European elite. They are products of the EU system of multi-level governance – people with diverse backgrounds thrown together to make joint decisions. Their *a priori* preferences are divergent.

Low on ladder of institutional capacity. If preferences are diverse, composite actors may try to produce intentional, unitary action by making preferences converge. Fritz Scharpf distinguishes four possible paths to unify decision-making, and each of these presupposes different institutional capacities. In declining order of effectiveness they are: hierarchical direction, majority voting, negotiated agreement, and unilateral action. The first two are far more effective than the last two in dealing with conflicting preferences.[9] So Scharpf's categorization enables us to array composite actors on a "ladder of institutional capacity" from high to low.

The most effective means to resolve conflicts in bureaucracies is hierarchical direction. However, hierarchy is weak in the Commission. Although the Commission bureaucracy is formally a textbook case of a

---

[9] Scharpf warns us that this is so only in the case of conflicts based on divergent preferences. Hierarchy or majority voting may not be effective when conflicts are cognitive rather than evaluative, i.e. when individuals disagree because their information is different or because they hold different conceptions of cause and effect (Scharpf 1997b: 58–60). I start from the assumption that top officials have broadly speaking the same knowledge (or ignorance) of facts and causal relationships concerning European governance. So, when top officials diverge, it is because they have different preferences – not because their knowledge of the world varies.

Weberian hierarchical organization, there is in reality no hierarchical superior with sufficient authority to reward or sanction behavior. Instead, consociational practices are superimposed on hierarchical relationships. Promotions at the top depend on one's nationality and support from one's national government – not on merit or loyalty to the Commission hierarchy. The rule that adjacent positions in the hierarchy should go to people from different nationalities institutionalizes checks and balances between superiors and subordinates. Nationality pulls rational individuals concerned about maximizing career chances away from the Commission's self-interest.

However, the personnel reform launched after the 1999 Commission resignation crisis could change this (chapter 7). If commissioner Neil Kinnock, the architect of this meritocratic reform, gets his way, the Commission could gain capacity for intentional action – for inculcating its employees with its institutional interest. Kinnock wants to buttress Weberian principles in the organization. He favors merit and seniority in promotions, and ethos of impartiality, and explicit hierarchical direction. Top officials' careers may then be determined primarily by their performance in the Commission. The Commission could then monitor its employees' actions more accurately, and employ carrots and sticks to bring individual preferences in line with its (now unitary) preferences. In other words, the Commission would become a more "unitary actor" and, in the process, come to resemble national administrations more closely.[10]

A second path for effective conflict resolution in the face of divergent preferences is by majority voting. Yet bureaucracies arely decide by voting, and neither do Commission officials.[11]

This leaves the two less potent tools of conflict resolution available to the Commission. It may seek convergence of preferences through negotiation, which explains why Commission rhetoric consistently extols the virtues of coordination among commissioners, directorates-general, or units. If that fails, convergence may perhaps emerge spontaneously through unilateral moves by autonomous actors. But neither of these is effective in the Commission. In Fritz Scharpf's terms, the Commission

---

[10] The French civil service invented a vivid expression for this, now widely used beyond France – *esprit de corps*. It captures the idea that civil servants' preferences are in perfect harmony with their civil service's institutional interest (Page 1985). The expression is rarely used to characterize the fragmented and politicized – consociational – civil services of Belgium or Italy, and for good reason!

[11] With the exception of the College of commissioners, which decides by simple majority. The voting rule in the College is a curious exception in the EU system. Decision-making in the European Union rarely uses majoritarian rules (chapter 7). There are good reasons for this. Majoritarian institutions tend to exacerbate conflicts in culturally heterogeneous societies, and the European Union is a diverse polity (Lijphart 1984, 1999).

is low on the "ladder of institutional capacity," that is to say, conflict resolution depends to a large extent on non-binding rules and norms of operation. Non-hierarchical practices abound.

Deadlock is a likely outcome under non-hierarchical rules, unless one can resort to informal practices to circumvent this. In the Commission, cabinets are decisive in getting around non-hierarchy – they are the prime movers *and* fixers. Motivated sometimes by national interest and other times simply by a desire to bypass veto points and shorten decision time, cabinets cut through standard procedures. And so they help to bring closure in decision-making otherwise subject to gridlock. But they do this by further undermining the Commission's limited capacity for hierarchical direction.[12]

Top Commission officials work in an institutional setting that has the characteristics of a network. They are locked in semi-permanent relationships of mutual, though not necessarily symmetrical, dependence, in which each actor maintains the option to go it alone. The European Commission is not unique in displaying network features. Many national bureaucracies and private corporations have become less hierarchical over the past two decades. Organizational networking has overtaken hierarchy as the prevailing paradigm of modern governance in the public *and* private sector (Brans 1997; Metcalfe 1996b, 2000; O'Toole 1997; Rosenau and Czempiel 1992; Scharpf 1997b; Schulman 1993). The European Commission reflects therefore a broader phenomenon. To the extent that hierarchical direction is replaced by networking in modern bureaucracies, it becomes increasingly less useful to conceive of bureaucratic agents as unitary actors.

Top officials on non-hierarchy

Commission officials are, of course, well aware of limited unity in the Commission. A top official echoes the double handicap of fragmented political direction and weak mechanisms for committing officials to unitary preferences. Together, these enable top officials to shirk standard hierarchical rules and to minimize cooperation that could affect their autonomy:

---

[12] Adrienne Héritier makes a similar argument for the general EU policy-making process. Decision-making in the European Union is laborious, and so one would expect the diversity of interests and the consensus-forcing nature of European institutions to lead to gridlock or deadlock (Scharpf 1988). Yet this has not stopped rapid institutional and policy change over the past two decades. Why not? Héritier argues this has to do with the "widespread and ubiquitous use of informal strategies and process patterns that circumvent political impasses" – "subterfuge or escape routes" (Héritier 1999b: 1).

Interviewer: Some people claim that divisions between DGs often weaken the Commission in its dealings with other institutions; others argue that the Commission is usually very good at presenting a united front. What is your opinion?

Official: It starts at the top, is my answer. If you have a College of twenty politicians of different political colors, different national origins, put together without any natural political cohesion, you should not blame the DGs for want of unity. It starts there. Under those circumstances, the natural human tendencies to territoriality are reinforced rather than weakened. Given that, I don't think we do a bad job at presenting a united front. Nevertheless, it is true that there are huge tensions and territorial combats. These exist also at national level, but the structure of the European Commission makes this a particularly thorny problem. It saps efficacy from the organization if one spends far too much time talking over trivial things for territorial reasons. As lean-and-mean as we are organizationally, we should be concentrating on the "enemy" as it were.

I: There are a variety of mechanisms that could facilitate coordination. The Commission secretariat-general has the formal role of prime coordinator. Does it also have this role in practice?

O: One should not have too much faith in the possibility for a secretariat-general to really work in the structure I have described. It can only concentrate on things when it becomes a political priority that there be coordination or when something becomes clearly dysfunctional. But they are a relatively small service and they have to prioritize their coordinating functions. Actually, it would be very much resented if they leaned too heavily on others. So this is a delicate business for them. We have tried different things from time to time – with more or less success depending on circumstances. During the most recent Commission reorganization, for example, we tried not to talk in terms of heavy-duty inter-service groups. Instead, we decided there should be high-level coordination between directors-general, sort of networks of directors-general. Oh well . . . in my areas, only one has worked: [then-director-general for environment] Mr. X' network on the environment. It has worked because we managed to keep the meetings infrequent and at a high level and we talked about important things. And perhaps [it worked] because our DG was already, long before the Maastricht Treaty, thinking that we have to integrate environment into our policy-making. So there is not a natural tension but real cooperation involved. But many of the other networks have just fallen by the wayside. And this is partly because one sometimes does not understand problems sufficiently to assess whether coordination is necessary. For example, at the time when the Trans-European Networks were launched, everyone thought that huge coordination was needed between Energy, Telecommunications, and Transport. Even the commissioners decided that this was so obviously necessary that they created a commissioners' coordination group under [then-commissioner of transport] Kinnock, but it has a virtually blank agenda because there is not that much interrelationship between networks in Energy, Transport, and Telecommunications. One could also imagine the reverse situation, where people might feel coordination is really needed but it is blocked by an inextricable fundamental political conflict.

I: Do you need first and foremost, then, the political will to coordinate?

O: Yes.

I: And that political will is out of your hands?

O: Yes, you need a common political agenda, which we do not necessarily have. (Official #16)

Top officials often cite the cabinet system as the main source of the Commission's deficient capacity to resolve conflicts. It is part of the *raison d'être* of cabinets to help political decision makers circumvent hostile bureaucratic behavior; bending standard hierarchical practices is expected of them – up to a point. However, the cabinet system also provides officials, at higher and lower levels alike, with powerful incentives to circumvent hierarchy even in the absence of conflict between bureaucratic and political leadership. My conversation with the same official continues:

I: What about the cabinets? For some, they are a disruptive force, and for others they play a useful role in coordinating policy-making.

O: They are everything that people say about them – both good and bad. It goes back to the uniqueness of the European Community. [Former Commission president Walter] Hallstein tried to create a European civil service and, to a certain extent, succeeded. At the same time, the top levels of the civil service are influenced by all kinds of political intervention. A good relationship between a commissioner and her department is very important but, at the same time, difficult to achieve. I fully understand the tendency of commissioners to try to build up some counterweight to the directorate-general. Remember that they usually come from a national political environment, and typically they have had government experience in a huge national ministry. It seems natural that they feel the need to have some counterweight through their cabinet. Moreover, they also have to deal with the College of commissioners. So the idea that these commissioners have a staff, which is not only there to watch *me* in my directorate-general, but also to be responsible for what is going on elsewhere, is perfectly acceptable. My criticism is that, because of the obvious advantages of cabinets to commissioners and to cabinet members themselves, they have grown too big. Put it this way: my directorate-general has approximately 150 university-level administrators. And they are all involved in policy-making in a substantive policy area. This DG is divided into five directorates, and each directorate is divided into three or four units. So you are down to pretty small units, each of which is responsible for a huge policy area. Take maritime safety: there is one head of unit, and four or five people, not more. The director-general is supposed to have all of this under coherent control. My commissioner has seven university graduates in his staff. The obvious problem is that if they are not kept sufficiently busy by other business in the Community, they start to run the directorate-general. Email has made it very difficult to keep the department under control. These cabinet members may have a different agenda from the commissioner; they might not even know what they're doing because they could be young and inexperienced, never mind they are bright sparks. However, two young people on different ends of the internal E-net [one in the cabinet and the other in the services] can be cooking up all kinds of things.

I: The sensation of power.

O: And this can cause trouble. So I think cabinets are out of control. It is all right when you have a strongly managed cabinet. But it is really difficult when the cabinet is not strongly managed, and communication is going on in all kinds of ways outside formal communication channels. (Official #16)

The absence of a unitary Commission does not necessarily disable individual Commission officials. It may also empower them. A battle-proof top official – a player in a host of major dossiers over the past two decades, from cabinets as well as from the bureaucracy – emphasizes how skillful Commission entrepreneurs score successes by working between the cracks of the system. The strategy suits a loose network-type institutional environment: seek out like-minded allies, or create coalitions with actors who pursue separate, but compatible, goals. The official draws a sharp contrast between the standard approach in the Commission and the "hierarchical direction" strategy found in the private corporate sector:

The Commission only works because it is able to put hierarchy aside and say: "One has to respect hierarchy in formal terms, but, to get this job done, who do we need on board to do it?" We are task oriented and person oriented. That requires a great deal of flexibility and adaptability. The only way to pull this off is by token acceptance of the procedures and hierarchies. We formally respect them. But the only way to make this thing work effectively within the deadlines that are fixed by politics is to do it fast, and by relying on a certain key number of people who are basically committed to the goal that one wants to realize. In a private corporate organization, all employees are subjected to blanket indoctrination into the goals of whatever the organization is producing. Whether it concerns setting up a new production program, launching a fresh product, or introducing a novel technique, every single person goes through training that resembles a propaganda exercise. This does not happen in the Commission. Instead, you have to form allies in the cause of a particular advancement of the policy. You do that informally, and not even necessarily consciously in the beginning . . . . This [need to create coalitions] has varied over the years with different presidents. [Former Commission president Jacques] Delors was very concerned to have a total vision of policy, which he impregnated on the services of the Commission and on the other commissioners. In that sense, his approach was quite like in a private organization. He said: "*This* is the vision and you should use *this* vocabulary. You should talk about solidarity and cohesion." He wanted everyone to use a common vocabulary. That has somewhat changed now. I hope that it doesn't mean that the Commission will be less strong. I hope it is possible to have a lot more players producing better results in the aggregate than [a unitary player] with one vision can. (Official #39).

There are strong arguments for disaggregating the Commission and examining the preferences of the people within.

Values and interests

Top officials' preferences on EU governance cannot be reduced to utility maximization. They are instead a function of socialization – values – as well as utility-maximizing calculation – interests. But what is the relative causal weight of these two logics of preference formation? And how does the pull of values vs. interests vary from issue to issue?

Most rational choice analysts now accept that individuals may be motivated by values in addition to utility maximization (Levi 1997a, 1997b; Weingast 1995). According to Douglass North, for example,

the evidence we have with respect to ideologies, altruism, and self-imposed standards of conduct suggests that the trade-off between wealth and these other values is a negatively sloped function. That is, where the price to individuals of being able to express their own values and interests is low, they will loom large in the choices made; but, where the price one pays for expressing one's own ideology, or norms, or preferences is extremely high, they will account much less for human behavior. (North 1990: 22)

For North, as well as other rational choice analysts, the starting point remains that individuals are calculating human beings interested in maximizing utility. Values, norms, and identities are residual categories. They come into play only when the price for non-maximizing behavior is low (Levi 1997b; Weingast 1995). Yet, granting analytical priority to instrumental calculation is inconsistent with recent work in cognitive and social psychology. This work has shown that human capacity for calculation is far more limited than rational choice models presume (Chong 2000; Kinder 1998). These authors portray human beings for whom values and identities provide essential and *prior* cues – not residual afterthoughts – to help them figure out what may be in their interest. My Commission study is consistent with this research in social psychology in that it suggests greater mileage can be gained by turning the Northian logic on its head.

A further criticism concerns North's conception of utility maximization, which he defines in neoclassical terms as wealth maximization. Equating individuals' utility function with maximizing income, rents, or wealth may make sense when one is interested in understanding preferences for *economic* goods, as is the case in economics. However, when one wants to explain preferences for *political* good (for example, whether the European Union should be more or less supranational), a narrow focus on wealth maximization misses the point. Whereas money is the currency in economic transactions, authority is the currency in political transactions. Whatever substantive goals a political elite actor has, it is likely that political authority, the capacity to exercise legitimate power over other individuals, helps to realize them. So utility-maximizing political actors may be expected to be primarily interested in sustaining their position in authority (Levi 1997b; Marks and Hooghe 2000). Whether a focus on sustaining one's position in authority also brings greater wealth depends on the rules of the game in a particular political setting (Marks and Hooghe 2000). Politics is a different game from economics.

In his integrative model of preference formation, Dennis Chong gives values and interests more equal standing as sources of human motivation. He proposes that values or dispositions dominate when incentives are weak or indistinguishable, whereas incentives govern when values or dispositions are weak or contradictory (Chong 2000: 45–65). Chong argues convincingly that *homo sociologicus* and *homo economicus* both exist. On the basis of my study, I venture one step further, and I put forward general principles that govern when one is likely to outshine the other.

Belief consistency. There is broad support in social and cognitive psychology literature for the view that individuals are motivated by the desire to hold consistent beliefs. Belief consistency presumes that the more a new object of preference formation resembles existing objects, the more an individual is likely to extend existing stable beliefs to the new object (Feld and Grofman 1988; Feldman 1988; George 1969, 1979; Jennings 1992; Sears 1993; Sears and Funk 1991; Sears and Valentino 1997).

One reason for the preeminence of belief consistency is that it dramatically reduces information costs for individuals trying to make up their mind on new issues (Chong 2000; Simon 1985). It enables them to avoid complex utility calculations, and that is all the more important because, in most cases, it is not obvious how overarching political and social issues may affect one's utility. For example, a top official could make an educated guess about how a shift to a market-liberal European Union would affect his professional career. An official in market-oriented services may anticipate benefits from such a shift because there may be more demand for competition policy or EU product regulation. However, he may also draw the opposite conclusion, because in a market-liberal European Union the Commission may face across-the-board cuts. That is why factors measuring personal career utility are weakly associated with top officials' preferences on European regulated capitalism vs. market liberalism. Even highly sophisticated individuals often lack the information to make reasonable calculations.

Even when it is possible to calculate the perceived trade-off between belief consistency and utility, individuals appear inclined to forgo career benefits in favor of belief consistency. The more encompassing and basic an issue, the more they are likely to prefer belief consistency to immediate career benefit (Elster 1990).[13] But they may even do so when an issue is more circumscribed. For example, a rational top Commission official in the current Commission-skeptical climate is likely to support an administrative and managerial Commission, because that is most likely to improve her career options. Media and national governments praise Commission actors who focus on management and, moreover, the Commission itself has altered its incentive structure by giving priority for promotion to candidates with managerial inclination and skills. However, as I show in chapter 6, many top officials choose *not* to adopt these utility-maximizing preferences. They oppose an administrative and managerial Commission for ideological reasons, because it would undercut broadly social democratic policies. Belief consistency is the default option.

Closeness and salience of beliefs. For belief consistency to be an option in the first place, old and new objects must be close; that is, they must be linked in some intelligible way. For example, issues concerning the basic political character of the EU – how authority should be allocated territorially, and how Europe's economy should be regulated – echo issues that have shaped political cleavages in national politics. Thus top officials can draw on a stock of embedded preferences when confronted with related questions at the European level.

In contrast, such conceptual affinity between the EU and national levels is far less obvious for Commission issues. Questions concerning the role and internal organization of the Commission in a multi-level, multinational EU polity do not have immediate parallels in individual countries. The role of the Commission makes sense only by reference to the EU's own institutional history. The most powerful socialization agents – national institutions and political parties – do not embody stable political beliefs on objects that are conceptually linked to this EU issue.

New objects must not only be conceptually close to old objects. The predispositions they evoke must also be salient in order to structure preferences, and that is primarily a function of a composite actor's position

---

[13] This is consistent with Jon Elster's argument that rational choice "is more powerful when applied to medium-sized problems like the purchase of a car or of a house." But " 'large problems,' in which the choice can be expected to have wide-ranging consequences, ... tend to fall outside the scope of the theory. Preference rankings over big chunks of life tend to be incomplete, and subjective probabilities over events in the distant future tend to be unreliable" (Elster 1990: 40).

on the ladder of institutional capacity. Predispositions linked to ideology and territory – rooted in political parties and national institutions – are powerful influences on top officials' preferences because political parties and national institutions are vibrant forces in political life. Top officials cannot avoid taking cues from their political party, or the national institution closest to their identity, when these institutions take a stance on basic issues.

Beliefs that do not help to make sense of a new reality (closeness) and beliefs that are not deeply held or institutionalized (salience) are unlikely to shape preferences. They are also unlikely to prevent people from thinking and behaving in a utility-maximizing fashion.

Survival and utility maximization. Rational utility maximization is most likely to trump other factors when an individual's life chances are at stake (Chong 2000; Sears 1993; Sears and Funk 1991). Here I depart from North's neoclassical focus on wealth maximization (North 1990). Political rulers' greatest fear in stable democracies is electoral defeat. I have reason to believe that top officials' greatest dread in the Commission is to have their career destroyed.

Hence utility maximization strongly predicts top officials' preferences on a consociational or Weberian Commission. Top officials know from experience that the criteria for professional success in the Commission differ dramatically between these two versions of Commission organization. They have compelling utilitarian reasons for supporting a system that employs criteria for which they enjoy a comparative advantage. There are calculable pay-offs for Commission officials under each system. A strict policy of national quotas punishes candidates with the "wrong" nationality, and it punishes those who lack strong national connections.[14] A merit-based promotion policy has its losers too. It disadvantages candidates from new member states – because they lack knowledge and

---

[14] I recall a conversation with a well-respected Danish director, who regretted that he had never been able to reach the highest rank. His hopes were dashed a few years before I interviewed him when the one Danish A1 position was given to a much younger, and politically better connected, compatriot. The Danish director, a veteran of the Danish enlargement wave, has now retired. I also remember encounters with two A2 officials of Greek nationality in their early fifties, both with a successful track record in the Commission. They rated their chances for promotion to director-general as essentially nil because the two Greek DG posts (one director-general and one deputy director-general) had recently been taken up by two Greek parachutists, after heavy-handed lobbying by Athens. Yet, the Commission resignation crisis in 1999 changed the outlook for Greeks. One Greek A1 official (the director-general) fell victim to the Commission reshuffling in 1999, and so, unexpectedly, a window of opportunity opened up. In the summer of 2000, a Greek A2 official with over fifteen years of Commission experience was promoted to director-general. Hereafter, the window of opportunity closed anew for all other Greek officials.

socialization – as well as candidates from administrative or educational systems that are out of tune with Commission norms.[15] The costs and benefits of consociationalism or Weberianism in the Commission are large and transparent. As Chong emphasizes, "people are more likely to act instrumentally when the incentives are apparent, there are large [personal] consequences to their decisions, and there is a clear relationship between means and ends" (Chong 2000: 62–3). With their professional future so directly at stake, belief consistency becomes a luxury for top officials. Survival concentrates the mind on utility.

This argument about the relative influence of socialization and utility maximization is general in scope and logical in form. Socialization is the predominant influence for large, new issues that are intelligibly connected to longstanding preferences on related issues. The institutional contexts that are most powerful in exerting socialization are those that are relatively high on the ladder of institutional capacity. Utility maximization is most influential when the issue is more narrowly circumscribed, and perceived to have high and transparent stakes for an individual's life chances. For top officials, reform of the Commission is such a concern.

Top officials on EU governance

Let us now summarize the main findings of chapters 4 to 7, which each examine top Commission officials' preferences on one dimension of EU governance. I relate the findings to the framework on preference formation presented in figure 1.1 (see figure 8.2). As we will see, the results are consistent with the general principles of preference formation outlined above.

Four dimensions

Supranationalism versus intergovernmentalism. The widespread assumption that the Commission is a greenhouse for supranationalism has little basis in reality. It is *not* the case that the longer one works in the Commission, the more supranationalist one becomes.

As chapter 4 shows, institutional settings outside the Commission are the best predictors of officials' preferences concerning the allocation of authority in the European Union. Two kinds of socialization experiences are very strong: length of prior service in a national administration, and

[15] The Kinnock reforms recognize this potential cultural bias. In the *White Paper on Reforming the Commission*, the passage on merit-based promotion explicitly states, "tests should take account of the multi-cultural dimension of the European Union. In this way, equal treatment of candidates from all member states will be ensured" (*White Paper on Reforming the Commission*, March 28, 2000: 27).

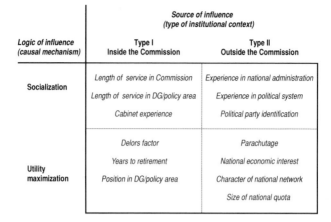

Logic of influence (causal mechanism)	Source of influence (type of institutional context)	
	Type I Inside the Commission	Type II Outside the Commission
Socialization	Length of service in Commission Length of service in DG/policy area Cabinet experience	Experience in national administration Experience in political system Political party identification
Utility maximization	Delors factor Years to retirement Position in DG/policy area	Parachutage National economic interest Character of national network Size of national quota

Figure 8.2 Top officials and preference formation on EU governance.

the constitutional character (federal or unitary) of an official's country of origin. Those from unitary countries are likely to be intergovernmentalist, as are former national civil servants. A third influence – party identification – is also significant. All three variables tap socialization outside the Commission.

Three utility variables survive controls, but utility maximization is much weaker than socialization. Officials who belong to strongly networked nationalities in Brussels tend to embrace intergovernmentalism. Officials from countries that benefit most from EU funding are likely to support supranationalism. Only one variable that taps the immediate Commission environment has some predictive value: top officials in Commission strongholds – directorates-general with the power of the purse or extensive autonomous competence – are more supranationalist than their colleagues in policy areas under Council control.

In sum, top officials' preferences on supranationalism versus intergovernmentalism are shaped mainly by contexts external to the Commission. On balance, socialization variables clearly outweigh utility variables. Predictors for supranationalism are located on the right-hand side of figure 8.2, and the weightiest of these are concentrated in the upper-right corner.

European regulated capitalism versus market liberalism. Variables tapping socialization outside the Commission play a major role in explaining preferences on European regulated capitalism versus market liberalism (chapter 5), as they do for supranationalism. By far the strongest influence is prior identification with a political party. Commission officials identifying with left parties usually support regulated capitalism whereas those identifying with right parties tend to favor market capitalism. In addition, prior service in a national administration reduces the appetite for European regulated capitalism.

Utility maximization has a limited impact on a subset of officials. Officials from countries that benefit most from EU funding tend to support European regulated capitalism, as do those who work in policy areas central to European regulated capitalism.

Once again, the experience that matters is that beyond the Commission, in a political party, in one's prior work environment, or in one's country. I have argued that the Commission is low on the ladder of institutional capacity, which helps us understand why it has great difficulty instilling a common viewpoint among its employees. Socialization influences are much more important than utility maximization. This is consistent with my expectation that individuals are more likely to be guided by values than by interests on large issues such as the role of government in the economy. The influences shaping preferences on regulated capitalism versus market liberalism are located on the right-hand side, predominantly in the upper-right corner, of figure 8.2.

Administrative – managerial Commission versus executive – initiating Commission. Contrasting influences come to the fore when one explains preferences on institutional and organizational issues (chapter 6). Should the Commission remain an executive body – a principal with initiative – or should it become more like a standard civil service – an administrative and managerial agent? This is a thorny issue for top officials. Their views are often only weakly crystallized, and this shows in the results. This dimension is the least well explained of the four dealt with in this book.

The range of experiences that influence top officials' preferences is more diverse than on each of the other dimensions. Three influences internal to the Commission are strongest. Top officials with long tenure in office are less likely to support an administrative and managerial role. This is the one and only instance where Commission socialization significantly shapes top officials' preferences on EU governance. There are also two factors that tap utility maximization in the Commission. Officials recruited by Jacques Delors prefer an administrative and managerial Commission because they want to safeguard "their" 1992 program.[16] Younger

---

[16] In chapter 1, I cautiously characterize this Delors factor as a hybrid of socialization and utility influence. But the evidence in chapter 6 leads me to conclude that the utility logic based on career concerns is more compelling than the impact of internalized values. The hypothesized direction of the relationship is the same for utility and socialization: Delors recruits tend to support an administrative and managerial role for the Commission.

officials oppose administrative management because career incentives are slanted in favor of initiating policy entrepreneurs rather than managers. The future role of the Commission has transparent implications for a top official's career; though a change in the Commission's role is unlikely to cost him his job, promotion, or pay, it would significantly alter the content and status of the job. So one would expect utility maximization to gain importance.

The strong impact of influences inside the Commission does not mean that factors external to the Commission do not matter. One socialization influence – party identification – and one utility variable – national interest – are significantly associated with preferences on the role of the Commission. Those on the political left, as well as those from countries that benefit most from EU funding, resist administration and management.

In sum, top officials' preferences on whether the Commission should be principal or agent are explained by experiences inside as well as outside the Commission; their views are partly a reflection of socialized values and partly a rational utility-calculating response to career incentives. In terms of figure 8.2, this explanation draws power from all four corners in about equal proportion.

Consociational Commission versus Weberian Commission. Career utility trumps socialization when one seeks to understand top officials' preferences on how the Commission should reconcile national diversity with a common European purpose in its own organization (chapter 7). Should the Commission be Weberian – merit based, detached from national differences, and expressing a common European interest – or consociational – with national quotas, responsive to national interests, and less concerned about an overarching European objective? This issue has direct implications for top officials' careers – perhaps even their survival as top Commission officials.

Two influences associated with nationality describe by far the largest proportion of the explained variance, and they do so for utilitarian reasons. First, officials from large countries tend to support a consociational Commission, because their chances for promotion seem less sharply circumscribed by national quotas.[17] Second, officials from strongly networked nationalities in Brussels are likely to support a consociational Commission, because they are best placed to exploit personnel practices that encourage national lobbying.

---

[17] This is more a matter of perception than of objective reality, but these perceptions can stir strong emotions.

The third-strongest variable taps utility inside the Commission. Officials in policy areas that require ongoing close interaction with national representatives are more likely to support a consociational Commission. These "soft policy areas" concern environmental, cultural, educational, and consumer policy. Utility maximization predominates.

One can summarize the general pattern simply: when preferences bear directly on issues of professional survival or success, internalized beliefs give way to utility concerns. Most factors with explanatory bite come from the bottom half of figure 8.2, and career incentives outside the Commission (bottom-right) weigh more heavily than those inside the Commission.

Concluding remarks

Clear patterns emerge from these four studies. First, contexts external to the Commission are more decisive for preferences than are contexts within the Commission: party, country, and prior work environment leave a deeper imprint on Commission officials' basic preferences than do their location in a particular directorate-general or cabinet. This is reflected in table 8.1, where I report, for each of the four dimensions, coefficients of determination (R^2) for two rival linear regression models, one limited to variables tapping external contexts and the other limited to variables tapping the Commission context. The results are unambiguous: external influences are much stronger than experiences inside the Commission. Only for top officials' views on the role of the Commission does the causal power of the "internal" model match that of the "external" model.

Top officials are neither utility-maximizing calculators nor products of socialization. They are both. But the causal weight of socialization

Table 8.1 *Explanatory power of external and internal models of preference formation (coefficients of determination, R^2)*

Top officials' preferences on . . .	External model (contexts outside the Commission)	Internal model (contexts inside the Commission)	Full model
Supranationalism	.35	.04	.38
European regulated capitalism	.38	.13	.42
Administrative management in Commission	.16	.14	.31
Consociational accommodation in Commission	.27	.12	.40

Table 8.2 *Explanatory power of socialization and utility models of preference formation (coefficients of determination, R^2)*

Top officials' preferences on . . .	Socialization model	Utility maximization model	Full model
Supranationalism	.29	.18	.38
European regulated capitalism	.38	.08	.42
Administrative management in Commission	.13	.11	.31
Consociational accommodation in Commission	.20	.34	.40

and utility vary markedly – and intelligibly – depending on the issue. This is summarized in table 8.2, where I report, for each of these four dimensions, the coefficient of determination for rival socialization and utility maximization models.

Taking the findings of table 8.1 and 8.2 together, there are distinct differences between the models explaining preferences on broader regime issues and those engaging preferences on institutional and organizational issues. The more encompassing and basic an issue for the EU polity, the more likely it is that officials' preferences are consistent with socialized values. When one seeks to explain officials' preferences on basic questions, such as the territorial allocation of authority between the EU and member states and relations between market and state, the best predictors are party identification and territorial identities or practices. On basic issues of European governance, utility maximization is a poor guide. Conversely, the more specific and delineated an issue for the EU polity, the more utility maximization prevails. Hence, when it comes to the role of and, especially, the internal organization of the Commission, career interests predict preferences.

When asked about her basic preferences on EU governance, a top Commission official is primarily motivated by the desire to hold consistent beliefs. Yet this default motivation of belief consistency makes way for utility calculation under particular conditions, namely, when her professional success is directly and calculably connected with fundamental choices on EU governance.

Most of the time, however, a top official is not in such a bind. She cares about the values and worldviews she holds, and she uses her position at the heart of the European Union to make these values count for those she identifies with – Europe, her country, her party, or more generally the community that matters to her. As one director-general puts it:

I have never thought of Europe as an end in itself. I have always considered Europe to be a means to achieve certain political ends – in my country, in the world, I have never been disappointed in Europe, because I never expected Europe to solve all our problems. It is not up to Europe to solve our problems. Europe is like a playground of Lego blocks where one stacks pieces upon one another, and that makes it possible to build a nice house. (Official #25)

Appendix I: Statistics

Table A.1 *Officials by DG in the Commission*

Service in the Commission	All top officials		Interviews		Questionnaires	
	%	No.	%	No.	%	No.
DG I (External economic relations, USA, Far East, WTO)	4.9	10	5.8	8	6.6	7
DG Ia (External political relations, Eastern Europe, CFSP)	4.9	10	6.6	9	6.6	7
DG Ib (External: Latin America, Mediterranean)	3.4	7	2.9	4	3.8	4
DG II (Economics & finance)	4.9	10	5.8	8	6.6	7
DG III (Industry)	4.9	10	2.2	3	1.9	2
DG IV (Competition)	4.9	10	3.7	5	2.8	3
DG V (Social affairs)	4.4	9	2.9	4	2.8	3
DG VI (Agriculture)	7.8	16	8.8	12	8.5	9
DG VII (Transport)	3.4	7	2.9	4	2.8	3
DG VIII (Development)	4.9	10	7.3	10	3.8	4
DG IX (Personnel)	2.9	6	2.2	3	0.9	1
DG X (Culture, audiovisual)	2.4	5	3.7	5	3.8	4
DG XI (Environment)	3.4	7	4.4	6	4.7	5
DG XII (Research)	5.9	12	4.4	6	3.8	4
DG XIII (Telecommunications)	4.4	9	2.9	4	3.8	4
DG XIV (Fisheries)	2.9	6	1.5	2	1.9	2
DG XV (Internal market)	3.4	7	3.7	5	2.8	3
DG XVI (Regional policy)	3.9	8	5.8	8	5.7	6
DG XVII (Energy)	3.5	6	0.7	1	0.9	1
DG XIX (Budget)	2.4	5	4.4	6	4.7	5
DG XX (Financial affairs)	2.4	5	0.7	1	0.9	1
DG XXI (Customs, taxes)	2.4	5	3.7	5	4.7	5
DG XXII (Education, training)	1.9	4	2.9	4	3.8	4
DG XXIII (Tourism, SME)	2.4	5	1.5	2	0.9	1
DG XXIV (Consumer affairs)	1.5	3	0.7	1	0.9	1
Secretariat-General	5.4	11	7.3	10	8.5	9
Spokesperson Service	0.5	1	0.7	1	0.9	1
Total	100.0	204	100.1	137	99.8	106
Chi-square			22.485		24.507	
Degrees of freedom			25		25	
Alpha			.608		.490	

Source: American Chamber of Commerce, *Guide to EU Institutions*, Brussels, 1996.

Table A.2 *Officials by nationality*

Nationality	All top officials		Interviews		Questionnaires	
	%	No.	%	No.	%	No.
Austrian	3.4		2.9	4	2.8	3
Belgian	4.3		5.1	7	5.7	6
Danish	2.5		5.8	8	5.7	6
Dutch	5.1		7.3	10	7.5	8
Finnish	2.5		1.5	2	1.9	2
French	14.0		20.4	28	17.9	19
German	14.4		8.0	11	8.5	9
Greek	4.3		4.4	6	2.8	3
Irish	2.3		2.9	4	3.8	4
Italian	14.0		14.6	20	15.1	16
Luxembourg	1.2		0.7	1	0.9	1
Portuguese	4.3		5.1	7	3.8	4
Spanish	10.2		5.1	7	3.8	4
Swedish	3.6		2.9	4	2.8	3
British	14.1		13.1	18	17.0	18
Total	100.2	204	99.8	137	100.0	106
Chi-square			20.387		16.510	
Degrees of freedom			14		14	
Alpha			.118		.283	

Table A.3 *Personal and professional characteristics of top officials (%)*

Characteristic	Interviews ($n = 137$)	Questionnaires ($n = 106$)
Position		
Director-general	13.1	14.2
Deputy director-general	14.6	11.3
Director	65.0	66.0
(Principal) advisor	6.6	7.5
Cabinet chef	0.7	0.9
Seniority in the Commission		
Less than 5 years	13.1	13.2
5–15 years	29.2	28.3
16–25 years	33.6	34.0
More than 25 years	24.1	24.5
Gender		
Women	6.5	6.6
Men	93.5	93.4
Education		
No university	1.5	1.9
Social sciences (including law)	73.1	72.4
Arts	10.4	10.5
Sciences	14.2	15.2
Transnational education		
No	61.2	63.8
In other European countries	23.1	18.1
In North America	13.4	16.2
In Europe & North America	2.2	1.9
Prior career (most important occupation)		
Commission as first job	18.0	16.0
Elected political mandate	6.0	4.7
Civil service	37.6	37.7
National (includes diplomacy)	25.6	29.2
EU (includes permanent representation)	12.0	8.5
Expertise	38.4	41.6
International organizations	4.5	3.8
Central bank/courts	5.3	4.7
University, research, journalism	16.5	18.9
Business, banking, professions	11.3	12.3
Trade unions, public interest groups	0.8	1.9
Civil service		
None	38.5	38.5
Less than 5 years	11.9	11.5
5–15 years	30.4	29.8
More than 15 years	19.3	20.2
Commission cabinet		
None	65.7	65.1
Less than 5 years	16.8	17.9
5 years or more	17.5	17.0
Parachutage		
No	56.9	55.7
Yes	43.1	44.3

Table A.4 *Dependent variables: descriptive statistics*

Variable	N	Mean	Median	S.D.	Minimum	Maximum	Description[a]
Supranationalism	105	2.56	2.33	.67	1.33	4.00	Index of items 1, 3, and 4
European regulated capitalism	105	3.22	3.50	.67	1.00	4.00	Index of items 6 and 7
Administrative management	105	2.53	2.50	.72	1.00	4.00	Index of items 11 and 12
Consociational accommodation	105	2.78	3.00	.79	1.00	4.00	Index of items 15 and 16

[a] The item numbers refer to the statements in table 3.1.

Table A.5 *Dependent variables: correlations*

Variable	(1)	(2)	(3)
Supranationalism (1)	1.000		
European regulated capitalism (2)	.24**	1.000	
Administrative management (3)	−.17*	.05	1.000
Consociational accommodation (4)	−.21**	−.06	−.05

$**p < .01$ $*p < .05$ (two-tailed)

Table A.6 *Independent socialization variables: descriptive statistics*

Variable	N	Mean	Median	S.D.	Minimum	Maximum	Description
Commission Socialization	105	18.00	21.00	10.70	1	38	Number of years in Commission
ERC Socialization	105	4.80	0.00	7.90	0	33	Number of years in DGs for European regulated capitalism
Cabinet Experience	105	0.35	0.00	0.48	0	1	1: worked in Commission cabinet
National Administration	105	6.00	3.00	7.20	0	28	Number of years in national civil service
Weak Weberian	105	0.12	0.00	0.33	0	1	1: worked in consociational national administration
Medium Weberian	105	0.24	0.00	0.43	0	1	1: worked in medium Weberian national administration
Strong Weberian	105	0.22	0.00	0.42	0	1	1: worked in strongly Weberian national administration
Private Sector	105	0.24	0.00	0.43	0	1	1: worked in private sector
Federalism	105	3.80	4.00	2.90	0	10	index 0–12: extent of federalism in home country
Country Size	105	40.00	57.00	25.70	0.4	79.3	Population of home country in millions
Corporatism	105	5.90	4.00	4.00	1	14	Rank 1–14: extent of corporatism in country
Socialist	105	0.24	0.00	0.43	0	1	1: socialist/social democrat
Christian Democrat	105	0.11	0.00	0.32	0	1	1: Christian democrat
Conservative	105	0.06	0.00	0.23	0	1	1: conservative
Liberal	105	0.17	0.00	0.38	0	1	1: liberal or centrist
Young Socialist	105	0.12	0.00	0.33	0	1	1: socialist born 1940 or after
Young Christ Democrat	105	0.07	0.00	0.25	0	1	1: Christian democrat born 1940 or after
Young Liberal	105	0.11	0.00	0.32	0	1	1: liberal born 1940 or after

Table A.7 *Independent socialization variables: correlations*

Variable	(1)	(2)	(3)	(4)	(5)	(6)	(7)	(8)	(9)	(10)	(11)
Commission Socialization (1)	1.00										
ERC Socialization (2)	.23**	1.00									
Cabinet Experience (3)	.29***	.01	1.00								
National Administration (4)	-.58***	-.25**	-.25**	1.00							
Weak Weberian (5)	-.21**	-.14	-.04	.05	1.00						
Medium Weberian (6)	-.48***	-.23**	-.13	.39***	-.21**	1.00					
Strong Weberian (7)	-.01	.09	-.05	.40***	-.20**	-.30***	1.00				
Private Sector (8)	-.09	-.21**	-.13	-.14	.13	-.05	-.03	1.00			
Federalism (9)	.22**	-.05	.19*	-.23**	.13	.02	-.33***	-.13	1.00		
Country Size (10)	.46***	.03	.21**	-.24**	-.25**	-.31***	.21***	-.19*	.37***	1.00	
Corporatism (11)	-.31***	-.13	-.13	.18*	.10	.50***	-.43***	.08	.31***	-.53***	1.00
Socialist (12)	.07	.15	.10	-.17*	-.01	-.05	-.13	-.10	.15	.24**	-.12
Christian Democrat (13)	.05	-.06	.11	-.05	.05	.01	-.12	.08	.09	-.36***	.25***
Conservative (14)	-.06	.02	-.01	.11	.03	-.04	.07	.15	-.22**	.00	-.10
Liberal (15)	-.20**	-.18*	-.07	.02	.06	.04	-.06	.16	-.01	-.09	.13
Young_Socialist (16)	-.16*	.15	.09	-.13	.12	-.07	-.06	-.01	.03	.08	-.10
Young_Christ Democrat (17)	-.13	-.06	.04	.04	.02	.12	-.05	.12	-.02	-.31***	.22**
Young_Liberal (18)	-.13	-.15	-.01	-.04	-.04	.01	-.12	.15	-.00	-.01	.07

*p < .10; **p < .05; ***p < .01 (two-tailed)

Table A.8 *Independent utility maximization variables: descriptive statistics*

Variable	N	Mean	Median	S.D.	Minimum	Maximum	Description
Age	104	55.60	56.00	5.40	45	66	Age = 1996 – year of birth
Power-DG	105	4.60	5.00	2.00	1	9	Index 1–9: extent of autonomous power/purse of current DG
ERC-DG	105	0.35	0.00	0.48	0	1	1: currently position in DG for European regulated capitalism
Admin/Management-DG	105	0.41	0.00	0.49	0	1	1: current position in DG for management, implementation or adjudication
Soft-DG	105	0.23	0.00	0.42	0	1	1: currently position in DG for soft policy
National Economic Benefit	105	0.64	0.25	1.00	0.11	4	EU structural funds as % of GDP for home country
National Quota	105	7.70	10.00	2.90	2	10	Votes for home country in Council of Ministers
National Clubness	105	1.30	2.00	0.82	0	2	Index 0–2: cohesiveness of national networking in Brussels
Hybrid variables (recruitment)							
Delors Factor	105	0.50	1.00	0.50	0	1	1: recruited during 1986–1994
Parachutage	105	0.42	0.00	0.50	0	1	1: parachuted (into A2 or A1 position)

Table A.9 *Independent utility maximization variables: correlations*

Variable	(1)	(2)	(3)	(4)	(5)	(6)	(7)	(8)	(9)
Age (1)	1.00								
Power-DG (2)	-.07	1.00							
ERC-DG (3)	-.14	.53***	1.00						
Admin/Management-DG (4)	.03	.40***	.24**	1.00					
Soft-DG (5)	-.04	-.17*	.55***	-.08	1.00				
National Economic Benefit (6)	-.15	-.11	.12	-.08	.18*	1.00			
National Quota (7)	.18*	.05	-.11	.07	-.29***	-.34***	1.00		
National Clubness (8)	-.02	-.02	.04	.05	-.04	-.18*	.22**	1.00	
Parachutage (9)	-.20**	.06	.14	.04	.18	.12	-.34***	.04	1.00
Delors Factor (10)	-.23**	.10	.13	.21**	-.01	.21**	-.06	-.10	-.01

$* p < .10; ** p < .05; *** p < .01$ (two-tailed)

Appendix II: Description of independent variables

Commission Socialization

Years in Commission service. *Source:* Biographical data from *The European Companion* (London: DPR Publishing, 1992, 1994); *Euro's Who's Who* (Brussels: Editions Delta, 1991); and from interviews by the author.

ERC-Soc

I calculate how many years each official spent in DGs dealing with European regulated capitalism. I use a restrictive definition of services for European regulated capitalism: social regulation (social policy, culture, environment, vocational training and education, consumer services: DGs V, X, XI, XXII, XXIV) and redistribution (agriculture, third world development, fisheries, regional policy: DGs VI, VIII, XIV, XVI). *Source:* biographical data and interviews.

Cabinet Experience

A dummy, with a value of 1 for those who served in a Commission cabinet. *Source*: biographical data and interviews.

National Administration

Years in national service. These concern positions in the executive branch of the state and hierarchically subordinate to central government: civil servants in line ministries, diplomats (excluding EU postings), and government ministers (but not national parliamentarians). For public officials with some autonomy from central authorities (courts, central bank, parliament, public companies, local government) or in positions with a strong European component (European desks in foreign affairs or near the head of government), I divide the number of years by two. *Source:* Biographical data and interview data.

Type of National Administration: Strong/Medium/Weak Weberian

Three dummies that tap strong/medium/weak Weberian bureaucratic tradition. I compare bureaucracies along four dimensions developed by Edward Page, and use these comparisons to categorize bureaucratic traditions along a consociational–Weberian dimension. My main sources are Edward Page (1985, 1995) and Page and Wright (1999a). I allocate values to former state officials only by nationality.

	Cohesion	Autonomy from political control	Caste-like character	Non-permeability of external interests	Summary
Austria	Weak	Weak	Weak	Weak	Weak
Belgium	Weak	Weak	Weak	Weak	Weak
Denmark	Weak	Strong	Weak	Weak	Medium
Finland	Weak	Weak	Weak	Weak	Weak
France	Strong	Medium	Strong	Strong	Strong
Germany	Weak	Medium	Strong	Weak	Medium
Greece	Weak	Weak	Weak	Weak	Weak
Ireland	Strong	Strong	Weak	Strong	Strong
Italy	Weak	Weak	Weak	Weak	Weak
Luxembourg	Weak	Weak	Weak	Weak	Weak
Netherlands	Weak	Medium	Weak	Weak	Medium
Portugal	Weak	Medium	Weak	Strong	Medium
Spain	Weak	Medium	Weak	Strong	Medium
Sweden	Weak	Strong	Weak	Weak	Medium
United Kingdom	Strong	Strong	Strong	Strong	Strong

Private Sector

A dummy that takes a value of 1 for top officials with prior experience in industry or banking. *Source:* Biographical data and interview data.

Federalism

A composite index of four variables to measure the extent of regional governance, developed by Gary Marks and myself (Hooghe and Marks 2001: appendix 2). This index ranges from 0 (centralized authority) to 12 (dispersed authority), and it combines measures for the extent of constitutional federalism, autonomy for special territories in the national state, the role of regions in central government, and the presence or absence of direct regional elections. Values reflect the situation in 1990. I allocate values to top officials according to their home country.

	Constitutional federalism (0–4)	Special territorial autonomy (0–2)	Role of regions in central goverment (0–4)	Regional elections (0–2)	Summary score (0–12)
Austria	4	0	2	2	8
Belgium/Lux	3	1	2	1	7
Denmark	0	1	0	0	1
Finland	0	1	0	0	1
France	2	0.5	0	2	4.5
Germany	4	0	4	2	10
Greece	0	0	0	0	0
Ireland	0	0	0	0	0
Italy	2	0	0	2	4
Netherlands	1	0	0	2	3
Portugal	1	1	0	0	2
Spain	3	2	0	2	7
Sweden	0	0	0	0	0
United Kingdom	1	0	0	0	1

Country Size

I use the population size of the country of origin of each senior Commission official. Values are expressed in millions.

Corporatism

This is based on an index of corporatism developed by Markus Crepaz for the early 1990s, which relies on twelve judgments made by experts attempting to quantify corporatism (Crepaz 1992). Crepaz does not include Portugal, Spain, and Greece, and so I add my own estimates for these countries separately. I transpose Crepaz' standardized scores into rankings, whereby the most corporatist EU member state has a value of 14 and the least corporatist a value of 1. Countries in descending extent of corporatism: Austria, Sweden, the Netherlands, Denmark, Germany, Finland, Belgium, Ireland, Portugal, Spain, France, Italy, Greece, the United Kingdom.

Capitalism

This is a four-category ranking reflecting a decreasing degree of non-market coordination in the economy (Kitschelt et al. 1999; Soskice 1999; for Southern Europe: Esping-Andersen 1999; Rhodes and van Apeldoorn

1997). The four categories consist of national coordinated market economies (CME) (value 4: Scandinavian countries), sectoral CME (3: Germany, Austria and Benelux), partial CME or family-oriented CME (2: France, Italy, Spain, Greece, and Portugal), and liberal ME (1: Ireland and the UK).

Party Identification

This variable consists of a set of dummies for the main party families: *Socialist, Christian Democrat, Conservative,* and *Liberal.* To model a generational effect I add interaction terms consisting of a generation dummy with three of the four party family dummies: *Young_Socialist, Young_Christ Democrat,* and *Young_Liberal.* A top official scores a value of 1 for *Young_Socialist* if he is socialist and born in 1940 or later. *Source:* self-reporting by officials during interview.

Age

Age of each official in 1996, the mid-point of the interview period. *Source:* biographical data and interviews.

Power-DG

This is a composite index of two formal measures of Commission discretion or power and one reputational measure. I employ two formal indicators collected by Edward Page (1997). Page measures three types of secondary legislative activity by the Commission: regulations, directives, and decisions that require Council approval; regulations, directives, and decisions that do not require Council approval; initiation of European Court of Justice cases by the Commission. The last two indicate the extent to which the Commission has discretion to make rules or make others comply with EU rules. As there are no official statistics on legislative output per DG, Page uses keywords (author; form; year; subject) to scan the Justis CD-Rom for legislation over the period 1980–94 (over 30,000 pieces), and allocates output to the DG that is the most plausible author. I did a manual recount for 1980–94 for some policy areas, and arrived at a comparable breakdown. Amendments to Page's data pertain to DGs created since 1994. So the first indicator concerns regulatory Commission output as a proportion of total legislative output: a value of 1 if 1–20 percent, 2 for 21–40 percent, 3 for 41–60 percent, 4 for 61–80 percent, and 5 for 81–100 percent. The second formal indicator concerns autonomy in adjudication, which is based on the absolute number of Court cases initiated by a DG: a value of 0 when no cases, 1 if fewer than fifty cases, and 2 if fifty or more cases. *Sources:* Page (1997); European Commission (n.d.).

For the reputational indicator, I use a question posed to the interviewed top officials, which asks them to name the three or four most powerful DGs or services in the Commission at the time of the interview. DGs with a high reputation (mentioned by 50 percent or more) obtain a value of 2, those with a medium reputation (mentioned by 5–49 percent) 1, and the remainder 0. I then add up the scores for these three indicators to create Power-DG. Values range between 1 and 9. I allocate scores to officials depending on the DG they work for at the time of the interview. *Source:* biographical data and interviews.

Services	Value
DG VI	9
DG IV	8
DG XVI	7
DG V, III	6
DG I, VIII, X, XI, XIV, XV, XXI	5
DG IX, Ia, SG, VII, XX	4
DG XVIII, Spokesperson, Ib, II, XXIV	3
DG XIII, XIX, XXII, XXIII	2
DG XII	1

ERC-DG

A dummy that takes a value of 1 for officials who work in an ERC-friendly DG (see above) at the time of the interview.

Admin/Management-DG

A dummy that takes a value of 1 for officials in DGs with tasks that are primarily routine administration, implementation, or adjudication. This is consistent with the definition of managerial roles by Edward Page (1997). I categorize as Admin/Management DGs: administrative services in the Commission (DG IX, XIX, and XX); heavily implementation-oriented services (DG VI, VIII, XIV, and XVI), and adjudication services (DG IV, XV, and XXI). All other DGs are categorized as predominantly initiative-oriented services. *Source:* biographical data and interviews.

Soft-DG

A dummy that takes a value of 1 for officials who work in a DG concerned with policy areas that use most frequently benchmarking, soft law, peer group pressure, technical reporting, and other soft policy instruments. EU case studies have identified the use of these policy instruments primarily in the socio-cultural area. I categorize as Soft-DGs: DG V, VIII, X, XI, XII, XXII, and XXIV. *Source:* biographical data and interviews.

National Economic Benefit

I use EU structural intervention for 1994–9 as a percentage of GDP in 1994 prices for each member state. *Source:* European Commission, *First Report on Economic and Social Cohesion 1996* (Brussels: DG XVI, 1996, 144, table 24). EU structural intervention (structural funds and cohesion fund) represents 0.51 percent of EU GDP for this period. Four cohesion countries receive a higher proportion: Portugal (3.98%), Greece (3.67%), Ireland (2.82%), and Spain (1.74%). I allocate scores to officials by nationality.

National Quota

I use as indicator the number of votes in the Council of Ministers for officials' country of origin, which is the proxy for estimating the national

	National economic benefit (% GDP)	National quota
Austria	0.19	4
Belgium	0.18	5
Denmark	0.10	3
Finland	0.40	3
France	0.22	10
Germany	0.21	10
Greece	3.67	5
Ireland	2.82	3
Italy	0.42	10
Luxembourg	0.15	2
Netherlands	0.15	5
Portugal	3.98	5
Spain	1.74	8
Sweden	0.37	4
United Kingdom	0.25	10

quota of Commission jobs. The variable ranges between 2 and 10. I allocate scores to officials by nationality.

National Clubness

This is an index composed of assessments on three indicators. First, strong cultural cohesion is characteristic of the Austrian, Dutch, Irish, Portuguese, and three Scandinavian nationalities (Abélès, Bellier, and McDonald 1993). The Irish in particular have a strong reputation in Brussels for social networking. Second, the organizational and financial resources of the French, British, German, and to a lesser extent the Spanish and Italian communities are greater than those of any other nationality. The wealthier, Northern communities are usually able to mobilize more resources than those from Southern Europe. Third, clubness can be promoted by intentional national policy. One indicator is direct national intervention. This can happen through the government; this is particularly strong for the French, British, German, and Spanish. French and British governments/civil services closely monitor personnel policy in the Commission and consider postings in Brussels as an integral part of the training for their best and brightest (Lequesne 1993). For the French, this is part of a more general policy to organize French citizens scattered over European and international institutions. Another route is via party-political connections. This is an important channel for German officials. National political parties tend to divide senior German posts in Brussels among themselves – in line with domestic practice. Party connections are also important for the Irish, the Austrians, and to some extent the Finnish. For Spaniards, national and party-political channels sometimes work at cross-purposes, which explains the medium score for Spain. Proactive governmental or party-political lobbying is much less prominent for the Dutch, Scandinavians, and to a lesser extent the Portuguese, largely because the merit-focused culture of these countries creates the perception that such networking strategies are inappropriate. The three remaining nationalities score low. In the Greek case, this is largely due to the ineffectiveness of government or party-political intervention. Belgians and Italians tend to display alienation from their clientelistic home base (interviews). A final indicator of national clubness is the extent to which Commission cabinets give priority to the career concerns of their compatriots. For senior appointments, commissioners of the relevant nationality are usually consulted, but some take such consultation more seriously than others. As a pointer to the importance attached to personnel issues, I have coded the number

	Community cohesion	Organizational resources	Government/ party policy	Cabinet resources	Summary
Austria	Strong	Medium	Strong	Very low	Strong
Belgium	Weak	Weak	Weak	Low	Weak
Denmark	Strong	Medium	Medium	Very low	Medium
Finland	Strong	Medium	Medium	Very low	Medium
France	Medium	Strong	Strong	High	Strong
Germany	Weak	Strong	Strong	Very high	Strong
Greece	Weak	Weak	Weak	Very low	Weak
Ireland	Strong	Medium	Strong	High	Strong
Italy	Weak	Medium	Weak	High	Weak
Luxembourg	Medium	Weak	Medium	Low	Medium
Netherlands	Strong	Medium	Medium	Low	Medium
Portugal	Strong	Weak	Medium	High	Medium
Spain	Medium	Medium	Medium	High	Medium
Sweden	Strong	Medium	Medium	Very high	Strong
United Kingdom	Weak	Strong	Strong	Very high	Strong

and rank of those responsible for personnel in each commissioner's cabinet under the Santer Commission. German, Swedish, and British cabinets devote most resources; followed by French, Italian, Irish, Portuguese, and Spanish cabinets; then by Belgian, Dutch, and Luxembourg cabinets; and finally by Austrian, Danish, Greek, and Finnish cabinets. *Source:* American Chamber of Commerce in Belgium, *EU Information Handbook* (Brussels, 1997). On the basis of these four streams of evidence, I divide the nationalities into three categories: weak clubness (Belgians, Greeks, Italians); medium clubness (Danish, Dutch, Finnish, Luxemburgers, Portuguese, Spanish); and strong clubness (Austrians, British, French, Germans, Irish, and Swedish). I allocate scores to officials by nationality.

Parachutage

A dummy that takes a value of 1 for officials who were appointed from outside the Commission into an A1 or A2 position. *Source:* biographical data and interviews.

Delors Factor

A dummy that takes a value of 1 for officials recruited to top positions during 1986–94, and a value of 0 for those appointed before or after.

Jacques Delors was in office from January 1985 through December 1994, though he was losing influence by 1993. One must also allow for time lags between the recruitment of officials and the start of the job. So I take 1986 as the starting date and the end of 1994 as a cut-off point. *Source:* biographical data and interviews.

Appendix III: Survey material

1. BIOGRAPHICAL PREPARATION SHEET
2. HOME QUESTIONNAIRE
3. INTERVIEW QUESTIONNAIRE

1.   Biographical Preparation Sheet

NAME: .... **CURRENT POSITION:** ....
Interview number: ....**Date of interview:** ....

1. **Country of origin:** ....
2. **Date of birth:** ....
3. **Education**
   Main degree
   0 Non-university (Bach Ms)
   1 Law-economics-politics
   2 Arts: ....
   3 Sciences: ....
   International university education
   0 None
   1 Other European institutes: ....
   2 North America: ....
   3 Europe and North America: ....
   4 Other
4. **Finish education/start career:** ....
5. **Date of entrance in EU:** ....
6. **Basis of recruitment**
   0 Internal recruitment (exam)
   1 External recruitment
   2 Enlargement fast track
   3 Pre-1965
7. **Career before entrance (1 = first half of career/ 2,3 = second half of career) Dates**
   1...................................
   2...................................
   3...................................
8. **CEC cabinet experience: NO**
   YES: ....
   ....
   ....
9. **Start of current job:** ....
10. **Previous positions in EU administration**
    of which leading (deputy head of unit and higher)
    1..
    2..
    3..
    4..

2.   Home Questionnaire

I.   Activities of Senior Commission Officials

1. We would like to know how often you meet in person the following positions in a *typical month* of your work year.

	Daily	Several times a week	Weekly	1–2 times a month	Less than once a month	
Your Commissioner						
Members of her/his Cabinet						
Commission President or his cabinet						
Other DGs, deputy DGs, or directors collectively						
Other DG, deputy or director individually						
Own service: collective meetings DG, deputies, directors						
Own service: DG, deputy or director individually						
Chefs d'unité collectively						
Chef d'unité individually						
A8–A5 officials individually						
European Parliament						
Council of Ministers						
Coreper/Council working group						
Committee of Regions and/or ECOSOC						
National minister						
Regional minister						
National civil servants						
Regional civil servants						
Regional offices in Brussels						
Trade unions						% European: % National:
Industry						% European: % National:
Environmental, consumer groups						% European: % National:
Press						

2. We would like to ask you to complete the table below. This refers to time spent in a *typical month* on various duties. Please indicate roughly *how many hours* or *% of your time* (whatever is more convenient) you are able to spend on each activity.

Time in Brussels	
Time outside Brussels	

Time in Brussels

Organization, planning and supervision of work, coordination in own DG	
Personnel management	
Preparation of documents for a higher authority	
Promotion of new ideas and policies	
Negotiation of normative acts with Council or Parliament	
Solving implementation problems with member states etc.	
Coordination with other DG's	
PR relations with people or bodies outside the Commission	
Other:	

Time outside Brussels

Negotiation of normative acts with Council or Parliament	
Solving implementation problems	
Promotion of new ideas and policies	
PR relations with people or bodies outside the commission	
Other:	

II.   Please express your opinions on the following statements by circling the appropriate symbol.

"Yes" (++)   *means – I agree without reservation*
"Yes, but…" (+)   *means – I agree, but with reservation*
"No, but…" (−)   *means – I disagree, but with reservation*
"No" (−−)   *means – I disagree without reservation*

	Yes	Yes, but	No, but	No
1 Commission civil servants should be prepared to risk a battle if they want to get things done.	++	+	−	− −
2 Senior civil servants should set aside strong personal convictions for the sake of a united position of the Commission.	++	+	−	− −
3 Europe should be more than a common market.	++	+	−	− −
4 A passable compromise is always better than a stand-off between two brilliant plans.	++	+	−	− −
5 It is imperative that the European Commission become the true government of the European Union.	++	+	−	− −
6 Great ideological principles never provide answers to the problems of Europe's citizens.	++	+	−	− −
7 European Union policy is too much influenced by big business.	++	+	−	− −
8 Commission civil servants should carry out the plans of the Commission president and his equipe with absolute loyalty.	++	+	−	− −
9 There are too many politicians with grand ambitions, and too few policy makers with valuable expertise in the Commission.	++	+	−	− −
10 A Commission which tolerates this much infighting among its staff will eventually destroy itself.	++	+	−	− −
11 The role of the Commission is to practice the art of the possible, not of designing grand ideals and plans.	++	+	−	− −
12 The Commission should hire fewer economists and lawyers, and more specialists in policy areas.	++	+	−	− −
13 The best advice on a proposed policy usually comes from the interests directly affected.	++	+	−	− −

continue

	Yes	Yes, but	No, but	No
14 The strength of Europe lies not in more power for Brussels, but in effective government at the lowest possible level.	++	+	−	− −
15 To get things done, it is often necessary for a senior civil servant to bend procedural conventions and informal rules.	++	+	−	− −
16 The Commission should concentrate on administering things efficiently.	++	+	−	− −
17 The Commission should support the European Parliament's bid for full legislative powers, even if the price would be to lose its monopoly of initiative.	++	+	−	− −
18 Senior civil servants should be willing to express their ideological convictions, even if they risk conflict with their colleagues.	++	+	−	− −
19 The Commission cannot function properly without a vision, a set of great priorities, a blueprint for the future.	++	+	−	− −
20 Too many Commission civil servants let their nationality interfere in their professional judgments.	++	+	−	− −
21 No united Europe without a mature European cohesion policy.	++	+	−	− −
22 The member states, not the Commission nor the European Parliament, ought to remain the central pillars of the European Union.	++	+	−	− −
23 I don't mind a politician's methods if he manages to get the right things done.	++	+	−	− −

continue

	Yes	Yes, but	No, but	No
24 It is usually best to stick to one's own opinions even though many other people may have a different point of view.	++	+	–	– –
25 The egoistic behaviour of some member states threatens the very survival of the European project.	++	+	–	– –
26 The Commission acts too much as an administration, and not enough as the government of Europe.	++	+	-	–
27 Rather than producing press releases or travelling through Europe on promotion campaigns, Commission civil servants had better get on with their work in quietude.	++	+	-	–
28 The Commission should concentrate on maintaining the internal market.	++	+	–	– –
29 Pressure groups and special interests, like trade unions, farmers' organizations, industry, environmental lobbyists, and so on, disturb the proper working of European government.	++	+	–	– –
30 It hurts the Commission's legitimacy that certain DGs tend to be dominated by particular nationalities, such as agriculture by the French, competition by the Germans, regional policy by the Spanish, environment by the north...	++	+	–	– –
31 The highly legalistic approach in many Commission services is very detrimental to innovative policy making.	++	+	–	– –
32 Europe has developed a unique model of society, and the Commission should help to preserve it: extensive social services, civilized industrial relations, negotiated transfers among groups to sustain solidarity, and steer economic activity for the general welfare.	++	+	–	– –

Do you have further comments?

Your comments on the questionnaire?

Thank you very much for your time. We guarantee of course absolute anonimity.

Could you please send this questionnaire to:
Prof Liesbet Hooghe
University of Toronto
Department of Political Science
100 St. George Street
Toronto M5S 1A1
Canada   Or: Fax 1-416-978 5566

3.   Interview Questionnaire

Interview number:......
target: 45–60 minutes

I. *One of the things we are most interested in is how European civil servants first became involved in European political life (rather than national life) [keep this very short].*

What was the most important reason for your interest in European affairs? What is your earliest recollection of being interested? [age]

Why did you decide to come to the Commission?

Before you came to Brussels – were you active in organizations supporting or contesting European integration (European movement, Bruges group etc.)? Are you still active now?

Have you been active in local or national politics? Are you still active now?

Now I would like to ask you about life as a senior civil servant in the Commission.
II. You came with your own policy plans, ideas ... to this job as a senior civil servant of the European Commission. Now in the first weeks, did you feel you would be able to pursue those goals, or did you feel constrained?
> Not at all constrained
> Constrained to a minor extent
> Constrained
> Heavily constrained

Which two of the following constraints did you experience most strongly in those early weeks:
> Your Commissioner
> Commission president or his cabinet
> Other DGs
> Your staff in your own DG
> Member states
> Organized interests
> Other:

Have you changed your opinion since then?
    No
    Yes – Which two now? . . . .

a   External appointments
You have probably a vivid recollection of your first weeks in the Commission. What are, briefly, your one or two most memorable experiences about starting to work in the Commission? What struck you as "typical Commission"?

b   Internal promotions: check whether promoted in new policy area
Your promotion to an A1-A2 civil servant carried new responsibilities. Did you experience this as a quite different job from your previous one, or was the difference not so big? (If the former): Could you recall one or two experiences from the first weeks which illustrate the difference?

1.

2.

III. Thinking about your role as a senior civil servant in the Commission, what would you say are the two or three most important duties and responsibilities involved?

1.

2.

3.

What do you consider to be the specific contribution of your work as a senior Commission civil servant to the government of the European Union [distinct from that of the Council, the political Commission, the European Parliament...]? What is within your power to make the government of the European Union work?

What is the one thing you would miss most if you left the Commission?

IV. What single achievement are you proudest of?

Is there another achievement which you recall with particular satisfaction? [keep very brief]

V. Here is a list with tasks a number of senior civil servants have set themselves. [Form A] Could you rank them in order of your priorities [you may want to scrap one or two]?

> Mediate conflicts in the Council, between Council and Parliament
> Identify new policy problems and devise new policies
> Defend the Commission's prerogatives vis-à-vis Council and
>   Parliament
> Fight public interventionism and overregulation
> Provide expertise in a specific policy area
> Combat pure market ideology and promote social values
> Respect divergent national interests and be accessible for fellow
>   nationals
> Promote a positive working environment in the DG

VI. *Can we turn from your personal activities and talk about the Commission as an organization: the functioning of the civil service, its relationship with the political Commission, with other institutions and actors?*

VI.1 Some people claim that divisions between DGs often weaken the Commission in its dealings with other institutions; others argue that the Commission is usually very good at presenting a united front vis-à-vis the Council, Parliament etc.

-Which side is closer to reality?

>   Divisions   United front

-What about your opinion? Would you like to see more or less of a united front on the Commission's part?

> More united front
> Less united front
> About the same

-What about the role of the Commission Secretariat?

-And the meetings of the chefs de cabinet?

-Do you expect an effect on the autonomy of your DG of the new Santer formula – groups of Commissioners, eg for transport, external affairs, economic and social cohesion?

VI.2. Some people claim that the Commission is very hierarchical, discouraging initiative from lower-ranking officials and making collaboration between individuals, units, and DGs difficult; others argue that the Commission is much more flexible than national administrations, rewarding people with innovative policy ideas.

-Which side is closer to reality?

      Hierarchical, not innovative   Flexible, innovative

-Should the brightest policy innovators, whatever their level of seniority, get more space (and better career prospects), you think, or are you against fast-track, special arrangements for a small number of people?

      More space for policy innovators
      Less space
      About the same

-Should there be more horizontal links in and between DGs to help coordination? Was the practice, encouraged under Delors, of standing and ad hoc committees (inter-service meetings), task forces, project groups a good idea? Example of success or disaster?

-How do you, in practice, try to optimalize coordination in your DG?

VI.3. Some people claim that several DGs are dominated by particular nationalities or groups of countries; others say there is no problem of national capture.

-Which side is closer to reality?

      National capture   No national capture

-Do you think that the Commission should pay more attention to the risks of national capture?

-What is your opinion on secondment formulae?

Totally negative
Rather negative
Positive within limits (temporary solution, limited to %)
Very positive

-On the senior appointments, do you find the March 1993 ruling by the Court of First Instance a wise or a dangerous precedent? The ruling annulled the appointments of two directors at A2 level in DG XIV on the grounds that the applicants were chosen not because of their qualifications but because the countries from which they came (Italy and Spain) were owed the jobs.

Wise   Dangerous

-What about other forms of capture? By big industry, the unions, agro-industry...

VI.4. Some people argue that partisan politics is quite important in the civil service, with some DGs pro-market, and others sympathetic to social-democratic ideals; others consider the Commission as above partisan politics.

-Which side is closer to reality?

Partisan   Above party politics

-Should the Commission try harder to stand above party politics and ideology, and stick to its technical duties, in your opinion?

Try harder
Try less hard
About the same

VI.5. As in national administrations, DGs have quite different reputations.

-Which would be the three to four most powerful DGs in 1995, you think? Which two or three are the weakest in your opinion?

1.

2.

3.

-Is your current rank ordering different from, say, five years ago?

-Is there a particular "rising star"?

-And in terms of efficiency and efficacy, which two to three do you find best?

1.

2.

3.

VII. What are, for you, very briefly, the two or three most important problems facing the European Union today?

1.

2.

3.

Would you have mentioned those same problems when you started this position in the Commission?

VIII. Let's talk for a moment about ... (most important problem which has directly to do with EU) [keep to five–seven minutes].

VIII.1. What do you think are the main sources or causes of this problem?

VIII.2. Briefly, what can be done about this problem in your view?

VIII.3. What, you think, could the European Union do better than national governments on this problem? What could the Commission do in particular?

VIII.4. Is that what most decision makers think, or do you hold a minority view? [Let him name the other parties: colleagues, political Commission, member states, other European institutions, interest groups, public...] Would you be prepared to compromise between the position of the other parties and your own?

VIII.5. Tell me, since you have been in your current position as a senior Commission civil servant, are there any groups or organizations outside the Commission whose views help you to think about this problem, whose views you value?
[Probe: Are there any others?]

-What about? [If not mentioned]

      National governments
      Industry (European Round Table ...)
      European Parliament
      Trade unions
      Social movements (Greenpeace, WWF ...)
      Academia/independent think tanks

VIII.6. If you had the power to take the decisions, would you consult with the various groups involved, or do what you think best?

      Definitely consult.
      Consult, but go ahead.
      Definitely go right ahead.

IX. And finally your own plans? Do you expect to round off your professional career in your current position in the European Commission?

Yes   No   Don't know   No reply

If no:
Are there any further positions in the Commission/European institutions you would like to seek some time in the future? [Eg. Change to another DG, become DG, stand for European Parliament, become political Commissioner, European chef de cabinet, national minister for European Affairs, etc etc.]

If no:
-Do you have plans to move on to functions outside European politics? National politics, national administration, international organizations, private sector, corporate organizations, academia?

-Have you been approached for this position?

Thank you for your time.

References

Abélès, Marc, and Irène Bellier. 1996. "La Commission européenne: du compromis culturel à la culture politique du compromis." *Revue Française de Science Politique* 46: 431–56.

Abélès, Marc, Irène Bellier, and Maryon McDonald. 1993. "Approche anthropologique de la Commission européenne." Brussels: Report for the European Commission (unpublished).

Aberbach, Joel, and Bert Rockman. 1998 "Image IV Revisited – Executive and Political Roles." *Governance* 1: 1–25.

1995. "The Political Views of U.S. Senior Federal Executives, 1970–1992." *Journal of Politics* 57: 838–52.

Aberbach, Joel, Bert Rockman, and Robert Putnam, eds. 1981. *Bureaucrats and Politicians in Western Democracies.* Cambridge, MA: Harvard University Press.

Albert, Michel. 1993. *Capitalism against Capitalism.* London: Whurr Publishers.

Allison, Graham. 1969. "Conceptual Models and the Cuban Missile Crisis." *American Political Science Review* 63: 689–718.

Almond, Gabriel A. 1956. "Comparative Political Systems." *Journal of Politics* 18: 391–409.

Anderson, Benedict. 1983. *Imagined Communities: Reflections on the Origins and Spread of Nationalism.* London: Verso.

Anderson, Christopher J. 1998. "When in Doubt, Use Proxies. Attitudes toward Domestic Politics and Support for European Integration." *Comparative Political Studies* 31: 569–601.

Anderson, Christopher J., and Matthew Gabel. 2000. "The Structure of Citizen Attitudes and the European Political Space." In: Gary Marks and Marco Steenbergen, eds. "Dimensions of Contestation in the European Union." Unpublished ms.

Anderson, Jeffrey. 1995. "The State of the (European) Union: From the Single Market to Maastricht, from Singular Events to General Theories." *World Politics* 47: 441–65.

1999. "European Integration and Political Convergence since Maastricht: the View from the Member States." Paper presented at the European Community Studies Association's Sixth Biennial International Conference, Pittsburgh, June 2–5.

Ansell, Christopher K., Craig Parsons, and Keith Darden. 1997. "Dual Networks in European Regional Development Policy." *Journal of Common Market Studies* 35: 347–75.

Aspinwall, Mark, and Gerald Schneider. 2000. "Same Menu, Separate Tables: the Institutionalist Turn in Political Science and the Study of European Integration." *European Journal of Political Research* 38: 1–36.

Bache, Ian. 1998. *The Politics of European Union Regional Policy.* Sheffield: Sheffield Academic Press.

Bawn, Kathleen. 1995. "Political Control versus Expertise: Congressional Choices about Administrative Procedures." *American Political Science Review* 89: 62–73.

Beck, Paul, and M. Kent Jennings. 1991. "Family Traditions, Political Periods, and the Development of Partisan Orientation." *Journal of Politics* 53: 742–63.

Bellier, Irène, 1995. "Une culture de la Commission européenne? De la rencontre des cultures et du multilinguisme des fonctionnaires." In: Yves Mény, Pierre Muller, J.-L. Quermonne, eds. *Politiques publiques en Europe.* Paris: L'Harmattan, 49–60.

Bendor, Jonathan, and Thomas H. Hammond. 1992. "Rethinking Allison's Models." *American Political Science Review* 86: 301–22.

Beyers, Jan, and Guido Dierickx. 1997. "Nationality and European Negotiations: the Working Groups of the Council of Ministers." *European Journal of International Relations,* 3: 435–71.

Biersteker, Thomas J. 1999. "Locating the Emerging European Polity: beyond States or State?" In Jeffrey Anderson, ed. *Regional Integration and Democracy: Expanding on the European Experience.* Boulder, CO: Rowman & Littlefield, 21–44.

Blais, André, and Stéphane Dion, eds. 1991. *The Budget-Maximizing Bureaucrat: Appraisals and Evidence.* Pittsburgh, PA: University of Pittsburgh Press.

Boissieu, Christian de, and Jean Pisani-Ferry. 1998. "The Political Economy of French Economic Policy in the Perspective of EMU." In: Barry Eichengreen and Jeffry Frieden, eds. *Forging an Integrated Europe.* Ann Arbor: University of Michigan, 49–89.

Bomberg, Elizabeth. 1998. *Green Parties and Politics in the European Union.* London: Routledge.

Bornschier, Volker, ed. 2000. *State-Building in Europe: The Revitalization of Western European Integration.* Cambridge: Cambridge University Press.

Börzel, Tanja. 1997. "Policy Networks: A New Paradigm for European Governance." Robert Schuman Working Papers, RSC 97/19.

Börzel, Tanja A., and Thomas Risse. 2000. "Who Is Afraid of a European Federation? How to Constitutionalize a Multi-Level Governance System?" In: Christian Jörges, Yves Mény, and J. H. H. Weiler, eds. *What Kind of Constitution for What Kind of Polity? Responses to Joschka Fischer.* Florence: European University Institute, Robert Schuman Centre, 45–59.

Bourtembourg, C. 1987. "La Commission des Communautés Européennes: Son personnel." In: Sabino Cassese, ed. *The European Administration.* Paris: International Institute of Administrative Sciences.

Brans, Marleen. 1997. "Challenges to the Practice and Theory of Public Administration in Europe." *Journal of Theoretical Politics* 9: 389–415.

Brewer, Gene, and Robert Maranto. 1998. "Comparing the Roles of Political Appointees and Career Executives in the U.S. Federal Executive Branch."

Paper presented at the Annual Meeting of the American Political Science Association, Boston, MA, September 3–6.

Calvert, Randall, Mathew McCubbins, and Barry Weingast. 1989. "A Theory of Political Control and Agency Discretion." *American Journal of Political Science* 33: 588–611.

Cameron, David R. 1997. "Economic and Monetary Union: Underlying Imperatives and Third-Stage Dilemmas." *Journal of European Public Policy* 4: 455–85.

1998. "Creating Supranational Authority in Monetary and Exchange-Rate Policy: the Sources and Effects of EMU." In: Wayne Sandholtz and Alec Stone Sweet, eds. *European Integration and Supranational Governance.* Oxford: Oxford University Press, 188–216.

Campbell, Colin. 1995. "Does Reinvention Need Reinvention?" *Governance* 8: 479–504.

Campbell, Colin, and Guy B. Peters. 1988. "The Politics/Administration Dichotomy: Death or Merely Change?" *Governance* 1: 79–99.

Caporaso, James. 1996. "The European Union and Forms of State: Westphalian, Regulatory or Post-Modern?" *Journal of Common Market Studies* 34: 29–52.

Checkel, Jeffrey. 1998. "The Constructivist Turn in International Relations Theory." *World Politics* 50: 324–48.

Chong, Dennis. 1996. "Values versus Interests in the Explanation of Social Conflict." *University of Pennsylvania Law Review* 144: 2079–134.

2000. *Rational Lives: Norms and Values in Politics and Society.* Chicago: University of Chicago Press.

Christensen, Dag Arne. 1996. "The Left-Wing Opposition in Denmark, Norway, and Sweden: Cases of Europhobia?" *West European Politics* 19: 526–46.

Christensen, Tom. 1991. "Bureaucratic Roles: Political Loyalty and Professional Autonomy." *Scandinavian Political Studies* 14: 303–20.

Christoph, James. 1993. "The Effects of Britons in Brussels: the European Community and the Culture of Whitehall." *Governance* 6: 518–37.

Chryssochoou, Dimitris. 1998. *Democracy in the European Union.* London and New York: Tauris Academic Studies.

Cini, Michelle. 1996. *The European Commission: Leadership, Organisation and Culture in the Commission.* Manchester: Manchester University Press.

Claude, Inis L.J. 1956. *Swords into Plowshares: The Problems and Progress of International Organization.* London: University of London Press.

Cocks, Peter. 1980. "Towards a Marxist Theory of European Integration." *International Organization* 34: 1–30.

Coen, David. 1997. "The Evolution of the Large Firm as a Political Actor in the European Union." *Journal of European Public Policy* 4: 91–108.

Coleman, William. 1998. "From Protected Development to Market Liberalism: Paradigm Change in Agriculture." *European Journal of Public Policy* 5: 632–51.

Collier, David, and James E. Mahon. 1993. "Conceptual 'Stretching' Revisited: Adapting Categories in Comparative Analysis." *American Political Science Review* 87: 845–55.

Committee of Independent Experts.1999. *First Report [to the European Parliament] on Allegations Regarding Fraud, Mismanagement and Nepotism in the European Commission*, published on March 15 1999 (http://www.europarl. eu.int/experts).

Conover, Pamela Johnston. 1991. "Political Socialization: Where's the Politics?" In: William Crotty, ed. *Political Science: Looking to the Future*, vol. III. Evanston, IL: Northwestern University Press, 125–54.

Conover, Pamela Johnston, and Stanley Feldman. 1984. "How People Organize the Political World: A Schematic Model." *American Journal of Political Science* 28: 95–126.

Converse, Philip E. 1964. "The Nature of Belief Systems in Mass Publics." In: David E. Apter, ed. *Ideology and Discontent*. New York: Free Press of Glencoe, 206–61.

1976. *The Dynamics of Party Support: Cohort-analyzing Party Identification*. Beverly Hills, CA: Sage.

Coombes, David. 1970. *Politics and Bureaucracy in the European Community: A Portrait of the Commission of the E.E.C.* London: George Allen & Unwin.

Cowles-Green, Maria. 1995. "Setting the Agenda for a New Europe: the ERT and EC 1992." *Journal of Common Market Studies* 33: 501–26.

Cox, Robert, and Harold Jacobson. 1973. *The Anatomy of Influence: Decision Making in International Organizations*. New Haven: Yale University Press.

Cox, Robert. 1996. "The Executive Head: an Essay on Leadership in International Organization." In: Robert Cox, with Timothy J. Sinclair, eds. *Approaches to World Order*. Cambridge: Cambridge University Press, 317–48.

Craig, Paul, and Grainne De Burca, eds. 1999. *The Evolution of EU Law*. Oxford: Oxford University Press.

Cram, Laura. 1994. "The European Commission as a Multi-Organization: Social Policy and IT Policy in the EU." *Journal of European Public Policy* 1: 195–217.

1997. *Policy Making in the EU: Conceptual Lenses and the Integration Process*. London: Routledge.

Crepaz, Markus. 1992. "Corporatism in Decline? An Empirical Analysis of the Impact of Corporatism on Macro-Economic Performance and Industrial Disputes in 18 Industrialized Democracies." *Comparative Political Studies* 25: 139–68.

Crouch, Colin, and Wolfgang Streeck. 1997. "The Future of Capitalism Diversity." In: Colin Crouch and Wolfgang Streeck, eds. *Political Economy of Modern Capitalism: Mapping Convergence and Diversity*, London: Sage, 1–19.

Dahl, Robert. 1999. "Can International Organizations be Democratic? A Skeptic's View." In: Ian Shapiro and Casiano Hacker-Cordon, eds. *Democracy's Edges*. Cambridge: Cambridge University Press, 19–36.

Dalton, Russell, and Richard Eichenberg. 1998. "Citizen Support for Policy Integration." In: Wayne Sandholtz and Alec Stone Sweet, eds. *European Integration and Supranational Governance*. Oxford: Oxford University Press, 250–82.

Dargie, Charlotte, and Rachel Locke. 1999. "The British Senior Civil Service." In: Edward C. Page and Vincent Wright, eds. *Bureaucratic Elites in Western European States: A Comparative Analysis of Top Officials*. Oxford: Oxford University Press, 178–204.

Dehousse, Renaud. 1992. "Integration v. Regulation? On the Dynamics of Regulation in the European Community." *Journal of Common Market Studies* 30: 383–402.

——— 1995. "Institutional Reform in the European Community: Are There Alternatives to the Majority Avenue?" *West European Politics* 18: 118–36.

——— 1997. "Regulation by Networks in the European Community: The Role of European Agencies." *Journal of European Public Policy* 4: 246–61.

Delors, Jacques. 1992. *Our Europe. The Community and National Development.* Translated from the French. London: Verso.

Derlien, Hans-Ulrich. 1994. "Karrieren, Tätigkeitsprofil und Rollenverständnis der Spitzenbeamten des Bundes: Konstanz und Wandel." *Verwaltung und Fortbildung* 22: 255–74.

——— 1998. "The German Bureaucratic Elite and Their Political Masters: Information Flow and Mutual Role Expectations." Paper presented at the Annual Meeting of the American Political Science Association, September 3–6.

Deutsch, Karl, et al. 1957. *Political Community: North-Atlantic Area.* New York: Greenwood Press.

Dierickx, Guido. 1998. "De Euro-Belgische ambtenaren. Een paradoxale prestatie." *Res publica* 40: 219–29.

Dierickx, Guido, and Jan Beyers. 1999. "Belgian Civil Servants in the European Union. A Tale of Two Cultures." *West European Politics* 22: 198–222.

Dierickx, Guido, and Philippe Majersdorf. 1993. *La culture politique des fonctionnaires et des hommes politiques en Belgique.* Brugge: Vandenbroele.

Dinan, Desmond. 1994. *Ever Closer Union? An Introduction to the European Community.* London: Macmillan.

——— 1999. "Governance and Institutions: A Transitional Year." In: Geoffrey Edwards and Georg Wiessala, eds. *The European Union: Annual Review 1998/1999.* Oxford: Blackwell Publishers, 37–62.

Dogan, Mattei. 1975. *The Mandarins of Western Europe: the Political Roles of Top Civil Servants.* London: Sage.

Dogan, Mattei, and Dominique Pelassy. 1984. *How to Compare Nations. Strategies in Comparative Politics.* Chatham, NJ: Chatham House Publishers, Inc.

Downs, Anthony. 1967. *Inside Bureaucracy.* Boston: Little, Brown.

Duchêne, François. 1994. *Jean Monnet: the First Statesman of Interdependence.* New York: Norton.

Dunleavy, Patrick. 1991. *Democracy, Bureaucracy and Public Choice: Economic Explanations in Political Science.* London: Harvester Wheatsheaf.

Ebbinghaus, Bernhard. 1999. "The Europeanization of Labour Unions." Paper presented at the Annual Meeting of the American Political Science Association, Atlanta, September 1–5.

Ebbinghaus, Bernhard, and Jelle Visser. 1997. "European Labor and Transnational Solidarity: Challenges, Pathways, and Barriers." In: Jytte Klausen and Louise A. Tilly, eds. *European Integration in Social and Historical Perspective: 1850 to the Present.* Boulder, CO: Rowman & Littlefield, 195–221.

ECSA Forum. 1997. "Does the European Union Represent an *n* of 1?" (James Caporaso, Gary Marks, Andrew Moravcsik, and Mark Pollack). *ECSA Review* 10(3).

Edwards, Geoffrey, and David Spence, eds. 1994. *The European Commission.* London: Cartermill.

Egeberg, Morten. 1995. "Organization and Nationality in the European Commission Services." *Arena Working Paper,* Oslo University, 13/95.

Eijk, Cees van der, and Mark Franklin, eds. 1995. *Choosing Europe? The European Electorate and National Politics in the Face of Union.* Ann Arbor: University of Michigan Press.

Elazar, Daniel. 1987. *Exploring Federalism.* Alabama: University of Alabama Press.

Elster, Jon. 1989. *Solomonic Judgements: Studies in the Limitations of Rationality.* Cambridge: Cambridge University Press.

1990. "When Rationality Fails." In: Karen Schweers Cook and Margaret Levi, eds. *The Limits of Rationality.* Chicago: University of Chicago Press, 19–51.

1994. "Rationality, Emotions, and Social Norms." *Synthese* 98: 21–49.

Ertman, Thomas. 1997. *Birth of the Leviathan: Building States and Regimes in Medieval and Early Modern Europe.* Cambridge: Cambridge University Press.

Esping-Andersen, Gøsta. 1999. "Politics without Class: Postindustrial Cleavages in Europe and America." In: Herbert Kitschelt, Peter Lange, Gary Marks, and John Stephens, eds. *Continuity and Change in Contemporary Capitalism.* Cambridge: Cambridge University Press, 293–316.

European Commission. 1996. *Top Decision Makers Survey: Summary Report.* Brussels: Directorate-General X.

1997. *Eurobarometer 46.* Brussels: Directorate-General X.

n.d. [2000]. *The European Union: A View from the Top. Top Decision Makers and the European Union.* Waver: EOS Gallup, Europe.

n.d. *Directory of EU Legislation in Force until Dec. 1994.* Brussels: European Commission, CD-Rom.

Falkner, Gerda. 1996. "The Maastricht Protocol on Social Policy: Theory and Practice." *Journal of European Social Policy* 6: 1–16.

1998. *EU Social Policy in the 1990s: Towards a Corporatist Policy Community.* New York: Routledge.

1999. "Corporatism, Pluralism and European Integration: the Impact on National Interest Intermediation." Paper presented at the 6th Biennial Conference of the European Community Studies Association, Pittsburgh, June 2–5.

Featherstone, Kevin. 1988. *Socialist Parties and European Integration: a Comparative History.* Manchester: Manchester University Press.

Feld, Scott L., and Bernard Grofman. 1988. "Ideological Consistency as a Collective Phenomenon." *American Political Science Review* 82: 773–88.

Feldman, Stanley. 1988. "Structure and Consistency in Public Opinion: the Role of Core Beliefs and Values." *American Journal of Political Science* 32: 416–40.

Financial Times, January 7, 1999. "Whistle-blowing."

Fioretos, Karl-Orfeo. 1998. "Anchoring Adjustment: Globalization, Varieties of Capitalism, and the Domestic Sources of Multilateralism." Ph.D. thesis defended at Columbia University, Department of Political Science.

Franchino, Fabio. 1999. "The Determinants of Control of the Commission's Executive Functions." European Integration Online Papers (EIoP), 3, 2; http://eiop.or.at/eiop/texte/1999-002a.htm.

2000. "Control of the Commission's Executive Functions: Uncertainty, Conflict and Decision Rules." *European Union Politics* 1: 63–92.

Gabel, Matthew. 1998a. "Research Note: the Endurance of Supranational Governance. A Consociational Interpretation of the European Union." *Comparative Politics* 30: 463–75.

1998b. "Public Support for European Integration: an Empirical Test of Five Theories." *Journal of Politics* 60: 333–54.

1998c. *Interests and Integration: Market Liberalization, Public Opinion and European Union.* Ann Arbor: University of Michigan Press.

Gabel, Matthew, and Simon Hix. 2000. "Defining the EU Political Space: an Empirical Study of the European Elections Manifestos, 1979–1999." In: Gary Marks and Marco Steenbergen, eds. "Dimensions of Contestation in the European Union." Unpublished ms.

Garrett, Geoffrey. 1992. "International Cooperation and Institutional Choice: the European Community's Internal Market." *International Organization* 46: 533–60.

Gaulle, Charles de. 1971. *Memoirs of Hope: Renewal, 1958–62; Endeavor, 1962– [Mémoires d'espoir].* Translated by Terence Kilmartin. London: Weidenfeld & Nicolson.

George, Alexander. 1969. "The Operational Code: a Neglected Approach to the Study of Political Leaders and Decision-Making." *International Studies Quarterly* 23: 190–222.

1979. "The Causal Nexus between Cognitive Beliefs and Decision-Making Behavior: the Operational Code." In: L. Falkowski, ed. *Psychological Models in International Politics.* Boulder, CO: Westview Press, 95–124.

Glenn, Norval. 1980. "Values, Attitudes, and Beliefs." In: Orville G. Brim, Jr. and Jerome Kagan, eds. *Constancy and Change in Human Development.* Cambridge, MA: Harvard University Press, 596–640.

Golub, Jonathan. 1996. "State Power and Institutional Influence in European Integration: Lessons from the Packaging Waste Directive." *Journal of Common Market Studies* 34: 313–39.

Gorges, Michael J. 1996. *Euro-Corporatism? Interest Intermediation in the European Union.* New York: University Press of America.

Götz, Klaus H. 1999. "Senior Officials in the German Federal Administration: Institutional Change and Positional Differentiation." In: Edward C. Page and Vincent Wright, eds. *Bureaucratic Elites in Western European States: A Comparative Analysis of Top Officials.* Oxford: Oxford University Press, 147–77.

Grande, Edgar. 2000. "Post-National Democracy in Europe." In: Michael Greven and Louis Pauly, eds. *Democracy beyond the State? The European Dilemma and the Emerging Global Order.* Boulder, CO: Rowman & Littlefield, 115–38.

Grant, Charles. 1994. *Delors: Inside the House that Jacques Built.* London: Nicholas Brealey.

Grant, Wyn. 1997. "BSE and the Politics of Food." In: Patrick Dunleavy, Andrew Gamble, Ian Holliday, and Gillian Peele, eds. *Developments in British Politics.* London: Macmillan.

Greenwood, Justin. 1997. *Representing Interests in the European Union*. London: Macmillan.

Greven, Michael T. 2000. "Can the European Union Finally Become a Democracy?" In: Michael T. Greven and Louis W. Pauly, eds. *Democracy beyond the State? The European Dilemma and the Emerging Global Order*. Boulder, CO: Rowman & Littlefield, 35–61.

Greven, Michael T., and Louis W. Pauly, eds. 2000. *Democracy beyond the State? The European Dilemma and the Emerging Global Order*. Boulder, CO: Rowman & Littlefield.

Grieco, Joseph. 1995. "The Maastricht Treaty, Economic and Monetary Union and the Neorealist Research Programme." *Review of International Studies* 21: 21–40.

Haan, Jakob de, and Sylvester C.W. Eijffinger. 2000. "The Democratic Accountability of the European Central Bank." *Journal of Common Market Studies* 38: 393–408.

Haas, Ernst. 1958. *The Uniting of Europe*. Stanford, CA: Stanford University Press.

1960. "International Integration: the European and the Universal Process." *International Organization* 4: 607–46.

1964. *Beyond the Nation-State: Functionalism and International Organization*. Stanford, CA: Stanford University Press.

1975. *The Obsolescence of Regional Integration Theory*. Berkeley, CA: Institute of International Studies.

Haas, Peter 1992. "Introduction: Epistemic Communities and International Policy Coordination." *International Organization* 46: 1–36.

Hall, Peter 1993. "Policy Paradigms, Social Learning, and the State – The Case of Economic Policymaking in Britain." *Comparative Politics* 25: 275–96.

Hall, Peter, and Rosemary Taylor. 1996. "Political Science and the Three New Institutionalisms." *Political Studies* 44: 936–57.

Hanley, David, ed. 1994. *Christian Democracy in Europe: A Comparative Perspective*. New York: Pinter Publishers.

Hayes-Renshaw, Fiona, and Helen Wallace. 1997. *The Council of Ministers of the European Union*. London: Macmillan.

Held, David. 1991. "Democracy, the Nation-State and the Global System." In: David Held, ed. *Political Theory Today*. Stanford, CA: Stanford University Press, 197–235.

1995. *Democracy and the Global Order: from the Modern State to Cosmopolitan Governance*. Stanford, CA: Stanford University Press.

Héritier, Adrienne. 1996. "The Accommodation of Diversity in European Policy Making and Its Outcomes: Regulatory Policy as a Patchwork." *Journal of European Public Policy* 3: 149–67.

1999a. "Elements of Democratic Legitimation in Europe: an Alternative Perspective." *Journal of European Public Policy* 6: 269–82.

1999b. *Policy-Making and Diversity in Europe: Escaping Deadlock*. Cambridge: Cambridge University Press.

Hix, Simon. 1994. "The Study of the European Community: the Challenge to Comparative Politics." *West European Politics* 17: 1–30.

——— 1998. "The Study of the European Union II: the 'New Governance' Agenda and Its Rival." *Journal of European Public Policy* 5(1): 38–65.

——— 1999. "Dimensions and Alignments in European Union Politics: Cognitive Constraints and Partisan Responses." *European Journal of Political Research* 35(1): 69–106.

Hix, Simon, and Christopher Lord. 1997. *Political Parties in the European Union.* London: Macmillan.

Hoffmann, Stanley. 1966. "Obstinate or Obsolete? The Fate of the Nation State and the Case of Western Europe." *Daedalus* 95: 892–908.

——— 1982. "Reflections on the Nation-State in Western Europe Today." *Journal of Common Market Studies* 21: 21–37.

Hoffmann, Stanley, and Robert Keohane, eds. 1991. *The New European Community: Decisionmaking and Institutional Change.* Boulder, CO: Westview.

Hollis, Martin, and Steve Smith. 1986. "Roles and Reasons in Foreign Policy Decision Making." *British Journal of Political Science* 16: 269–86.

Hood, Christopher. 1998a. "Individualized Contracts for Top Public Servants: Copying Business, Path-dependent Political Re-engineering or Trobriand Cricket?" *Governance* 11: 443–62.

——— 1998b. *The Art of the State: Culture, Rhetoric, and Public Management.* Oxford: Clarendon Press.

Hooghe, Liesbet. 1996. "Building a Europe with the Regions: the Changing Role of the European Commission." In: Liesbet Hooghe, ed. *Cohesion Policy and European Integration: Building Multilevel Governance.* Oxford: Oxford University Press/Clarendon Press, 89–128.

——— 1997. "A House with Differing Views: the European Commission and Cohesion Policy." In: Neill Nugent, ed. *At the Heart of the Union: Studies of the European Commission.* London: Macmillan, 89–108.

——— 1998. "EU Cohesion Policy and Competing Models of European Capitalism." *Journal of Common Market Studies* 36: 457–77.

——— 1999a. "Images of Europe: Orientations to European Integration among Senior Officials of the Commission." *British Journal of Political Science* 29: 345–67.

——— 1999b. "Supranational Activists or Intergovernmental Agents? Explaining Political Orientations of Senior Commission Officials to European Integration." *Comparative Political Studies* 32: 435–63.

Hooghe, Liesbet, and Gary Marks. 1999. "The Making of a Polity: the Struggle over European Integration." In: Herbert Kitschelt, Peter Lange, Gary Marks, and John Stephens, eds. *Continuity and Change in Contemporary Capitalism.* Cambridge: Cambridge University Press, 70–97.

——— 2001. *Multi-level Governance and European Integration.* Boulder, CO: Rowman & Littlefield.

Hooghe, Liesbet, Gary Marks, and Carole Wilson. 2000. "Party Positions on European Integration: New Politics versus Left/Right." In Gary Marks and Marco Steenbergen, eds. "Dimensions of Contestation in the European Union." Unpublished ms.

Höreth, Marcus. 1999. "No Way out of the Beast? The Unsolved Legitimacy Problem of European Governance." *Journal of European Public Policy* 6: 249–68.

Huber, Evelyne, and John D. Stephens. 2001. *Development and Crisis of the Welfare State: Parties and Policies in Global Markets.* Chicago: University of Chicago Press.

Imig, Doug, and Sidney Tarrow. 1997. "From Strike to Euro-Strike: the Europeanization of Social Movements and the Development of a Euro-Polity." Harvard University Weatherhead Center for International Affairs Working Paper, No. 97–10.

    eds. 2001. *Contentious Europeans: Protest and Politics in the New Europe.* Boulder, CO: Rowman & Littlefield.

Inglehart, Ronald. 1967. "An End to European Integration." *American Political Science Review* 6: 91–105.

Ingraham, Patricia W. 1998. "Making Public Policy. The Changing Role of the Higher Civil Service." In: B. Guy Peters and Donald J. Savoie, eds. *Taking Stock: Assessing Public Sector Reforms.* Montreal: McGill-Queen's University, 164–86.

Jachtenfuchs, Markus, and Beate Kohler-Koch. 1995. "Regieren im Dynamischen Mehrebenensystem." In: Markus Jachtenfuchs and Beate Kohler-Koch, eds. *Europäische Integration.* Opladen: Leske & Budrich.

    1997. "The Transformation of Governance in the European Union." Updated version of MZES Working Paper No. 11, http://userpage.fuberlin.de.

Jennings, M. Kent. 1992. "Ideological Thinking among Mass Publics and Political Elites." *Public Opinion Quarterly* 56: 419–41.

Joerges, Christian, Yves Mény, and J.H.H. Weiler, eds. 2000. *What Kind of Constitution for What Kind of Polity? Responses to Joschka Fischer.* Florence: Robert Schuman Centre for Advanced Studies, European University Institute.

Johnston, Iain. 1998. "Socialization in International Institutions: the Asean Way and IR Theory." Paper prepared for a conference on "The Emerging International Relations of East Asia" sponsored by the University of Pennsylvania/Dartmouth College, October.

Kato, Junko. 1996. "Review Article: Institutions and Rationality in Politics – Three Varieties of Neo-Institutionalism." *British Journal of Political Science* 26: 553–82.

Katz, Richard. 1997. "Representational Roles." *European Journal of Political Research* 32: 211–26.

Katzenstein, Peter. 1985. *Small States in World Markets: Industrial Policy in Europe.* Ithaca, NY: Cornell University Press.

Keohane, Robert. 1984. *After Hegemony: Cooperation and Discord in the World Political Economy.* Princeton, NJ: Princeton University Press.

Keohane, Robert O., and Joseph S. Nye, Jr. 2000a. "Globalization: What's New? What's Not? (And So What?)." *Foreign Policy* 118: 104–19.

2000b. "The Club Model of Multi-lateral Cooperation and Problems of Democratic Legitimacy." Paper prepared for the American Political Science Association, Washington D.C., August 31–September 3.

Kersbergen, Kees van. 1997. "Between Collectivism and Individualism: the Politics of the Centre." In: Hans Keman, ed. *The Politics of Problem-Solving in Postwar Democracies*. London: Macmillan, 113–40.

——— 1999. "Contemporary Christian Democracy and the Demise of the Politics of Mediation." In: Herbert Kitschelt, Peter Lange, Gary Marks, and John Stephens, eds. *Continuity and Change in Contemporary Capitalism*. Cambridge: Cambridge University Press, 346–70.

Kille, Kent J., and Roger Scully 1997. "Institutional Leadership and International Collaboration: Evidence from the United Nations and the European Union." Paper delivered at the Annual Meeting of the American Political Science Association, August 28–31.

Kinder, Donald R. 1998. "Opinion and Action in the Realm of Politics." In: Daniel T. Gilbert, Susan T. Fiske, and Gardner Lindzey, eds. *The Handbook of Social Psychology*, vol. II, 4th edn. New York: Oxford University Press, 778–867.

Kinder, Donald R., and David O. Sears. 1985. "Public Opinion and Political Action." In: Gardner Lindzey and Elliot Aronson, eds. *Handbook of Social Psychology*, vol. II: *Special Fields and Applications*. New York: Random House, 659–741.

Kitschelt, Herbert, Peter Lange, Gary Marks, and John Stephens, eds. 1999. *Continuity and Change in Contemporary Capitalism*. Cambridge: Cambridge University Press.

Kohler-Koch, Beate. 1996. "Catching up with Change: the Transformation of Governance in the European Union." *Journal of European Public Policy* 3: 359–80.

Kohler-Koch, Beate, and R. Eising, eds. 1999. *The Transformation of Governance in the European Union*. London: Routledge.

Kreher, Alexander. 1997. "Agencies in the European Community: a Step towards Administrative Integration in Europe." *Journal of European Public Policy* 4: 225–45.

Laffan, Brigid. 1996. "From Policy Entrepreneur to Policy Manager: the Challenge Facing the Commission." *Journal of European Public Policy* 4: 422–38.

Lane, Jan-Erik ed. 1997a. *Public Sector Reform: Rationale, Trends and Problems*. London: Sage.

——— 1997b. "Introduction: Public Sector Reform: Only Deregulation, Privatization and Marketization?" In: Jan-Erik Lane, ed. *Public Sector Reform: Rationale, Trends and Problems*. London: Sage, 1–16.

——— 1997c. "Democracy, Sovereignty and the European Union." *West European Politics* 20: 201–8.

Lankowski, Carl. 1997. "Europe's Ambiguous Unity." In: Alan Cafruny and Carl Lankowski, eds. *Europe's Ambiguous Unity: Conflict and Consensus in the Post-Maastricht Era*. Boulder, CO: Lynne Rienner, 1–17.

Leibfried, Stephan, and Paul Pierson, eds. 1995. *European Social Policy: between Fragmentation and Integration.* Washington D.C.: Brookings Institution.

1996. "Social Policy." In: Helen Wallace and William Wallace, eds. *Policy-Making in the European Union.* Oxford: Oxford University Press, 185–207.

Lequesne, Christian. 1993. *Paris–Bruxelles: Comment ce fait la politique européenne de la France.* Paris: Presses universitaires de la Fondation nationale des sciences politiques.

Levi, Margaret. 1997a. *Consent, Dissent and Patriotism.* Cambridge: Cambridge University Press.

1997b. "A Model, a Method and a Map: Rational Choice in Comparative and Historical Analysis." In: Mark I. Lichbach and Alan S. Zuckerman, eds. *Comparative Politics: Rationality, Culture and Structure.* Cambridge: Cambridge University Press, 19–41.

Lewis, Jeffery. 1998. "Is the 'Hard Bargaining' Image of the Council Misleading? The Committee of Permanent Representatives and the Local Elections Directive." *Journal of Common Market Studies* 36: 479–504.

Liefferink, Duncan. 1997. *European Environmental Policy: The Pioneers.* Manchester: Manchester University Press.

Liegl, Barbara, and Wolfgang C. Müller. 1999. "Senior Officials in Austria." In: Edward C. Page and Vincent Wright, eds. *Bureaucratic Elites in Western European States: A Comparative Analysis of Top Officials.* Oxford: Oxford University Press, 90–120.

Lijphart, Arend. 1969. "Consociational Democracy." *World Politics* 21: 207–25.

1984. *Democracies: Patterns of Majoritarian and Consensus Government in Twenty-One Countries.* New Haven, CT: Yale University Press.

1999. *Patterns of Democracy: Government Forms and Performance in Thirty-Six Countries.* New Haven, CT: Yale University Press.

Lijphart, Arend, Ronald Rogowski, and R. Kent Weaver. 1993. "Separation of Powers and Cleavage Management." In: R. Kent Weaver and Bert A. Rockman, eds. *Do Institutions Matter? Government Capabilities in the United States and Abroad.* Washington D.C.: Brookings Institution, 302–44.

Lindberg, Leon N. 1963. *The Political Dynamics of European Economic Integration.* Stanford, CA: Stanford University Press.

Lindberg, Leon N., and Stuart A. Scheingold. 1970. *Europe's Would-Be Polity: Patterns of Change in the European Community.* Englewood Cliffs, NJ: Prentice-Hall.

Lipset, Martin Seymour, and Stein Rokkan. 1967. "Cleavage Structures, Party Systems and Voter Alignments: an Introduction." In: Martin Seymour Lipset and Stein Rokkan, eds. *Party Systems and Voter Alignments: Crossnational Perspectives.* New York: Free Press, 1–64.

Lodge, Juliet. 1994. "Transparency and Democratic Legitimacy." *Journal of Common Market Studies* 32: 343–68.

Lodge, Milton, and Marco Steenbergen. 1995. "The Responsive Voter: Campaign Information and the Dynamics of Candidate Evaluation." *American Political Science Review* 89: 309–26.

Lustick, Ian. 1997. "Lijphart, Lakatos, and Consociationalism." *World Politics* 50: 88–117.

McCubbins, Mathew, Roger Noll, and Barry Weingast. 1987. "Administrative Procedures as Instruments of Political Control." *Journal of Law, Economics and Organization* 3: 243–77.

McDonald, Maryon. 1997. "Identities in the European Commission." In: Neill Nugent, ed. *At the Heart of the Union: Studies of the European Commission.* London: Macmillan, 27–48.

McGuire, William J. 1993. "The Poly-Psy Relationship. Three Phases of a Long Affair." In: Shanto Iyengar and William J. McGuire, eds. *Explorations in Political Psychology.* Durham, NC: Duke University Press, 9–35.

MacMullen, Andrew. 1997. "European Commissioners, 1952–95." In: Neill Nugent, ed. *At the Heart of the Union. Studies of the European Commission.* London: Macmillan, 27–48.

McRae, Kenneth, ed. 1974. *Consociational Democracy: Political Accommodation in Segmented Societies.* Toronto: McClelland & Steward.

Majone, Giandomenico. 1989. *Evidence, Argument and Persuasion in the Policy Process.* New Haven, CT: Yale University Press.

1991. "Crossnational Sources of Regulatory Policy Making in Europe and the United States." *Journal of Public Policy* 11: 79–101.

1992. "Market Integration and Regulation: Europe after 1992." *Metroeconomica* 43: 131–56.

1993. "The European Community: between Social Policy and Social Regulation." *Journal of Common Market Studies* 31: 153–69.

1994a. "The European Community as a Regulatory State." Lectures given at the Academy of European Law, July.

1994b. "The Rise of the Regulatory State in Europe." *West European Politics* 17: 77–101.

1995. "The Development of Social Regulation in the European Community: Policy Externalities, Transaction Costs, Motivational Factors." *Aussenwirtschaft* 50: 79–110.

1996. *Regulating Europe.* London: Routledge.

1997."The New European Regulatory Agencies: Regulation by Information." *Journal of European Public Policy* 4(2): 262–75.

1998. "Europe's 'Democratic Deficit': The Question of Standards." *European Law Journal* 4: 5–28.

2000. "The Credibility Crisis of Community Regulation." *Journal of Common Market Studies* 38: 273–302.

Mann, Michael. 1993. "Nation-States in Europe and Other Continents: Diversifying, Developing, Not Dying." *Daedalus* 13: 115–40.

Mansbridge, Jane, 1990. "The Rise and Fall of Self-Interest in the Explanation of Political Life." In: Jane Mansbridge, ed. *Beyond Self-Interest.* Chicago: University of Chicago Press, 3–22.

March, James, and Johan Olsen. 1984. "The New Institutionalism: Organizational Factors in Political Life." *American Political Science Review* 78: 734–49.

1989. *Rediscovering Institutions. The Organizational Basis of Politics.* New York: Free Press.

Marks, Gary. 1992. "Structural Policy in the European Community." In: Alberta Sbragia, ed. *Euro-Politics: Institutions and Policy Making in the "New" European Community*. Washington: Brookings Institution, 191–224.

1993. "Structural Policy and Multilevel Governance in the EC." In: Alan Cafruny and Glenda Rosenthal, eds. *The State of the European Community: Volume 2*. Boulder, CO: Lynne Rienner, 391–410.

1996a. "An Actor-Centered Approach to Multilevel Governance." *Regional and Federal Studies* 6: 20–38.

1996b. "Exploring and Explaining Variation in EU Cohesion Policy." In: Liesbet Hooghe, ed. *Cohesion Policy and European Integration: Building Multilevel Governance*. Oxford: Oxford University Press/Clarendon Press, 388–422.

Marks, Gary, and Doug McAdam. 1995. "Social Movements and the Changing Structure of Political Opportunities in the European Union." *West European Politics* 19: 249–78.

Marks, Gary, and Liesbet Hooghe. 2000. "A Critique of Neoclassical Theory." *Journal of Common Market Studies* 38: 795–816.

Marks, Gary, and Marco Steenbergen. 2000. "Political Contestation in the European Union." In: Gary Marks and Marco Steenbergen, eds. "Dimensions of Contestation in the European Union." Unpublished ms.

Marks, Gary, and Carole Wilson. 1998. "National Parties and the Contestation of Europe." In: Thomas Banchoff and Mitchell P. Smith, eds. *Legitimacy and the European Union*. New York: Routledge, 113–33.

2000. "The Past in the Present: a Cleavage Theory of Party Positions on European Integration." *British Journal of Political Science* 30: 433–59.

Marks, Gary, Liesbet Hooghe, and Kermit Blank. 1996. "European Integration since the 1980s. State-Centric versus Multi-Level Governance." *Journal of Common Market Studies* 34: 343–78.

Marks, Gary, Carole Wilson, and Leonard Ray. Forthcoming. "National Political Parties and European Integration." *American Journal of Political Science*.

Marks, Gary, Jane Salk, Leonard Ray, and François Nielsen. 1996. "Competencies, Cracks and Conflict: Regional Mobilization in the European Union." *Comparative Political Studies* 29: 164–92.

Marsh, David, and R.A.W. Rhodes, eds. 1992. *Implementing Thatcherite Policies: Audit of an Era*. Philadelphia, PA: Open University Press.

Martin, Lisa. 1993. "International and Domestic Institutions in the EMU Process." *Economics and Society* 5: 125–44.

2000. *Democratic Commitments: Legislatures and International Cooperation*. Princeton, NJ: Princeton University Press.

Mattli, Walter. 1999. *The Logic of Regional Integration. Europe and Beyond*. Cambridge: Cambridge University Press.

Mazey, Sonia. 1992. "Conception and Evolution of the High Authority's Administrative Practices." In: E.V. Heyen, ed. *Yearbook of European Administrative History: Early European Community Administration*. Baden-Baden: Nomos, 31–47.

Mazey, Sonia, and Jeremy Richardson. 1993. "EC Policy Making: an Emerging European Policy Style?" In: D. Liefferink, Philip Lowe, and A.P.J. Mol, eds. *European Integration and Environmental Policy*. Scarborough, Ontario: Belhaven Press, 114–25.

Mearsheimer, John. 1990. "Back to the Future: Instability in Europe after the Cold War." *International Security* 15: 5–56.

Meer, Frits M. van der, and Jos C.N. Raadschelders. 1999. "The Senior Civil Service in the Netherlands." In: Edward C. Page and Vincent Wright, eds. *Bureaucratic Elites in Western European States: A Comparative Analysis of Top Officials*. Oxford: Oxford University Press, 205–28.

Mény, Yves, Pierre Muller, and Jean-Louis Quermonne, eds. 1994. *Politiques publiques en Europe*. Paris: L'Harmattan.

Mény, Yves. 1993. *Government and Politics in Western Europe: Britain, France, Italy and Germany*. Oxford: Oxford University Press.

Merkel, Wolfgang. 1999. "Legitimacy and Democracy: Endogenous Limits of European Integration." In: Jeffrey Anderson, ed. *Regional Integration and Democracy*. Boulder, CO: Rowman & Littlefield, 45–67.

Metcalfe, Les. 1992. "Après 1992: la Commission pourra-t-elle gérer l'Europe?" *Revue française d'administration publique* 63: 401–12.

——— 1996a. "Building Capacities for Integration: the Future Role of the Commission." *EIPASCOPE* 2: 2–8.

——— 1996b. "The European Commission as a Network Organization." *Publius* 26: 43–62.

——— 2000. "Reforming the Commission: Will Organizational Efficiency Produce Effective Governance?" *Journal of Common Market Studies* 38: 817–41.

Michelmann, Hans J. 1978a. "Multinational Staffing and Organisational Functioning in the Commission of the European Communities." *International Organization* 32: 477–96.

——— 1978b. *Organisational Effectiveness in a Multinational Bureaucracy*. Farnborough, UK: Saxon House.

Migué, Jean-Luc, and Gerard Bélanger. 1974. "Toward a General Theory of Managerial Discretion." *Public Choice* 17: 27–43.

Milner, Helen. 1997. *Interests, Institutions and Information: Domestic Politics and International Relations*. Princeton, NJ: Princeton University Press.

Milward, Alan. 1992. *The European Rescue of the Nation-State*. Berkeley: University of California Press.

Milward, Alan, and V. Sørensen. 1993. "Interdependence or Integration? A National Choice." In: A. Milward, R. Ranieri, F. Romero, and V. Sørensen, eds. *The Frontier of National Sovereignty: History and Theory, 1945–1992*. New York: Routledge.

Mitrany, David. 1966 [1943]. *A Working Peace System*. Chicago: Quadrangle.

Moe, Terry. 1984. "The New Economics of Organization." *American Journal of Political Science* 28: 739–77.

——— 1990. "The Politics of Structural Choice: toward a Theory of Public Bureaucracy." In: Oliver E. Williamson, ed. *Organization Theory: from Chester Barnard to the Present and Beyond*. Oxford: Oxford University Press, 116–53.

——— 1991. "Politics and the Theory of Organization." *Journal of Law, Economics, and Organization* 7: 106–29.

1997. "The Positive Theory of Public Bureaucracy." In: Dennis C. Mueller, ed. *Perspectives on Public Choice: a Handbook.* Cambridge: Cambridge University Press, 455–80.

Monnet, Jean. 1962. "A Ferment of Change." *Journal of Common Market Studies* 1: 203–11.

1978. *Memoirs.* London: Collins.

Monroe, Kristen Renwick. 1996. *The Heart of Altruism. Perceptions of a Common Humanity.* Princeton, NJ: Princeton University Press.

Moravcsik, Andrew. 1993. "Preferences and Power in the European Community: a Liberal Intergovernmentalist Approach." *Journal of Common Market Studies* 31: 473–524.

1994. "Why the European Community Strengthens the State: Domestic Politics and International Cooperation." Center for European Studies Working Paper Series #52. Paper presented at the Annual Meeting of the American Political Science Association, New York, September 1–4.

1998. *The Choice for Europe: Social Purpose and State Power from Messina to Maastricht.* Ithaca, NY: Cornell University Press.

1999. "A New Statecraft? Supranational Entrepreneurs and International Cooperation." *International Organization* 53: 267–306.

Morris, David S. 1998. "Moving from Public Administration to Public Management." In: Michael Hunt and Barry O'Toole, eds. *Reform, Ethics and Leadership in Public Service: Festschrift in Honour of Richard A. Chapman.* London: Ashgate, 55–68.

Morrisroe, Darby. 1998. "The State of 'State Offices' in Washington: a Critical Assessment." Paper presented at the Annual Meeting of the American Political Science Association, Boston, September 3–6.

Murphy, Craig N. 1994. *International Organization and Industrial Change: Global Governance since 1850.* Cambridge: Polity Press.

Nelsen, Brent, and Alexander Stubb, eds. 1998. *The European Union: Readings on the Theory and Practice of European Integration.* Boulder, CO: Lynne Rienner.

Neunreither, Karl-Heinz. 1972. "Transformation of a Political Role: Reconsidering the Case of the Commission of the European Communities." *Journal of Common Market Studies* 10: 233–48.

1995. "Citizens and the Exercise of Power in the European Union: towards a New Social Contract?" In: Allan Rosas and Esko Antola, eds. *A Citizen's Europe: in Search of a New Order.* London: Sage, 1–18.

Nicoll, Sir William. 1996. " The 'Code of Conduct' of the Commission towards the European Parliament." *Journal of Common Market Studies* 34(2): 277–81.

Niskanen, William A. 1971. *Bureaucracy and Representative Government.* New York: Aldine-Atherton.

1994. *Bureaucracy and Public Economics.* Aldershot, UK: Edward Elgar.

Noel, Emile. 1973. "The Commission's Power of Initiative." *Common Market Law Review* 10: 123–5.

Nordlinger, Eric. 1972. *Conflict Regulation in Divided Societies.* Cambridge, MA: Center for International Affairs, Harvard University.

Nørgaard, Asbjørn Sonne. 1996. "Rediscovering Reasonable Rationality in Institutional Analysis." *European Journal of Political Research* 29: 31–57.

North, Douglass. 1990. *Institutions, Institutional Change, and Economic Performance.* Cambridge: Cambridge University Press.

Nugent, Neill. 1995. "The Leadership Capacity of the European Commission." *Journal of European Public Policy* 2: 603–23.

   1999. *The Government and Politics of the European Union.* 4th edn. Durham, NC: Duke University Press.

Nye, Joseph, ed. 1968. *International Regionalism.* Boston: Little Brown.

Offe, Claus. 2000. "The Democratic Welfare State in an Integrating Europe." In: Louis W. Pauly and Michael T. Greven, eds. *Democracy beyond the State: the European Dilemma and the Emerging Global Order.* Boulder, CO: Rowman & Littlefield, 63–90.

Olson, Mancur. 1982. *The Rise and Decline of Nations: Economic Growth, Stagflation, and Social Rigidities.* New Haven, CT: Yale University Press.

Ostrom, Elinor. 1986. "An Agenda for the Study of Institutions." *Public Choice* 48: 3–25.

   1991."Rational Choice Theory and Institutional Analysis." *American Political Science Review* 85: 237–43.

O'Toole, Larry J., Jr. 1997. "Treating Networks Seriously: Practical and Research Based Agendas in Public Administration." *Public Administration Review* 57: 45–51.

Page, Edward C. 1985. *Political Authority and Bureaucratic Power.* Whitstable, UK: Harvester Press.

   1995. "Administering Europe." In: Jack Hayward and Edward Page, eds. *Governing the New Europe.* Durham, NC: Duke University Press, 257–85.

   1997. *People Who Run Europe.* Oxford: Clarendon/Oxford University Press.

Page, Edward C., and Vincent Wright, eds. 1999a. *Bureaucratic Elites in Western European States. A Comparative Analysis of Top Officials.* Oxford: Oxford University Press.

   1999b. "Conclusion: Senior Officials in Europe." In: Edward C. Page and Vincent Wright, eds. *Bureaucratic Elites in Western European States: A Comparative Analysis of Top Officials.* Oxford: Oxford University Press, 266–79.

   1999c. "Introduction." In: Edward C. Page and Vincent Wright, eds. *Bureaucratic Elites in Western European States: A Comparative Analysis of Top Officials.* Oxford: Oxford University Press, 1–12.

Peters, B. Guy. 1992. "Bureaucratic Politics and the Institutions of the European Community." In: Alberta Sbragia, ed. *Euro-Politics: Institutions and Policy Making in the "New" Europe.* Washington, D.C.: Brookings Institution, 75–122.

   1994. "Agenda-Setting in the European Community." *Journal of European Public Policy* 1: 9–26.

   1996. "Models of Governance for the 1990s." In: Donald F. Kettl and H. Brinton Milward, eds. *The State of Public Management.* Baltimore, MD: Johns Hopkins University Press, 15–44.

Peters, B. Guy, and Donald J. Savoie, eds. 1995. *Governance in a Changing Environment.* Montreal: McGill-Queen's University Press.

1998. *Taking Stock: Assessing Public Sector Reforms*. Montreal: McGill-Queen's University Press.

Peterson, John. 1995a. "Decision Making in the European Union: towards a Framework for Analysis." *Journal of European Public Policy* 2: 69–94.

1995b. "Playing the Transparency Game: Consultation and Policy Making in the European Commission." *Public Administration* 73: 473–92.

1997a. "States, Societies and the European Union." *West European Politics* 20: 1–23.

1997b. "The European Union: Pooled Sovereignty, Divided Accountability." *Political Studies* 45: 559–78.

1999. "The Santer Era: the European Commission in Normative, Historical and Theoretical Perspective." *Journal of European Public Policy* 6: 46–55.

Peterson, John, and Elizabeth Bomberg. 1999. *Decision-Making in the European Union*. London: Macmillan.

Pierre, Jon, and Peter Ehn. 1999. "The Welfare State Managers: Senior Civil Servants in Sweden." In: Edward C. Page and Vincent Wright, eds. *Bureaucratic Elites in Western European States: A Comparative Analysis of Top Officials*. Oxford: Oxford University Press, 229–48.

Pierson, Paul. 1996."The Path to European Integration: a Historical Institutionalist Analysis." *Comparative Political Studies* 29: 123–63.

Pinder, John. 1968. "Positive Integration and Negative Integration: Some Problems of Economic Union in the EEC." *The World Today* 24: 88–110.

Pollack, Mark. 1995. "Creeping Competencies: the Expanding Agenda of the European Community." *Journal of Public Policy* 14: 97–143.

1997. "Delegation, Agency, and Agenda Setting in the European Community." *International Organization* 51: 99–134.

1999. "A Blairite Treaty: Neoliberalism and Regulated Capitalism in the Treaty of Amsterdam." In Karl-Heinz Neunreither and Antje Wiener, eds. *European Integration After Amsterdam: Institutional Dynamics and Prospects for Democracy*. Oxford: Oxford University Press, 266–89.

2000. "The End of Creeping Competence? EU Policy-Making since Maastricht." *Journal of Common Market Studies* 38: 519–38.

Pollitt, Christopher. 1993. *Managerialism and the Public Services: Cuts or Cultural Change in the 1980s?* Oxford: Basil Blackwell.

Posner, Barry Z., and Warren H. Schmidt. 1994. "An Updated Look at the Values and Expectations of Federal Government Executives." *Public Administration Review* 54: 20–4.

Putnam, Robert. 1973. *The Beliefs of Politicians: Ideology, Conflict and Democracy in Britain and Italy*. New Haven, CT: Yale University Press.

1976. *The Comparative Study of Political Elites*. Englewood Cliffs, NJ: Prentice-Hall.

Radaelli, Claudio. 1999. *Technocracy in the European Union*. New York: Longman.

Reif, Karl-Heinz, and Ronald Inglehart, eds. 1991. *Eurobarometer: the Dynamics of European Integration. Essays in Honor of Jacques-René Rabier*. London: Macmillan.

Rhodes, Martin. 1992. "The Future of the 'Social Dimension': Labour Market Regulation in Post-1992 Europe." *Journal of Common Market Studies* 30: 23–51.

1995. "A Regulatory Conundrum: Industrial Relations and the Social Dimension." In: Stephan Leibfried and Paul Pierson, eds. *European Social Policy: between Fragmentation and Integration*. Washington. D.C.: Brookings Institution, 78–122.

1996. "Delivering Welfare: Repositioning Non-Profit and Co-operative Action in Western European Welfare States." *Journal of Common Market Studies* 34: 478.

Rhodes, Martin, and Bastiaan van Apeldoorn. 1997. "Capitalism versus Capitalism in Western Europe." In: Martin Rhodes, Paul Heywood, and Vincent Wright, eds. *Developments in West European Politics*, New York: St. Martin's Press, 171–89.

Rhodes, Rod, Ian Bache, and Stephen George. 1996. "Policy Networks and Policy-Making in the European Union: a Critical Appraisal." In: Liesbet Hooghe, ed. *Cohesion Policy and European Integration: Building Multilevel Governance*. New York: Oxford University Press/Clarendon Press, 367–87.

Richards, David. 1997. *The Civil Service under the Conservatives 1979–97: Whitehall's Political Poodles*. Brighton: Sussex Academic Press.

Richardson, Jeremy, ed. 1996. *European Union: Power and Policy Making*. London: Routledge.

1997. "Interest Groups. Multi-Arena Politics and Policy Change." Paper presented at the Annual Meeting of the American Political Science Association, Washington D.C., August 28–31.

1998. "The EU as an Alternative Venue for Interest Groups." Paper presented at the Annual Meeting of the American Political Science Association, Boston, September 3–6.

Ringquist, Evan. 1995. "Political Control and Policy Impact in EPA's Office of Water Quality." *American Journal of Political Science* 39: 336–63.

Risse-Kappen, Thomas. 1996. "Exploring the Nature of the Beast: International Relations Theory and Comparative Policy Analysis Meet the European Union." *Journal of Common Market Studies* 34: 53–80.

Risse, Thomas. 1997. "Who Are We? A Europeanization of National Identities?" European University Institute paper.

Rockman, Bert, and Guy B. Peters, eds. 1996. *Agenda for Excellence 2: Administering the State*. Chatham: Chatham House Publishers.

Rohrschneider, Robert. 1994. "Report from the Laboratory: the Influence of Institutions on Political Elites' Democratic Values in Germany." *American Political Science Review* 88: 927–41.

1996. "Cultural Transmission versus Perceptions of the Economy. The Sources of Political Elites' Economic Values in the United Germany." *Comparative Political Studies* 29: 78–104.

Rosati, Jerel. 1981. "Developing a Systematic Decision-Making Framework: Bureaucratic Politics in Perspective." *World Politics* 33: 234–52.

Rose, Richard. 1991. "What Is Lesson-Drawing?" *Journal of Public Policy* 11: 3–30.

Rosenau, James, and E.-O. Czempiel, eds. 1992. *Governance without Government: Order and Change in World Politics.* Cambridge: Cambridge University Press.

Ross Schneider, Ben. 1993. "The Career Connection: a Comparative Analysis of Bureaucratic Preferences and Insulation." *Comparative Politics* 25: 331–50.

Ross, George. 1995a. "Assessing the Delors Era and Social Policy." In: Stephan Leibfried and Paul Pierson, eds. *European Social Policy: between Fragmentation and Integration.* Washington: Brookings Institute, 357–88.

1995b. *Jacques Delors and European Integration,* New York: Oxford University Press.

Rouban, Luc. 1999. "The Senior Civil Service in France." In: Edward C. Page and Vincent Wright, eds. *Bureaucratic Elites in Western European States: A Comparative Analysis of Top Officials.* Oxford: Oxford University Press, 65–89.

Safran, William. 1995. *The French Polity, 4th edn.* White Plains, NY: Longman.

Sandholtz, Wayne. 1996. "Membership Matters: Limits of the Functional Approach to European Institutions." *Journal of Common Market Studies* 34: 403–29.

Sandholtz, Wayne, and Alec Stone Sweet, eds. 1998. *European Integration and Supranational Governance.* Oxford: Oxford University Press.

Sandholtz, Wayne, and John Zysman. 1989. "1992: Recasting the European Bargain." *World Politics* 42: 95–128.

Sartori, Giovanni. 1991. "Comparing and Miscomparing." *Journal of Theoretical Politics* 3: 243–57.

Sbragia, Alberta. 1992. "Thinking about the European Future: the Uses of Comparison." In: Alberta Sbragia, ed. *Euro-Politics. Institutions and Policy Making in the "New" European Community.* Washington D.C.: Brookings Institute, 257–92.

1993. "The European Community: A Balancing Act." *Publius* 23: 23–38.

1996. "Environmental Policy." In: Helen Wallace and William Wallace, eds. *Policy-Making in the European Union.* Oxford: Oxford University Press, 235–55.

Scharpf, Fritz W. 1988. "The Joint-Decision Trap: Lessons from German Federalism and European Integration." *Public Administration* 66: 239–78.

1994. "Community and Autonomy: Multilevel Policy Making in the European Union." *Journal of European Public Policy* 1: 219–42.

1996. "Negative and Positive Integration in the Political Economy of European Welfare States." In: Gary Marks, Fritz Scharpf, Philippe Schmitter, and Wolfgang Streeck, eds. *Governance in the European Union.* London: Sage, 15–39.

1997a. "Demokratische Politik in der internationalisierten Ökonomie." Max-Planck Institut für Gesellschaftsforschung Köln, Working Paper 97/9.

1997b. *Games Real Actors Play: Actor-Centered Institutionalism in Policy Research.* Boulder, CO: Westview Press.

1998. "Interdependence and Democratic Legitimation." Max-Planck Institut für Gesellschaftsforschung Köln, Working Paper 98/2.

1999. *Governing in Europe: Effective and Democratic?* Oxford: Oxford University Press.

2000. "The Viability of Advanced Welfare States in the International Economy: Vulnerabilities and Options." *Journal of European Public Policy* 7, 190–228.

Schmidt, Manfred. 1998. "The Consociational State. Hypotheses Regarding the Political Structures and Political Performance Profile of the European Union." Paper presented at a conference on Consociationalism, Harvard University, May.

Schmitter, Philippe C. 1969. "Three Neofunctional Hypotheses about International Integration." *International Organization* 23: 161–6.

1970. "A Revised Theory of Regional Integration." *International Organization* 24: 836–68.

1996. "Imagining the Future of the Euro-Polity with the Help of New Concepts." In: Gary Marks, Fritz Scharpf, Philippe Schmitter, and Wolfgang Streeck, eds. *Governance in the European Union*. London: Sage, 121–50.

2000. *How to Democratize the European Union...And Why Bother?* Boulder, CO: Rowman & Littlefield.

Schmitter, Philippe C., and Terry Lynn Karl. 1991. "What Democracy Is...and Is Not." *Journal of Democracy* 2: 75–88.

Schneider, Gerald. 1997. "Choosing Chameleons: National Interests and the Logic of Coalition Building in the Commission of the European Union." Paper presented at the 5th Biennial Meeting of the European Community Studies Association, Seattle, May 28–June 1.

Schulman, P.R. 1993. "The Negotiated Order of Organizational Reliability." *Administration and Society* 25: 353–72.

Searing, Donald D. 1969. "The Comparative Study of Elite Socialization." *Comparative Political Studies* 1: 471–500.

1986. "A Theory of Political Socialization: Institutional Support and Deradicalization in Britain." *British Journal of Political Science* 16: 341–76.

1991. "Roles, Rules and Rationality in the New Institutionalism." *American Political Science Review* 32: 47–68.

1994. *Westminster's World: Understanding Political Roles*. Cambridge: Cambridge University Press.

Searing, Donald, Gerald Wright, and George Rabinowitz. 1976. "The Primacy Principle: Attitude Change and Political Socialization." *British Journal of Political Science* 6: 83–113.

Sears, David O. 1993. "Symbolic Politics: A Socio-Psychological Theory." In: Shanto Iyengar and William J. McGuire, eds. *Explorations in Political Psychology*. Durham, NC: Duke University Press, 113–49.

Sears, David O., and Carolyn L. Funk. 1991. "The Role of Self-Interest in Social and Political Attitudes." *Advances in Experimental Social Psychology* 24: 1–91.

Sears, David O., and Nicholas A. Valentino. 1997. "Politics Matters: Political Events as Catalysts for Preadult Socialization."*American Political Science Review* 91: 45–65.

Sedelmeier, Ulrich, and Helen Wallace. 2000. "Eastern Enlargement. Strategy or Second Thoughts?" In: Helen Wallace and William Wallace, eds. *Policy-Making in the European Union*. Oxford: Oxford University Press, 427–60.

Shapiro, Martin. 1997. "The Problems of Independent Agencies in the United States and the European Union." *Journal of European Public Policy* 4(2): 276–91.

Simon, Herbert A. 1947. *Administrative Behavior.* New York: Macmillan.

1985. "Human Nature in Politics: the Dialogue of Psychology with Political Science." *American Political Science Review* 79: 293–304.

Skogstad, Grace. 1998. "Ideas, Paradigms and Institutions: Agricultural Exceptionalism in the European Union and the United States." *Governance* 11: 463–90.

Soskice, David. 1999. "Divergent Production Regimes: Coordinated and Uncoordinated Market Economies in the 1980s and 1990s." In: Herbert Kitschelt, Peter Lange, Gary Marks, and John Stephens, eds. *Continuity and Change in Contemporary Capitalism.* Cambridge: Cambridge University Press, 101–34.

Spruyt, Hendrik. 1994. *The Sovereign State and Its Competitors.* Princeton, NJ: Princeton University Press.

Steiner, Jürg, and Thomas Ertman, eds. Forthcoming. *Consociational Democracy in Western Europe. Still or Again the Politics of Accommodation?* Oxford: Oxford University Press.

Steunenberg, Bernard. 1996. "Agency Discretion, Regulatory Policy Making and Different Institutional Arrangements." *Public Choice* 86: 309–39.

Stone Sweet, Alec, and Thomas Brunnell. 1996. "Constructing a Supranational Constitution: Dispute Resolution and Governance in the European Community." *American Political Science Review* 92: 63–82.

Stone Sweet, Alec, and Wayne Sandholtz. 1997. "European Integration and Supranational Governance." *Journal of European Public Policy* 4: 297–317.

1998. "Integration, Supranational Governance, and the Institutionalization of the European Polity." In: Wayne Sandholtz and Alec Stone Sweet, eds. *European Integration and Supranational Governance.* Oxford: Oxford University Press, 1–26.

Strauss, Anselm. 1987. *Qualitative Analysis for Social Scientists.* Cambridge: Cambridge University Press.

Streeck, Wolfgang. 1991. "Neo-Voluntarism: a New European Social Policy Regime?" In: Gary Marks, Fritz Scharpf, Philippe Schmitter, and Wolfgang Streeck, eds. *Governance in the European Union.* London: Sage, 64–94.

1996. "From Market-Making to State-Building? Reflections on the Political Economy of European Social Policy." In: Stephan Leibfried and Paul Pierson, eds. *European Social Policy: Between Fragmentation and Integration.* Washington D.C.: Brookings Institution, 389–431.

1998. "The Internationalization of Industrial Relations in Europe: Prospects and Problems." Max Planck Institut für Gesellschaftsforschung Köln, Discussion Paper 98/2.

Streeck, Wolfgang, and Philippe Schmitter. 1991. "From National Corporatism to Transnational Pluralism: Organized Interests in the Single European Market." *Politics and Society* 19: 133–64.

Suleiman, Ezra. 1975. *Politics, Power and Bureaucracy in France.* Princeton, NJ: Princeton University Press.

1984. *Bureaucrats and Policy Making.* New York: Holmes & Meier.

Suleiman, Ezra, and Henri Mendras, eds. 1995. *Le Recrutement des élites en Europe*. Paris: Editions La Découverte (Collections Recherches).

Taggart, Paul. 1998. "A Touchstone of Dissent: Euroscepticism in Contemporary Western European Party Systems." *European Journal of Political Research* 33: 363–88.

Tarrow, Sidney. 1995. "The Europeanisation of Conflict: Reflections from a Social Movement Perspective." *West European Politics* 18: 223–51.

1999. "Building a Composite Polity: Popular Contention in the European Union." Mimeo.

Taylor, Paul. 1991. "The European Community and the State: Assumptions, Theories and Propositions." *Review of International Studies* 17: 109–25.

1996. *The European Union in the 1990s*. Oxford: Oxford University Press.

Taylor, Shelley E. 1981. "The Interface of Cognitive and Social Psychology." In: John H. Harvey, ed. *Cognition, Social Behavior and the Environment*. Hillsdale, NJ: Lawrence Erlbaum, 189–211.

Teague, Paul, and John Grahl. 1992. *Industrial Relations and European Integration*. London: Lawrence & Wishart.

The Economist, December 19, 1998. "Charlemagne: Erkki Liikanen, Europe's Housekeeper."

Thelen, Kathleen. 1999. "Historical Institutionalism in Comparative Politics." *Annual Review of Political Science*. 2: 369–404.

Thomassen, Jacques, and Herman Schmitt. 1999. "Partisan Structures in the European Parliament." In: Richard Katz and Bernhard Wessels, eds. *The European Parliament, National Parliaments and European Integration*. Oxford: Oxford University Press.

Tilly, Charles. 1975. *The Formation of National States in Western Europe*. Princeton, NJ: Princeton University Press.

1990. *Coercion, Capital and European States A.D. 990–1990*. Oxford: Basil Blackwell.

Tsebelis, George. 1990. "Elite Interaction and Constitution Building in Consociational Democracies." *Journal of Theoretical Politics* 2: 5–29.

Tsebelis, George, and Geoffrey Garrett. 2000. "Legislative Politics in the European Union." *European Union Politics* 1: 9–36.

Tsebelis, George, and Amie Kreppel. 1998. "The History of Conditional Agenda-Setting in European Institutions." *European Journal of Political Research* 33: 41–71.

Tullock, Gordon. 1965. *The Politics of Bureaucracy*. Washington D.C.: Public Affairs Press.

Turner, Lowell. 1996. "The Europeanization of Labor: Structure before Action." *European Journal of Industrial Relations* 2: 325–44.

Verba, Sidney. 1965. "Conclusion: Comparative Political Culture." In: Lucien Pye and Sidney Verba, eds. *Political Culture and Political Development*. Princeton, NJ: Princeton University Press, 512–60.

Wallace, Helen, and William Wallace, eds. 2000. *Policy-Making in the European Union*. Oxford: Oxford University Press.

Wallace, Helen. 1993. "European Governance in Turbulent Times." *Journal of Common Market Studies* 31: 293–303.

——— 1996. "The Institutions of the EU: Experience and Experiments." In: Helen Wallace and William Wallace, eds. *Policy-Making in the European Union.* Oxford: Oxford University Press, 37–68.

——— 2000. "The Institutional Setting: Five Variations on a Theme." In: Helen Wallace and William Wallace, eds. *Policy-Making in the European Union.* Oxford: Oxford University Press, 3–37.

Wallace, William. 1996. "Rescue or Retreat? The Nation-State in Western Europe, 1945–93." *Political Studies* 42: 52–76.

Weaver, R. Kent. 1992. "Political Institutions and Canada's Constitutional Crisis." In: R. Kent Weaver, ed. *The Collapse of Canada?* Washington D.C.: Brookings Institution, 7–75.

Weingast, Barry. 1995. "A Rational Choice Perspective on the Role of Ideas: Shared Belief Systems and State Sovereignty in International Cooperation." *Politics and Society* 23: 449–64.

Weisberg, Herbert. 1998. "The Political Psychology of Party Identification." Paper prepared for the Annual Meeting of the American Political Science Association, Boston, MA, September 3–6.

Wessels, Wolfgang. 1998. "Comitology: Fusion in Action. Politico-Administrative Trends in the EU System." *Journal of European Public Policy* 5: 209–34.

Wilks, Stephen. 1996. "Regulatory Compliance and Capitalist Diversity in Europe." *Journal of European Public Policy* 3: 536–59.

Wintrobe, Ronald. 1997. "Modern Bureaucratic Theory." In: Dennis C. Mueller, ed. *Perspectives on Public Choice: a Handbook.* Cambridge: Cambridge University Press, 429–54.

Wood, Dan, and Richard Waterman. 1991. "The Dynamics of Political Control of the Bureaucracy." *American Political Science Review* 85: 801–28.

——— 1993. "The Dynamics of Political-Bureaucratic Adaptation." *American Journal of Political Science* 37: 497–528.

Worsham, Jeff, Mark Allen Eisner, and Evan J. Ringquist. 1997. "Assessing the Assumptions: a Critical Analysis of Agency Theory." *Administration and Society* 28(4): 419–40.

Wright, Vincent. 1994a. "Reshaping the State: the Implications for Public Administration." *West European Politics* 17: 102–37.

——— 1994b. *Privatization in Western Europe: Pressures, Problems and Paradoxes.* London: Pinter Publishers.

Yee, Albert S. 1997. "Thick Rationality and the Missing 'Brute Fact': the Limits of Rationalist Incorporations of Norms and Ideas." *Journal of Politics* 59: 1001–39.

Zaller, John. 1992. *The Nature and Origins of Mass Opinion.* Cambridge: Cambridge University Press.

Zürn, Michael. 2000. "Democratic Governance beyond the Nation-State." In: Michael Greven and Louis Pauly, eds. *Democracy beyond the State? The European Dilemma and the Emerging Global Order.* Boulder, CO: Rowman & Littlefield, 91–114.

Index